THE CHURCH CANTATAS OF J. S. BACH

By the same Author

REQUIEM : MUSIC OF MOURNING AND CONSOLATION

THE
CHURCH
CANTATAS
OF
J. S. BACH

ALEC ROBERTSON

PRAEGER PUBLISHERS
New York · Washington

BOOKS THAT MATTER

Published in the United States of America in 1972
by Praeger Publishers, Inc., 111 Fourth Avenue,
New York, N.Y. 10003

Library of Congress Catalog Card Number: 70-158094

Printed in Great Britain

To Donald Beswick

CONTENTS

vii

INTRODUCTION

In 1926 Constable & Co. published, in a limited edition, a book by a leading Bach scholar, Charles Sanford Terry, *Johann Sebastian Bach's Cantata Texts*, which contained his translations into English of all Bach's cantatas, sacred and secular. The church cantatas had made a profound impression on me when I first came to study them some thirteen years before and, as a result, formed a small group of singers and instrumentalists to perform privately, once a week, those of the cantatas that lay within our competence. The 1914 war brought this rewarding activity to an end, but in 1926, my love for the cantatas undiminished, I hastened to purchase Terry's book (reprinted by Holland Books in 1964). It has been a constant and much valued companion over the past years, during which I cherished the idea—now fulfilled—of one day writing a modest companion volume to it which would deal specifically with the music of the church cantatas and its religious implications and also be of use as a reference book—even for those who will have no regard for what the author has to say.

Terry expended much time and labour over a reconstruction of the Leipzig Liturgy as it was carried out during Bach's Cantorate at St Thomas's and devoted a long and most valuable introduction to it in his book.

His plan, the basic idea of which I have followed, was to set out the cantatas for Sundays and Feast Days in the order of the Lutheran Church Year—the First Sunday of Advent to the Twenty-Seventh Sunday after Trinity—with details of the Epistle and Gospel, retaining German for the titles of the cantatas and the opening lines of each succeeding number in them, giving the scoring in each case and also the genesis of the chorales used.

The *Hauptgottesdienst*, the principal Lutheran service on Sundays and Feast Days, was, up to the Administration of Holy Communion, primarily centred on the Gospel for the day. It dictated the choice of the simple motet sung at the start, the hymns (chorales), and the libretto of the *Hauptmusik*, or cantata, sung before the hour-long sermon which was the culminating point of this part of the service.

All this information is of the greatest importance for the understanding of the 'application' of the Gospel text by the librettists and of quotations often made of material from the Old and New Testaments or other sources.

I determined, in my book, to lay special emphasis on the religious significance of Bach's treatment of the librettos he set, not only in general but in regard to single words or sentences which he singled out for prominence.

Terry's very free translations, which were not intended to reproduce the literal meaning of the German text, certainly make the librettos, the majority of which have small literary merit, very readable: but, in accordance with prevailing opinion today, I decided to opt for literal translations. For these I turned to *The Cantatas of Johann Sebastian Bach* by my friend W. G. Whittaker who, alas, did not live to see the publication of his *magnum opus* by the Oxford University Press in 1959. Whittaker realized, of course, that though such translations would result in bad English they would at any rate reproduce the meaning of each German word as it appeared. In a few cases where the English translations, owing to the different construction of the German language, read particularly awkwardly the publishers have kindly allowed me to make small adjustments for the sake of intelligibility. Where two cantatas bear the same name the English translation has been varied for easier identification.

Whittaker planned the order of his book in quite a different way from Terry's, dealing with categories such as cantatas with borrowed material, wholly original cantatas, chorale cantatas, etc. His book is invaluable to students, but also holds much to interest the intelligent reader who need not feel bound to agree with Whittaker's views (or, for that matter, with mine in this book) about Bach's use of symbolism, pictorial or otherwise, which remains a controversial matter.

It has not been possible, in the space available to me, to include any music examples. I have also had to interpret the title of my book very strictly. This has meant the omission of all those cantatas not assigned to a particular Sunday or Feast Day, incomplete cantatas, those for weddings, funerals, civic occasions, the oratorios. This left me with 173 'liturgical' cantatas to deal with and even so I originally found myself greatly exceeding the furthest limit of words allowable!

The brief commentaries on each item—omitted when there seemed nothing special to say—do not profess to do much more than act as guideposts and as it was impossible, in most cases, to quote texts in full, especially those of recitatives, I have had to resort to paraphrases to give a general idea of them.

A discography has not been included since this so quickly gets out of date but I should mention that *Das Alte Werk*, as from the start of 1972, are issuing recordings of the entire range of Bach's church and secular cantatas in the numerical order of the *Bach Gesellschaft* Edition. Four to five albums, each containing two records, are to be released each year and made available through record dealers.

As regards the dating of the cantatas all Bach's biographers up to Karl Geiringer's excellent biography, published in 1966—which has all the latest information—have erred in ascribing the majority of the chorale cantatas to the years 1735–44, whereas the researches of Dr Alfred Dürr, head of the J. S. Bach Institute, founded at Göttingen in 1951, and his colleagues, have proved that these cantatas, for the most part, were composed between 1724 and 1725 and the majority of the whole series of the extant Leipzig works between 1723 and 1729.

I have used Dr Dürr's dating and in each case I have placed the earliest composed cantata first in my survey, headed by the Gospel and Epistle for the day (not repeated), and set out the rest, where there is more than one, in chronological order. The Gospel and Epistle sources I have taken from Terry and the biblical quotations are from the Revised Version of the Bible.

The cantatas were sung on alternate Sundays at St Thomas's and St Nicholas, the latter being given preference as its pastor was also the superintendent of St Thomas's School. Bach rehearsed his choir on Saturday afternoons. Out of the fifty-four singers, in 1730, seventeen formed the cantata choir, twenty the motet choir. Bach described the rest as 'no musicians at all', but presumably they could at least manage to take part in simple four-part chorales. For the twenty instrumental players he needed to augment his meagre resources he drew on a body of professionals who served the Leipzig churches and on the University students.

The service began at seven in the morning and lasted until noon, and at about seven-thirty the ill-fed and badly housed boys and young men of the first choir took their parts in the cantata, providing also the soloists, unless a visiting tenor or bass was able to assist for the arias. It is important to remember that Bach was the cantor, not, as is sometimes said, the organist of St Thomas's. Each church had its own organist.

Terry considers there is conclusive evidence that the congregation took part in the chorales that were within their competence. They had hymn books and they were provided with sheets which included from four to eight of the librettos.

I have been able, three times in my long life, to go through the whole series of the extant church cantatas and have constantly studied them and lived with them in between. There are, naturally, dull movements here and there, when Bach failed to be inspired by the text of a recitative or aria, though rarely of a chorus. His adaptations in the cantatas of previously existing material are usually so skilfully done that their origins could go unsuspected, but sometimes they do not fit the new circumstances at all well and awkwardness in the setting of the words betrays their origin and gives ammunition to rationalist musicians who wish to prove that Bach was no more religious than the cantor in the next town and regarded the composition of church cantatas merely as a routine job.

There is no need to enlarge on the appeal of the music but I cannot resist drawing attention to the astonishing melodic richness to be found in cantata after cantata, the satisfying harmonic foundations, the marvellous contrapuntal skills and the splendid vital rhythms. Some listeners, one hopes, may feel impelled to go further than immediate enjoyment of the music and make the effort, not always an easy task, to enter into the alien world of Lutheran theology and so reach a greater understanding of the religious significance of Bach's *personal* treatment of the texts of the librettos. That effort was pre-eminently made by W. G. Whittaker, an agnostic who, if sometimes unable to conceal his dislike of the librettists' typical dwelling on sin and repentance, shows a moving understanding of what those concepts meant to Bach, and of how his music transcends the triteness and brashness with which fundamental Christian dogmas are so often—though by no means always—handled by the librettists.

Above all there is Bach's inspiring faith in God, his tender and profound love of Christ, and his sublime approach to death as the key to eternal life, all concepts which he clothes in glorious music.

The whole matter is summed up in a splendid passage by Alfred Einstein in his *A Short History of Music* (Cassell, 1936). 'The art of the Bach cantata is an exposition of the foundations and principles of the Christian faith, and none more searching or more inexorable, deeper or more precise, has ever been. The temporal life and the eternal, works and faith, mortality and death, sin and repentance, suffering and salvation—all the emotions and inspirations of the Christian soul exalted this, the greatest of preachers since Luther, not to theological abstractions but to a passionate presentation by symbolic means of an incomparably vivid musical imagination.'

I am deeply grateful to Miss Annette Carter, my literary editor at Cassell's, for her invaluable help and advice in the preparation of this book, which involved checking details of the scoring and scriptural references in the cantatas and much else. I am also very grateful to my typists, Mrs Susan Larsen and Mrs Kay Savage, for deciphering my difficult handwriting.

xii

TECHNICAL TERMS AND ABBREVIATIONS

VOICES

S	Soprano	T	Tenor
A	Alto	B	Bass

INSTRUMENTS

Cembalo The harpsichord, very rarely used by Bach in the church cantatas.

Clar Clarino. A high-pitched trumpet.

Cont Basso continuo (formerly called 'thorough-bass' in English). Bach uses the Italian term for un-figured or figured bass parts. Figures placed below single bass notes indicate the harmonies to be played above them, e.g. $^6_3$ represents the third and sixth notes of a common chord. The keyboard instrument for the continuo is, unless otherwise specified, the organ. The realization (that is, the filling-in) of a continuo part on the organ, particularly in recitatives and arias, calls for great artistry and imagination. The other instruments Bach used in the continuo were the violoncello, violone and bassoon.

Cor
Cor da cacc Corno, corno da caccia. There is no consensus of opinion as to whether Bach used both these terms indifferently to indicate the Waldhorn, or French horn. C. S. Terry, in his book *Bach's Orchestra* (O.U.P., 1961), gives some evidence to the contrary, believing that at one time Bach in his use of these two terms distinguished the mellow tone associated with the Waldhorn from the more strident tone of the Jagdhorn. The latter was an instrument in use at princely courts, e.g. Weimar and Cöthen. Bach first specifies Corno alone in his scores at the cessation of his courtly service in 1723.

Cor da tirarsi	Corno da tirarsi. Terry suggests that this was not a particular instrument but a tromba da tirarsi (q.v.) with an adapted mouthpiece which produced horn tone.
Cornetto	An antique curved wooden wind instrument with a tone which has been likened to that of a well-trained chorister.
Fag	Fagotto. Bassoon.
Fl	Flute. In Bach's scores, and therefore in this book, this always indicated the flute à bec or Blockflöte, known in English as the recorder. The fact is often ignored in performance today.
Fl à bec	See Flute.
Fl trav	This is the transverse or horizontal flute we have in the modern orchestra.
Ob d'am	Oboe d'amore. An instrument with a pitch between the oboe and the oboe da caccia (q.v.)
Ob da cacc	Oboe da caccia. An alto oboe, in tone similar to the so-called cor anglais, the latter word being a corruption of *anglé*.
Org	Organ.
Te	Taille. A tenor oboe.
Timp	Timpani.
Tr	Tromba (trumpet).
Tr da tirarsi	A slide trumpet with the mechanism of a trombone.
Trb	Trombone.
Violetta	Another term for the viola.
Violone	An octave lower than the viol da gamba. Similar to the double-bass.
Vla	Viola.
Vla d'am	Viola d'amore. An instrument with six or seven strings and a number of wire strings beneath the fingerboard which vibrate in sympathy.
Vla da gamba	Viola da gamba. A bass viola.
Vln	Violin.
Vln picc	Violino piccolo. Smaller and higher in pitch than the violin.
V'cello	Violoncello.
V'cello picc	Violoncello piccolo, a five-stringed instrument with a compass between the viola and the violoncello.

CANTATA
The title 'cantata' without qualification signi-fies the normal form of these works in which there is usually a chorale at the end.

CHORALE CANTATA
The chorale cantata is based on a chorale first heard in the opening chorus and quoted in various ways thereafter.

SOLO CANTATA
Solo cantatas are works for one or more solo voices but they usually end with a chorale for chorus.

RECITATIVE
(1) *Secco* (dry). This type is accompanied only by a figured bass line indicating chords that punctuate the vocal line. (2) Accompanied. The vocal lines are accompanied by a written-out part for the chosen instruments.

RITORNELLO
The recurrence of an instrumental introduction to choral or solo numbers, coming between lines or complete verses. The material is usually developed and so differs from the rondo-refrain type. The term is sometimes applied to the introductory matter itself.

SEQUENCE
Repetition of a short phrase at a higher or, more rarely, lower pitch. Bach frequently uses this device in the cantatas, usually making two repetitions but occasionally three.

THE LIBRETTOS

The principal writers of texts used by Bach and especially composed as church cantatas were as follows:

Salomo Franck (1659–1725), civil servant; Erdmann Neumeister (1671–1756), Lutheran pastor; Marianne von Ziegler (1695–1760), poet; Christian Frederich Henrici (1700–1764), best known by his pen-name 'Picander', civil servant.

Bach's biographers ascribe a considerable number of other church cantata texts to Franck, Ziegler and Picander, but always with the qualification 'possibly' or 'probably', and this also applies to some cantatas in which it is thought Bach had a hand, or of which he may have been the author. I have usually limited myself to certainties. Particulars of other doubtfully ascribed cantatas, together with biographical notes about his chief librettists, can be found in *The Literary Background to Bach's Cantatas* by James Day (Dobson, 1961).

Epistle: Rom. XIII. 11–14 (Our salvation is nearer than we believe).
Gospel: Matt. XXI. 1–9 (Christ's entry into Jerusalem).

Nun komm, der Heiden Heiland (Come, Redeemer of our race).

Chorale Cantata BWV 61. Weimar, 1714. Libretto by Erdmann Neumeister.

The congregational hymn, 'Nun komm, der Heiden Heiland' ('Come, Redeemer of our race'), sung on this Sunday before the intoning of the Gospel reading, was Luther's adaptation of the Latin hymn 'Veni Redemptor gentium', and its plainsong, ascribed to St Ambrose. Bach uses it in the opening chorus of this cantata, twice in Cantata BWV 62, three times in Cantata BWV 36, as well as in many of his chorale preludes for organ, of which the one in the *Eighteen Preludes* (BWV 659) is the finest.

The librettist of this cantata, Erdmann Neumeister (1671–1756), on whom Bach drew for four other cantatas, was a Lutheran pastor. He published five sets of cantata texts in the 'new style'—that is the recitative and aria *da capo* style—and frankly admitted fashioning his librettos after the manner of Italian opera.

1 OVERTURE (Chorus)
(As above)
SATB. Vln i, ii (unis.), Vla i, ii, Fag, Org and Cont

Bach cast this movement in the three-fold form of the French Overture of the period, Slow—Fast—Slow, a plan he uses again in several other cantatas. The solemn processional theme on the orchestra must have been suggested to him by the words of the Gospel for this Sunday, which relates the triumphant entry of Christ into Jerusalem. He gives the first line of the chorale melody 'Come, Redeemer of our race', successively to sopranos, tenors and basses, these voices then uniting in the second line with the altos 'As the Virgin's child recognized'.

The choice of this Gospel out of season may have been determined by the fifth of the eight verses of Luther's hymn, 'From the Father cometh He, and returneth speedily; Down to Hell His word descends, till again in Heaven it ends'. The Christian is to remember that the new-born Child was to die for his salvation at

B

the hands of those—some of them at least—who shouted 'Hosanna' five days before they cried out 'Crucify'.

As the orchestra concludes the slow section the key changes from A minor to C major, the time from 4/4 to 3/4, the tempo being marked *Gai*. This fugal movement in which the chorus sing the third line of the chorale 'Of whom wonders all the world', ends with a return to the slow opening section at the fourth line '[that] God such birth to Him ordained'.

The chain of sequences in the fast section of this superb movement recalls those in the old French carol we know as 'Angels from the realms of Glory', but this must be pure coincidence.

2 RECITATIVE—ARIOSO
'Der Heiland ist gekommen' ('The Saviour now appeareth')
T. Org and Cont

The expressive arioso speaks of the radiant light and the blessings He brings to His own.

3 ARIA
'Komm, Jesu, komm zu deiner Kirche und gieb ein selig neues Jahr' ('Come, Jesus, come to thy Church and grant a blessed New Year')
T. Vln i, ii, Vla i, ii (unis.), Org and Cont

The melody of the introduction, warmly scored, is in the rhythm of a slow gigue. The soloist repeats the three opening bars and then develops the theme, with the work 'Come' touchingly isolated.

4 RECITATIVE
'Siehe, siehe, ich stehe vor der Tür und klopfe an' ('Behold, behold, I stand at the door and knock')
B. Vln i, ii, Vla i, ii, Org and Cont

This is one of Bach's finest recitatives. The text is from Revelations III. 20. The orchestral chords are marked *pizzicato* throughout, depicting the knocking on the door; the voice also illustrates it at 'and knock'.

5 ARIA
'Öffne dich, mein ganzes Herze' ('Open thyself, my whole breast')
S. V'celli with Org

This is the ardent and eager response that welcomes Jesus into the Christian heart. The middle section, in the minor, reflects that 'dust to dust returns' but this is not the end for those who are blessed with the Saviour's presence.

6 CHORALE

'Amen, Amen! Komm, du schöne Freudenkrone, komm und bleib nicht lange. Deiner wart' ich mit Verlangen' ('Amen, Amen! Come then, lovely joy-crown, come, and delay not long. For thee I wait with longing')
SATB. Vln i, ii (unis.), Vla i, ii, Fag with A.T.B. Org and Cont

For this chorale the librettist used the last four lines of Philipp Nicolai's hymn, with its associated melody (1599), 'Wie schön leuchtet der Morgenstern'. The melody lines are given to the soprano in long notes, the lower vocal parts have expressive extended phrases on 'Verlangen' ('longing') and in the last two bars the violins, who have a brilliant part all through, run up the scale to G in alt, picturing the rising of the morning star.

Nun komm, der Heiden Heiland (Now come, the heathens' Saviour).
Chorale Cantata BWV 62. Leipzig, 1724.

This cantata, which uses the same chorale as No. 61, has inevitably been overshadowed by its more attractive and poetic predecessor, but it has decided merits of its own. The libretto is based on Luther's hymn and uses the first and last verses in the opening and concluding movements and paraphrases of verses in the remaining movements.

1 CHORUS

(As above)
SATB. Ob i, ii, Vln i, ii, Vla, Cor with S. Cont

At the close of the festive orchestral introduction, the oboes unexpectedly bring in the first line of the chorale melody, the chorus, A.T.B., then singing it successively in diminution—that is notes of half the value of the long ones played by the horn. The sopranos sing the melody in long notes throughout.

2 ARIA

'Bewundert, O Menschen, dies grosse Geheimnis' ('Marvel, O men, at this great mystery')
T. Ob i, Vln i, Ob ii, Vln ii, Vla, Cont

3

At the tenor's singing of the line 'the Highest Lord appears to the world' the florid phrases rise up the scale to a high point of climax.

3 RECITATIVE

'So geht aus Gottes Herrlichkeit und Thron sein eingeborner Sohn' ('So departs from God's glory and throne his only-begotten Son')
B. Cont

Christ is here described as the lion of Judah come with joy to redeem the lost and sinning. 'A star of pleasing passing worth' (Psalm XIX. 5).

4 ARIA

'Streite, siege, starker Held' ('Fight, conquer, strong hero')
B. Vln i, ii, Vla (all unis.), Cont

Here and nowhere else in the cantatas the upper strings only are to be found throughout with the continuo. Bach provided them with no separate parts but simply put *sempre col Continuo*. The device illustrates vividly the strength of the Hero.

5 RECITATIVE

'Wir ehren diese Herrlichkeit und nahen nun zu Krippen' ('We honour this glory and come now to Thy cradle')
S.A. Vln i, ii, Vla, Cont

This simple little duet is exquisite. The first violins rise high above the voices as if illustrating the closing line 'The darkness frightens us not, we see Thine undying light'.

6 CHORALE

'Lob sei Gott, dem Vater, g'than' ('Praise to God the Father be given')
As No. 1. Insts. with voices. Cont

A simple harmonization of the doxology.

Schwingt freudig euch empor (Soar joyfully on high).

Cantata BWV 36. Leipzig, before 1731.

The use of secular musical material in a church work was as common in Bach's time as in the great age of polyphony. It went to ridiculous lengths in the sixteenth century and well merited the censure of the Council of Trent. Luther, and his helpers, drew freely and sensibly on popular song for some of his chorales. Bach considered that all his music, vocal and instrumental, sacred or secular, was composed for 'the greater glory of God and the refreshment of the spirit'. On some occasions—as we will find later on—he was careless over his adaptation of pre-existing material, either because he was short of time, or bored by the libretto he had to set. At other times we can only marvel at his skill in adaptation. The music of Nos. i, iii, v, vii of the present work appears in those of Bach's secular cantatas BWV 36 a, b, c. This one is based on 36a, 'Steigt freudig in die Luft', composed in 1726 for the birthday of the Princess of Anhalt-Cöthen. Picander's libretto for this has survived but the music is lost except for the numbers mentioned above.

PART I

1 CHORUS
(As above)
SATB. Ob d'am i, ii (unis), Vln i, ii, Vla, Org and Cont

This chorus seems to show Bach flinging his hat (or wig!) into the air for sheer joy at the coming of the Lord. Here the Gospel text of the entry into Jerusalem becomes relevant.

The voices enter one after the other, basses up to sopranos, but after the ritornello following the two opening lines the chorus shout, unaccompanied, 'Yet hold back': and though the music continues as joyfully as before the moral is drawn that though your hearts rise up to God in heaven they must pay their dues to His Son on earth.

2 CHORALE (Duet)
S.A. Ob d'am i, ii, with SA. Org and Cont

The chorale as in Cantatas BWV 61 and 62, 'Nun komm, der Heiden Heiland', is begun, after a general introductory bar, by the alto, and taken up a fourth higher by the soprano. After her first bar the two voices continue independently, echoing one another here and there. It is a lovely setting, dwelling tenderly on the Virgin Mary; then on 'the wonder of all the earth', the birth of Christ.

3 ARIA
'Die Liebe zieht mit sanften Schritten' ('Love guides with gentle steps')
T. Ob d'am solo, Org and Cont

A da capo aria expressing that the soul is eager, but shy and faltering, 'seeking his love as does a bride'.

5

4 CHORALE
'Zwingt die Saiten in Cythara' ('Pluck the strings in Cythara')
SATB. Ob d'am i, ii, Vln i, ii, Vla with voices: Org and Cont

Verse vi of Philipp Nicolai's hymn 'Wie schön leuchtet der Morgenstern' (1599) with its melody greets the coming of the heavenly bridegroom.

PART 2

5 ARIA
'Willkommen, werter Schatz' ('Welcome, precious treasure')
B. Vln i, ii, Vla, Org and Cont

The text of this aria in the secular cantata (BWV 36c) is the equivalent of 'Happy birthday to you [the Rector of St Thomas's School]' and so was easily changed into an anticipatory welcome to the birth of Jesus, 'Welcome, precious treasure'. The music is pleasing but unremarkable.

6 CHORALE
'Der du bist dem Vater gleich' ('Thou that art equal to the Father')
T. Ob d'am i, ii, Org and Cont

This is the sixth verse of Luther's hymn sung by the solo tenor in long notes.

7 ARIA
'Auch mit gedämpften, schwachen Stimmen wird Gottes Majestät verehrt' ('Even with subdued and weak voices God's majesty is revered')
S. Vln solo, Org and Cont

This is a delightful aria with a delicate and beautifully designed accompaniment.

Bach illustrates his liking for realistic description in the enchanting middle section of the aria 'For resounds only the spirit thereby'. 'Resounds' is sung to broken phrases with frequent *staccato* markings.

8 CHORALE
'Lob sei Gott, dem Vater, g'than' ('Praise to God the Father be given')
SATB. As No. 4. Insts. with voices, Org and Cont

The eighth and last verse of Luther's hymn (see p. 1).

FOURTH SUNDAY IN ADVENT

Epistle: Phil. IV. 4–7 (Rejoice in the Lord alway).
Gospel: John I. 19–28 (Make straight the way of the Lord).

Bereitet die Wege, bereitet die Bahn (Prepare the way, prepare the course).
Solo Cantata BWV 132. Weimar, 1715. Libretto by Salomo Franck.

This is Bach's only cantata for the Fourth Sunday in Advent. At Leipzig cantatas were sung only on the first Sunday, but in accordance with Luther's dislike of an invariable observance church authorities could, within reason, take their own line, and so this cantata had a place in the Weimar liturgy.

1 ARIA
(As above)
S. Ob, Vln i, ii, Vla, Cont

In answer to the question put by the Jews 'Who art thou?' John the Baptist replied by quoting the prophet Isaiah (XL. 3)—'I am the voice of one that crieth, Prepare ye in the wilderness the way of the Lord', and went on to prophesy the coming of the Messiah.

The instrumental introduction to the aria reflects, in its lovely dance-like melody and in its rising and falling scale passages, the joyful event that is to be. The soprano is given a long run on 'Bahn' ('the course') of seven and a half bars. One of the most satisfying features of Bach's writing is a perfect balance between musical and spiritual logic and so at the repeat of the opening words the same vocal pattern returns, but this time with the florid passages taken up higher. After the ritornello—which repeats the instrumental introduction in full—the text of the middle section is 'Prepare the ways and make the paths in faith and love to the Highest quite smooth'. The outstanding feature of this section is the highlighting of the words 'Messiah approaches' which are sung three times, each time unaccompanied.

2 RECITATIVE
'Willst du dich Gottes Kind und Christi Bruder, nennen?' ('Wouldst thou call thyself a son of God and Christ's [own] brother?')
T. Cont

7

Here the librettist becomes didactic. Bach passes from *secco* to *arioso* and concludes with a graphic description, in the bass of the continuo, of the words 'Roll away the heavy sin-stones' and a plea to unite the soul in faith with the Saviour.

3 ARIA
'Wer bist du?' ('Who art thou?')
B. V'cello, Cont

In this aria the question 'Who art thou?' is not the one addressed to John the Baptist by the Jews, as before, but to the Christian conscience, and so was intended to come home to the listening congregation. The austere music has an obsessive motif on the cello which is rarely absent throughout. Self-judgement comes in the second half of the grim aria '[Thou art] a child in Satan's net, a false, hypocritical Christian!' The word 'hypocritical' is set to a long and tortuous phrase and the soul struggling in Satan's net is graphically represented by downward leaps.

4 RECITATIVE
'Ich will, mein Gott, dir frei heraus bekennen' ('I will, my God, make full confession to Thee')
A. Vln i, ii, Vla, Cont

The text alludes to the baptism which once cleansed the newborn child of sin and restored it to grace. It ends with a prayer for pity on the soul who has broken her baptismal vows, but now with faith renewed, ardently desires to keep them.

5 ARIA
'Christi Glieder, ach bedenket, was der Heiland euch geschenket durch der Taufe reines Bad' ('Members of Christ, ah, consider, what the Saviour gave you through baptism's pure bath')
A. Vln solo, Cont

The wide ranging arabesques for the solo violin, rising up the scale and gradually and gently falling to a cadence before the voice comes in, represent, symbolically, the cleansing waters of baptism, the gift of 'the new robes of crimson and white silk'.

6 CHORALE
Bach supplied no concluding chorale but simply wrote 'chorale simplice stylo' in the autograph. The libretto, however, gives the text of the fifth verse of Elisabeth Kreutziger's hymn 'Herr Christ, der einig Gottes-Sohn' (1524) which begins 'Ertödt uns durch dein Güte'. The anonymous melody is well known in piano solo or duet transcriptions by the title 'Mortify us by Thy Grace'.

CHRISTMAS DAY

Epistle: Titus II. 11–14 (The grace of God has appeared to me).
Gospel: Luke II. 1–14 (The Nativity of Christ).

Christen, ätzet diesen Tag (Christians, engrave this [glad] day).

Cantata BWV 63. Leipzig 1723.

1 CHORUS
(As above)
SATB. Tr i, ii, iii, iv, Timp, Ob i, ii, iii, Fag, Vln i, ii, Vla, Org and Cont

The libretto—thought to be by Bach—is without chorale, aria, or biblical quotation. The large forces noted above are not used again until the concluding chorus.

The full brass at once repeat the first four bars of the joyous C major ritornello theme with which the movement, in 3/8 time, begins on the woodwind. The chorus burst in just after it reaches a full close, enthusiastically exclaiming 'Christians engrave this glad day in metal and marble'. The same pattern is repeated in the middle section, after the orchestral ritornello, at 'Come hasten to the manger', which leads to scintillating passages to illustrate the 'ray' in the line, 'The ray that shines out is for you the light of mercy'.

Bach—if it was he—recalls here the text of the alternative Epistle for the Feast, 'The people in darkness have seen a great light' (Isaiah I. 2–7). The *da capo* brings back the orchestral introduction and so the brass, silent all through the choral parts of the movement.

2 RECITATIVE
'O sel'ger Tag!' ('Oh blessed day!')
A. Vln i, ii, Vla, Org and Cont

The lengthy text rejoices in the coming of this great day in which the promise that God would appear in human flesh to defeat Satan and heal the world is fulfilled.

3 DUET
'Gott, du hast es wohlgefüget, was uns jetzo widerfährt' ('God, Thou hast it well ordained what now befalls us')
S.B. Ob solo, Org and Cont

The constant repetition of the first line of the text in the first section of this duet emphasizes deep gratitude for all it portends

9

and this is underlined by the exuberant oboe obbligato. The middle section enjoins continual trust in God's mercy bestowed on us. The oboe here is silent except for a very brief ritornello between the lines of the text.

4 RECITATIVE
'So kehret sich nun heut' das bange Leid, mit welchem Israel geängstet und beladen in lauter Heil und Gnaden' ('The fearful suffering endured by Israel today now turns into pure redemption and mercy')
T. Org and Cont

5 DUET
'Ruft und fleht den Himmel an, kommt, ihr Christen, kommt zum Reihen' ('Call and implore the heavens, come, ye Christians, come into the ranks')
A.T. Vln i, ii, Vla, Org and Cont

This duet, in 3/8 time, is a dance movement in Bach's most beguiling manner. The first violin has a series of downward plunging arpeggios in the strings' accompaniment to the round dance.

6 RECITATIVE
'Verdoppelt euch demnach, ihr heissen Andachtsflammen' ('Redouble, therefore, you hot flames of devotion')
B. Ob i, ii, iii, Vln i, ii, Vla, Fag, Org and Cont

Bach obeys the command by scoring this recitative in eight individual parts. It is one of his most imaginative short recitatives.

7 CHORUS
'Höchster, schau in Gnaden an' ('Highest, contemplate in mercy')
SATB. As at No. 1

A chorus as fine as that in No. 1. The brilliant orchestral introduction gives the impression of a vast multitude gathered together in praise and prayer to God.

An effective instance here, when the double fugue begins after the great outburst with the opening words, of the voices being left without accompaniment for five bars.

Gelobet seist du, Jesu Christ (Praised be thou, Jesus Christ).

Chorale Cantata BWV 91. Leipzig, 1724.

The libretto of this cantata is based on Luther's hymn (1524) with the above title. The first, second and last verses are set unaltered in Nos. 1, 2 and 7 and verses iii, iv, v, and vi in paraphrases by Picander. The melody of the hymn has an interesting history. It is first found as a tenth-century sequence 'Grates omnes reddamus' ('Let all give thanks') derived from the elaborate plainsong *Alleluia* of the Christmas Midnight Mass. In Germany in pre-Reformation times it was sung to a vernacular text, then became, in the fourteenth century, a popular '(kyrie) eleison', a spiritual folksong. Luther added six verses of his own to the single original one.

1 CHORUS
(As above)
SATB. Cor i, ii, Timp, Ob i, ii, iii, Vln i, ii, Va, Cont

The fine melody is put into a brilliant instrumental setting with rousing exchanges between horns and oboes. The sopranos sing the melody, mostly in long notes with the rest of the chorus breaking in a half-beat after the soprano's first note, as if impatient to join with the angels in the rejoicing at Christ's birth as man.

2 RECITATIVE AND CHORALE
'Der Glanz der höchsten Herrlichkeit' ('The splendour of the highest glory')
S. Cont

The recitative passages by Picander are interwoven with the second verse of the chorale, a device often used by Bach, but one which rarely fails to delight.

3 ARIA
'Gott, dem der Erdenkreis zu klein ist' ('God for whom the earth is too small')
T. Ob i, ii, iii, Cont

The aria, a paraphrase of verses iii–iv, has the dotted rhythm Bach frequently uses to depict royal state. 'Heaven and earth', the text declares, 'cannot encompass God and yet he is born in a humble manger.'

4 RECITATIVE
'O Christenheit, wohlan!' ('O Christendom awake!')
B. Vln i, ii, Vla, Cont

A paraphrase of verse v. 'Make thyself ready to receive thy creator, let thy heart be moved by this love. He comes to thee to call us to his throne and for this wretched world to meet Him.' The recitative passes at these last words into an astonishing upward chromatic scale for the voice on the word 'wretched'.

5 DUET
'Die Armut, so Gott auf sich nimmt' ('The poverty which God on himself takes')
S.A. Vln i, ii (unis.), Cont

The paraphrase of verse vi emphasizes that 'by his poverty we are made rich'. It makes salvation possible, the glory of the angels, the abundance of the treasures of heaven.

The dotted rhythm of solemnity hardly ceases throughout the duet, as if to underline the majesty of God made man. It comes only into the instrumental parts.

6 CHORALE
'Das hat er alles uns getan' ('This has he all to us done')
SATB. Ob i, ii, iii, Vln, i, ii, Vla, all with voices, Cor i, ii, Timp, Cont

The last verse of the hymn.

Unser Mund sei voll Lachens (Let our mouth be full of laughter).
Cantata BWV 110. 1725.

1 CHORUS
(As above)
SATB. Tr i, ii, iii, Timp, Fl trav i, ii, Ob, i, ii, iii, Fag, Vln i, ii, Vla, Org and Cont

The opening chorus is a supreme example of Bach's immense skill in adaptation. The orchestral part reproduces, with a few modifications and the addition of flutes to the scoring, the whole of the first movement of the D major Overture (BWV 1069). Bach imposes the four vocal parts above the start of the *allegro* (in 9/8) which is, of course, preceded and followed by the massive *grave* section (4/4).

The text of the chorus is based on Psalm cxxvi. 2, which is a cry of joy for the Lord's delivery of Sion from bondage. 'Then was our mouth filled with laughter and our tongue with singing.'

('Then said they amongst the nations' is omitted.) 'The Lord hath done great things for us.'

The chorus, if sung lightly—as it should be—shakes with joyous laughter.

2 ARIA

'Ihr Gedanken und ihr Sinnen' ('Ye thoughts and ye meditations')

T. Fl trav i, ii, Fag, Org and Cont

The text begs the 'thoughts and meditations' to detach themselves from the earth and mount swiftly heavenwards, remembering always what God has done.

3 RECITATIVE

'Dir, Herr, ist niemand gleich. Du bist gross . . . und kannst's mit der That beweisen.' ('Unto thee, Lord, is no man equal. Thou art great, . . . and [thou] canst it with deeds prove')

B. Vln i, ii, Vla, Org and Cont

The concluding cadence is one that Bach often uses to give special emphasis to the words, the leading note instead of ascending to the key note drops to the octave below.

4 ARIA

'Ach Herr, was ist ein Menschenkind?' ('Ah Lord, what is a child of man?')

A. Ob d'am solo, Org and Cont

The opening lines must have been suggested by Psalm VIII. 4: 'What is man that you should keep him in mind, mortal man that you care for him?'

The happy, laughing mood of the opening chorus is momentarily dispersed in the first section of the aria, which answers the question posed above with 'a worm whom thou cursest, when hell and Satan are round him'.

5 DUET

'Ehre sei Gott in der Hohe und Friede auf Erden und den Menschen ein Wohlgefallen' ('Glory be to God in the highest, and peace on earth and goodwill to men')

S.T. Org and Cont

For this brilliant and gorgeous duet Bach adapted the music to 'Virga Jesse floruit' (sung on Feasts of the Blessed Virgin Mary in the Roman rite) which is one of the four interpolated movements in the original version, in E flat, of his setting of the Latin

Magnificat (BWV 243), transposed from F to A and allotted to tenor and soprano soloists instead of bass. This duet was left incomplete in the *Magnificat* but what is missing can be supplied from this source. The text is, of course, from St Luke's Gospel II. 14.

6 ARIA

'Wacht auf! ihr Adern und ihr Glieder!' ('Awake ye veins and ye limbs')

B. Tr i, Ob i, ii, with Vln i, ii, Ob da cacc with Vla, Org and Cont

A stirring aria. The trumpet sounds the awakening call in the first bar and then the triumphant music breaks out. The call is to 'Sing such joy-songs as are pleasing to our God'. In the middle section, as the text dictates, the woodwind instruments are silent. 'And you, ye devotional strings shall prepare praise whereby themselves heart and spirit rejoice'.

7 CHORALE

'Alleluja! Alleluja! gelobt sei Gott! singen wir' ('Alleluia, Alleluia, praised be God. We sing')

SATB. As No. 3. Fl trav i, ii added. All with voices

The text is the fifth verse of Caspar Fuger's 'Wir Christenleut' (1592) with a melody attributed to his son (1593).

CHRISTMAS MONDAY

Epistle: Acts VI. 8–15; VII. 55–60 (Martyrdom of St Stephen).
Gospel: Matt. XXIII. 34–39 (Woe to Jerusalem that killeth the prophets) or
Luke II. 15–20 (The Shepherds at the manger).

Dazu ist erschienen der Sohn Gottes (Wherefore has appeared the Son of God).

Cantata BWV 40. Leipzig, Christmas Monday, 1723.

Whittaker describes this cantata as 'one of the most perfect, every number is of superb quality. It is, indeed, truly representative both of the composer's religious outlook and of his supreme inventive and imaginative powers'.

1 Chorus
(As above)
SATB. Cor i, ii, Ob i, ii, Vln i, ii, Vla, Cont

The short orchestral introduction, begun by the horns, joyously announces the appearance of God's Son, which the chorus proclaim in detached choral phrases. The text does not come from the Gospel of this Sunday but from the First Epistle of John III. 8, 'He that doeth sin is of the devil; for the devil sinneth from the beginning. To this end was the Son of God manifested, that He might destroy the works of the devil.' Bach vividly and dramatically depicts the battle.

2 Recitative
'Das Wort ward Fleisch und wohnet in der Welt' ('The Word was made flesh and dwells in the World')
T. Cont

The text of this recitative shows that Bach had St John's Gospel in mind. At 'The light of the world illuminates the orb of earth', Bach gives the verb a descriptive run up the scale, echoed by the continuo.

3 Chorale
'Die Sünd macht Leid' ('The sin brings sorrow')
SATB. Cor i, Ob i, ii, Vln i, ii and Vla, all with voices, Cont

This is the third verse of Caspar Fuger's hymn 'Wir Christenleut hab'n jetzund Freud' (1592) with the melody by Caspar Fuger Jnr (1593). It is peculiar in having the first line in each verse at once repeated.

4 ARIA
'Höllische Schlange, wird dir nicht bange?' ('Hellish serpent, dost thou not fear?')
B. Ob i, ii, Vln i, ii, Vla, Cont

This is one of Bach's finest arias. The obsessive rhythm depicting the serpent is present throughout the aria until the last line, 'Those who were lost are with eternal peace rejoiced'.

5 RECITATIVE
'Die Schlange, so im Paradies' ('The serpent who in Paradise')
A. Vln i, ii, Vla, Cont

The text speaks of the serpent who brought about the fall of man in Paradise, but it no longer excites fear. The Saviour takes its poison away. The declamation is superb and the nature of the lovely instrumental accompaniment is obviously related to the comforting assurance of the last line, 'therefore be comforted'.

6 CHORALE
'Schüttle deinen Kopf und sprich; fleuch, du alte Schlange' ('Shake thy head and say; away thou old serpent')
SATB. Cor i, Ob i, ii, Vln i, ii, and Vla, all with voices, Cont

This second verse of Paul Gerhardt's hymn, 'Schwing dich auf zu deinem Gott' (1653), with its associated melody (1680) magnificently harmonized, follows on the message of the recitative.

7 ARIA
'Christenkinder, freuet euch' ('Christian children rejoice')
T. Cor i, ii, Ob i, ii, Cont

Another wonderful aria. The opening words are set to fanfare-like phrases and the nature of the scoring depicts Christ as conqueror of sin. 'Let Satan furiously rage and storm, do not be afraid, Jesus will gather his chickens under his wing.'

8 CHORALE
'Jesu, nimm dich deiner Glieder ferner in Gnaden an' ('Jesu, take thee thy members further in mercy')
SATB. As No. 3

This is the fourth verse of Christian Keimann's hymn, 'Freuet euch, ihr Christen alle' (1646), with its associated melody (1646).

Christum wir sollen loben schon (Lord Christ we now Thy praises sing).
Chorale Cantata BWV 121. Leipzig, 1724.

1 CHORUS
(As above)
SATB. Cornetto, Ob d'am, Trb i, ii, iii, Vln i, ii and Vla, all with voices, Cont

The chorus is in the style of the then old-fashioned motet. The lower voices, therefore, come in one by one, with the first line of the chorale, breaking into florid phrases on the word 'praises'. The sopranos, after all this, introduce the chorale melody in long notes. The melody comes from a plainsong source, the words are the first verse of Coelius Sedulius's Christmas hymn 'A solus ortus cardine' (c. 450) in Luther's translation.

2 ARIA
'O du von Gott erhöhte Creatur, begreife nicht, nein, nein, bewund're nur' ('O thou by God exalted creature, understand not, no, no, admire only')
T. Ob d'am, Cont

This is a very tuneful aria of which the melody is borrowed from some untraceable source. Schweitzer called its declamation 'barbarous', but that is not likely to worry many people. The oboe d'amore accompaniment, when the voice comes in, is delicious.

3 RECITATIVE
'Der Gnade unermesslich's Wesen hat sich der Himmel nicht zur Wohnstatt auserlesen' ('Mercy's immeasurable being has not confined itself to Heaven as a dwelling')
A. Cont

A very expressive recitative which speaks of the unfathomable mystery of God becoming man and choosing a Virgin's womb as His dwelling.

4 ARIA
'Johannis freudenvolles Springen' ('John's joyful leaping')
B. Vln i, ii, Vla, Cont

The words are a paraphrase of verse 5 of the hymn which speaks of Mary greeting Elizabeth as related by St Luke (1. 41–45), 'When Elizabeth heard the salutation of Mary, the babe leaped in her womb'. And it is precisely that which Bach illustrates symbolically in this vivacious and gloriously melodious aria.

c   17

5 RECITATIVE

'Doch wie erblickt es dich in deiner Krippe?' ('Yet how sees it Thee in Thy crib?')

S. Cont

The recitative emphasizes thanksgiving. In the penultimate bar for the voice the soprano has a little fanfare of joy reaching a B natural above the stave—rare with Bach.

6 CHORALE

'Lob, Ehr und Dank sei dir gesagt' ('Praise, honour and thanks to Thee be said')

SATB. As at No. 1.

Verse viii of the hymn.

Selig ist der Mann, der die Anfechtung erduldet (Blessed is the man who endureth temptation).

Solo Cantata BWV 57. Leipzig, 1725.

It is difficult to explain why this cantata is so devoid of the joy proper to the season. This apart, it is in itself a beautiful work.

1 ARIA

(As above)

B. Ob i, ii, with Vln i, ii, Te with Vla, Org and Cont

The text comes from St James's Epistle i. 12, 'Blessed is the man that endureth temptation: for when he hath been approved, he shall receive the crown of life'. (The closing line 'which the Lord promised to them that love him' is omitted.) The libretto is a dialogue between Jesus and the Soul.

The aria forms a moving tribute to St Stephen, the first Christian martyr, who was stoned to death and whose feast day is on 26 December.

2 RECITATIVE

S: 'Ach! dieser süsse Trost erquickt auch mir mein Herz' ('Ah! this sweet comfort quickens also my heart')

S. Org and Cont

The Soul now draws attention to her sufferings in extravagant language such as 'I am a completely abandoned lamb, and must yield myself to the wolves' rage and cruelty. Ah! Jesus, but for comfort from thee courage and heart would be full of mourning.'

3 ARIA

'Ich wünschte mir den Tod wenn du, mein Jesu, mich nicht liebtest' ('I should wish for me death if Thou, my Jesus, me not lovedst')

S. Vln i, ii, Vla, Org and Cont

The mourning speech, long and full of pathos, has, I think, what can legitimately be called a 'tear motif' woven into the instrumental part, characterized by the two-note quaver groups combined with an imploring second theme.

The voice enters with a melody of its own which recalls the 'Agnus Dei' in the B minor Mass. At 'Ja, wenn du mich annoch betrübtest' ('Yea! if thou me yet grieved') the continuo bass has the 'tear motif' in the accompaniment to the imploring prayer which ends, 'So had I more than Hell's misery'.

4 RECITATIVE

'Ich reiche dir die Hand und auch mit das Herze' ('I reach my hand to thee and also my heart')

B.S. Org and Cont

The Soul is comforted by Jesus and assured that her fear will be defeated.

5 (ARIA)

'Ja! Ja! ich kann die Feinde schlagen' ('Yea, yea, I can the enemies strike')

B. Vln i, ii, Vla, Org and Cont

Jesus replies in this vigorous aria (a term Bach never uses when Jesus speaks in person), a battle piece set to defiant phrases.

6 RECITATIVE

'In meinem Schoss liegt Ruh und Leben, dies will ich dir einst ewig geben' ('In my bosom lies rest and life, this will I to thee some day for ever give')

S.B. Org and Cont

In her reply the Soul prays to be as favoured as Stephen was and longs for the desired end.

7 ARIA

'Ich ende behende mein irdisches Leben' ('I end swiftly my earthly life')

S. Vln solo, Org and Cont

The instrumental part is characterized by syncopated phrases

19

for the violin falling two octaves as if the Soul were 'fluttering down into the Saviour's bosom'.

Bach ends the rapturous aria with the words, 'Here hast thou the soul, what givest thou to me?' by underlining the question with a rise of a sixth.

8 CHORALE

'Richte dich, Liebste, nach meinem Gefallen und glaube' ('Conduct thyself, beloved, according to my pleasure, and believe') SATB. Ob i, ii, Vln i, ii, Te, Vla, all with voices, Org and Cont

A straightforward setting of the sixth verse of Ahasuerus Fritsch's hymn-dialogue 'Hast thou, Lord Jesus, thy countenance withdrawn from me?' (1668) to its associated melody (1665).

Epistle: Heb. i. 1–14 (Christ is preferred above the angels) or
Eccles. xv. 1–8 (Wisdom embraceth those that fear God).
Gospel: John i. 1–14 (In the beginning was the Word) or
John xxi. 15–24 (Jesus commandeth Peter to feed his lambs and sheep).

Sehet, welch eine Liebe (See now what love).
Cantata BWV 64. Leipzig, 1723.

1 CHORUS
'Sehet, welch eine Liebe hat uns der Vater erzeiget, dass wir
Gottes Kinder heissen' ('See now, what love the Father shows us,
that we are called Sons of God')
SATB. Cornetto, Trb i, ii, iii, Vln i, ii, Vla, all with voices, Org and Cont

This chorus is in the motet style, a finely fashioned fugue in
which 'See', proclaimed at once at the start by the whole chorus,
doubled by the instruments, is continually passed from voice to
voice. Great stress is laid on 'shows' in the form of lengthy runs.
Bach ends with a splendid gesture of love and faith. The chorus
shout 'See', there is a one-beat rest, then, 'Sons of God he deigns
to call us'.

2 CHORALE
'Das hat er alles uns getan' ('All this for us He has done')
SATB. Cornetto, Trb i, ii, Vln i, ii, Vla, Org and Trb iii with Cont

This is the seventh verse of the chorale 'Gelobt seist du, Jesu
Christ' ('Now praised be thou, Jesus Christ'), Luther's version
of the tenth-century sequence 'Grates omnes reddamus', the
melody of which is based on the 'Alleluia', in the Roman Rite,
of the Christmas Midnight Mass.

3 RECITATIVE
'Geh, Welt! behalte nur das Deine' ('Hence, world! Retain only
thine own')
A. Org and Cont

The Christian soul is set on heaven, not on the attractions of
worldly wealth, which are a snare and a delusion. The frequent
rushes up and down the scale in the accompaniment point the
moral. The alto ends with the words 'and so despairing earth I
sing', the last two words leading straight into the following
chorale.

4 CHORALE
'Was frag ich nach der Welt und allen ihren Schätzen?' ('What care I for the world and all its treasures?')
SATB. As at No. 1

This is the first verse of Georg Michael Pfefferkorn's hymn as above (1667). The anonymous melody is that of Johann Heerman's 'O Gott, du frommer Gott' (1679). In this harmonization of the melody, Bach gives the continuo a bass of unbroken quavers up to the cadence; a typical example of his 'walking' basses and eloquent here of confident faith.

5 ARIA
'Was die Welt in sich hält muss als wie ein Rauch vergehen' ('What the world keeps to itself must disperse like smoke')
S. Vln i, ii, Org and Cont

The constant sequential runs in the first violin part suggest the effervescent nature of material things.

Bach weaves an expressive little motif on the violins into the introductory bars of the aria and many times thereafter in the vocal and violins' parts and then, with lovely effect, in the middle section, where the words are 'But what Jesus gives to me and what my soul loves, remains firmly and eternally secure'.

6 RECITATIVE
'Der Himmel bleibet mir gewiss' ('Heaven remains to me assured')
B. Org and Cont

The text contains an allusion to one of the Gospels for the day, John xxi. 15–24, and then only remotely in the last lines. These paraphrase Jesus's reply to Peter's question, 'Lord, and what shall this man do?' 'If I will that he tarry till I come, what is that to thee?' The singer laments that he must tarry here on earth, a weary pilgrim awaiting his summons to pass through death's dark portal.

7 ARIA
'Von der Welt verlang ich nichts' ('From the world I demand nothing')
A. Ob d'am, Org, Cont

The text is very similar to that of all the previous numbers, a scorning of earth's vain glories by one assured of heaven and eternal life, but it is suffused with happiness. The lovely part for the oboe d'amore lends great charm to the aria.

8 CHORALE
'Gute Nacht, o Wesen' ('Good night [Farewell], O existence')
SATB. As No. 1

The first verse of Johann Franck's 'Jesu, meine Freude' (1653), a chorale which was modelled on a secular love song 'Flora, my joy, my soul's pasture'. This is a curious cantata for a congregation which had been celebrating materially as well as spiritually for the last three days, but a feast of fine and attractive music.

Ich freue mich in dir (In thee I do rejoice).
Chorale Cantata BWV 133. Leipzig, 1724.

The text of the chorale is based on Caspar Ziegler's hymn (1692) with the above title. Verses i and iv come in Nos. 1 and 6, the rest are paraphrased in the intermediate numbers.

1 CHORUS
(As above)
SATB. Ob d'am i, ii, with Vln ii and Vla, Vln i, Cornetto with S. Cont

The melody of the chorale, in the top part, is simply harmonized up to the sixth of the eight lines, 'Ach, wie ein süsser Ton' ('Ah, how sweet a sound'), when the sopranos sustain 'Ton' for three and a half bars, while the other voices move independently below.

The attraction of the movement is provided by the orchestral part in which the chief motif characterizes the 'sweet sound'.

Each line of the chorale is followed by a ritornello and indeed, the orchestral part could stand, without the chorale, as a *Sinfonia*. It is most exhilarating, a dance of joy.

2 ARIA
'Getrost! es fasst ein heil'ger Leib des Höchsten unbegreiflich's Wesen' ('Be comforted! A holy body encompasses the Highest's incomprehensible being')
A. Ob d'am i, ii, Cont

These words refer to the Gospel, St John i. 1–14, 'The Word became flesh'.

3 RECITATIVE
'Ein Adam mag sich voller Schrecken vor Gottes Angesicht

23

im Paradies verstecken' ('An Adam full of terror, may hide himself from God's face in Paradise')
T. Cont

Bach marks *adagio* for 'The all highest God comes in to us' then, at the opening tempo, 'and so affrights my heart not, it knows His pitying nature'.

4 ARIA
'Wie lieblich klingt es in dcn Ohren dies Wort: Mein Jesus ist geboren' ('How sweetly rings it in my ears this word; my Jesus is born')
S. Vln i, ii, Vla, Cont

The 'sweet sound' of the first verse of the chorale is now discovered to be 'My Jesus is born', to which Bach gives a phrase that might well have come from a chorale. The soprano has her own melody and it takes twenty-four bars for her to reveal what is 'Sweetly ringing in her ear'! The ringing of bells is realistically depicted by alternate open and stopped strings without continuo but with repeated notes on the viola, possibly to suggest a larger bell.

The time changes from 4/4 to 12/8 in the middle section of the aria. 'Who does not understand Jesus' name and in whom it does not penetrate the heart, must have a heart like rock.' This very ordinary sentence draws from Bach one of the finest pieces of sustained and exquisite lyrical writing in the whole range of the cantatas.

5 RECITATIVE
'Wohlan! des Todes Furcht und Schmerz erwägt nicht mein getröstet Herz' ('Well then! Death's fear and pain my comforted heart ignores')
B. Cont

Jesus will remember the loving heart even when it is in the grave.

6 CHORUS
'Wohlan! so will ich mich an dich, O Jesu, halten O Jesu! dir, nur dir, dir leb' ich ganz allein; auf dich, allein auf dich, O Jesu, schlaf' ich ein' ('So will I hold to Thee, O Jesus, O Jesus in Thee, only Thee, I live wholly in Thee, alone in Thee, O Jesus, I fall asleep')
SATB. As No. 1. Insts. with voices. Cont

This is the sixth and last verse of the hymn, simply harmonized.

Süsser Trost, mein Jesus kommt (Sweet comfort, my Jesus comes).
Solo Cantata BWV 151. Leipzig, 1725.

The libretto, by an unknown author, draws, for part of its text from the Epistle for the day—Hebrews 1. 1–14, in which St Paul speaks, *inter alia*, of Jesus 'Having become by so much better than the angels, as he hath inherited a more excellent name than they. For unto which of the angels said he at any time "Thou art my son, this day have I begotten thee".'

1 ARIA
(As above)
S. Fl trav, Ob d'am, Vln i, ii, Vla, Cont

This aria is in 12/8 time, which is nearly always indicative of something exceptional in Bach. The tempo is *molto adagio*, the upper strings, with the oboe d'amore, are marked *piano sempre*. Their gentle, lullaby rhythm underlines the soul's delight in the 'Sweet comfort' mediated by the Saviour, expressed in the exquisite arabesque phrases given to the flute. The opening measures, as we delightedly anticipate, are taken over by the soprano, with the flute momentarily silent but then entering again as she sings to a rising phrase 'Jesus now is born'. The ritornello with which the flute ends is even more ecstatic.

2 RECITATIVE
'Erfreue dich, mein Herz' ('Rejoice, my heart')
B. Cont

The recitative ends at 'God becomes a man and will on earth become even much poorer than we'.

3 ARIA
'In Jesu Demut kann ich Trost, in seiner Armuth Reichthum finden' ('In Jesu's humility can I find comfort, in His poverty, riches')
A. Ob d'am, Vln i, ii, Vla (all unis.), Cont

The aria meditates on the last words of the recitative and stresses that the Saviour's humility brings Him closer to us. The middle section speaks of the Saviour's healing hand which weaves garlands of blessings. Bach gives typical pictorial phrases to 'weaves'.

25

4 RECITATIVE
'Du teurer Gottessohn, nun hast du mir den Himmel aufge-
macht' ('Thou dear God's Son, now Thou hast for me the
heavens opened')
T. Cont

This recitative reiterates the message of St Paul's Epistle.

5 CHORALE
'Heut' schleusst er wieder auf die Tür zum schönen Paradies'
('Today he unlocks again the door to the beautiful Paradise')
SATB. Fl trav, Ob d'am, Vln i, ii, Vla, all with voices, Cont

This is verse viii of the hymn by Nicholas Herman 'Lobt Gott,
ihr Christen alle gleich' (1560) with the melody set by him in
1554 to a secular text.

Epistle: Gal. IV. 1–7 (Christ is sent to redeem those under the law).
Gospel: Luke II. 33–40 (Christ is born for the redemption of Israel).

Tritt auf die Glaubensbahn (Walk in the way of faith).
Solo Cantata BWV 152. Weimar, 1714. Libretto by Salomo Franck.

1 CONCERTO
Fl à bec, Ob, Vla d'am, Vla da gamba, Cont

The libretto comes from Salomo Franck's collection, *The offering of Christian devotion*, published in 1715, and possibly the date of this cantata. It is scored for two solo voices only, without choruses or chorales, following thus the pattern of cantata librettos first adopted by Erdmann Neumeister. Spitta called the cantata 'altogether one of the most remarkable of Bach's productions'. The concerto, in the style of the French overture, begins with an *Adagio* of only four bars 4/4 time, followed by an *Allegro ma non presto* in 3/8 time. This rather long but absolutely enchanting movement trips, rather than walks, happily along 'the way of faith'. The subject has a marked resemblance to that of the composer's more sedate organ fugue in A major (BWV 536).

2 ARIA
'Tritt auf die Glaubensbahn Gott hat den Stein geleget, der Zion hält und träget' ('Walk in the way of faith, God has the stone laid, which holds and carries Zion')
B. Ob, Cont

The words refer to verse 39 of the Gospel and tell of Anna, a prophetess, coming into the temple just after Simeon had uttered his Nunc Dimittis and blessed Mary and Joseph: she speaks of the redemption the child will bring to Israel.

3 RECITATIVE
'Der Heiland ist gesetzt in Israel zum Fall und Auferstehen' ('The Saviour now is set for the fall and rising again [of many] in Israel')
B. Cont

These are Simeon's words to Mary and Joseph after he has blessed them (St Luke II. 34). At 'fall and rise' Bach makes the singer leap down and up an octave. Spitta, shocked by Bach's naïve realism, thought the leaps seemed like a joke in bad taste!

There is a vivid description, also involving a wide compass, of a perverse stumbling into the stone which could lead to 'Hell's dark hole'. The arioso that follows speaks of the rock-like Corner Stone on which faith can build, sure of grace and salvation.

4 ARIA

'Stein, der über alle Schätze, hilf, dass ich zu aller Zeit durch den Glauben auf dich setze meinen Grund der Seligkeit' ('Stone, which is above all treasures, help [me] that I at all times through faith, on Thee may set my hope of blessedness')
S. Fl à bec, Vla d'am, Cont

One of Bach's loveliest arias, and one which should only be sung by a soprano whose tone will stay rock-steady on the long notes Bach gives to 'stone'. The melody has an affinity with the cradle-song in Part 2 of the *Christmas Oratorio* and makes one wonder if Bach here pictures the child, on whom salvation depended, asleep in his mother's arms, tenderly regarded by Joseph and Simeon.

5 RECITATIVE

'Es ärgre sich die kluge Welt, dass Gottes Sohn verlässt den Ehrenthron' ('Let the cunning world be angry, that the Son of God leaves the honour-throne')
B. Cont

There are two Biblical quotations in this recitative. 'I will destroy the wisdom of the wise' (1 Corinthians 1. 19), and 'If the blind guide the blind, both shall fall into a pit'. The continuo, not the voice, depicts these last words (Matt. xv. 14).

6 DUET

S: 'Wie soll ich dich, Liebster der Seelen umfassen' ('How shall I, Beloved of Souls, embrace Thee') B: 'Du musst dich verleugnen und Alles verlassen' ('Thou must thyself renounce and everything leave')
S.B. Fl and Ob (unis.), Cont

This is one of the dialogues between the Soul and Jesus so frequent in the cantata librettos. Spitta considered such duets were not properly church music at all and all the more so when, as here, set in dance rhythm, albeit marked *andante*.

The duet, despite Spitta, makes a delightful conclusion to the cantata.

Das neugebor'ne Kindelein (The newborn child).
Chorale Cantata BWV 122. Leipzig, 1724.

1 CHORUS
'Das neugebor'ne Kindelein, das herzeliebe Jesulein, bringt
abermal ein neues Jahr, der auserwählten Christen Schaar'
('The new-born Child, the dearly-beloved, little-Jesus, brings
once more a New Year to the chosen Christian flock')
SATB. Ob i, ii, with Vln i, ii, Te, with Vla, Cont

The libretto is based on the hymn by Cyriakus Schneegass
(1595). In Nos. 1, 4, and 6, verses i, iii and iv are unaltered. In
Nos. 2 and 3, verse ii is paraphrased. The melody is by Melchior
Vulpius (1609). This joyous chorus has the familiar pattern of
the chorale in the soprano in long notes, with the other parts
moving independently, and each line of the verse followed by a
ritornello.

2 ARIA
'O Menschen, die ihr täglich sündigt' ('Oh men, ye who daily
sin')
B. Cont

The exhortation is made more emphatic by being repeated to
its initial phrase. The text explains why we should be joyful. 'We
mortals, scarred by sin's dark blemish as angels now should
joyous be, for hear how jubilant they tell that God on earth
descends to dwell, so comfort take and care bid vanish.'

3 RECITATIVE
'Die Engel, welche sich zuvor vor euch, als vor Verfluchten,
scheuten, erfüllen nun die Luft im höhern Chor' ('The Angels,
who themselves formerly from you, as from th' accursed shrank,
fill now the air in the high chorus')
S. Fl i, ii, iii, Cont

At the words 'fill now the air', the three flutes begin to play the
melody of the chorale, at a high pitch; it indeed makes an angelic
effect.

4 TERZETT
'Ist Gott versöhnt und unser Freund' ('If God is our Friend and
Helper'). 'Oh wohl uns, die wir an ihn glauben' ('Oh happy we in
God confiding')
A.S.T. Vln i, ii, Vla, (all unis.), Cont

29

The solo alto sings the chorale in the middle part, soprano and tenor the text of the 'Arie'.

The two texts are complementary and the derision directed at Satan who dares to defy God, finds vivid expression in the soprano and tenor parts as the alto reaches the end of the first three lines of the chorale.

5 RECITATIVE

'Dies ist ein Tag, den selbst der Herr gemacht' ('This is the day the Lord himself hath made')
B. Vln i, ii, Vla, Cont

The first line of the text comes from Psalm CXVIII. 24. The libretto continues 'who sent his son all in a manger laid, O blessed time that is now fulfilled.'

6 CHORALE

'Es bringt das rechte Jubeljahr' ('Come, let us hail this happy year')
SATB. Ob. i, ii, Te, Vln i, ii, Vla, all with voices, Cont

A plainly harmonized sixth verse of the chorale.

Gottlob! nun geht das Jahr zu Ende (God be praised! now goes the year to [its] end).

Chorale Cantata BWV 28. Leipzig, 1725. Libretto by Erdmann Neumeister.

I ARIA

(As above)
S. Ob. i, ii, Te, Vln i, ii, Vla, Cont

It falls to the soprano first to give thanks for the year now ended and to greet the new year, bright with promise, that lies ahead. There is a constant alteration between the instrumental groups, oboes and strings, with reflective passages at 'Think, O Soul', thanking God for His goodness in the year past. This is emphasized in a six-fold repetition.

2 CHORUS

'Nun lob, mein Seel, den Herren' ('Now, my Soul, praise the Lord')
SATB. Cornetto, Ob i, ii, Te, Trb i, ii, iii, Vln i, ii, Vla, all with voices, Cont.

The first verse of Johann Graumann's chorale with the above title set to its associated melody (1540) and sung here in long notes by the sopranos. The first line is intoned by the tenors, with a counter-theme for altos and basses, the sopranos only then entering with the melody. At the close, the voices, over a firm pedal note for the instrumental basses and the continuo, proclaim 'The King creates justice and rights the wronged at last'.

3 ARIOSO
'So spricht der Herr' ('Thus saith the Lord')
B. Cont

Anything would come as something of an anticlimax after that great chorus and this *arioso* is no exception, but after the majestic and intricate music just heard its melodiousness falls pleasantly on the ear. The Lord says 'I shall take delight in doing you good. I will surely plant you in this land with all my heart and all my soul'.

4 RECITATIVE
'Gott ist ein Quell' ('God is a spring')
T. Vln i, ii, Vla, Cont

The strings give a sheen to this fine piece of declamation 'God is a spring, a light, a treasure . . . who God has, has all.'

5 DUET
'Gott hat uns im heurigen Jahre gesegnet' ('God has blessed us in the present year')
A.T. Cont

A most attractive duet.

6 CHORALE
'All solch dein Güt wir preisen' ('All such things of Thy goodness we praise')
SATB. As at No. 2

The melody of this chorale of praise and a prayer for peace in the New Year is the sixth verse of Paul Eber's hymn 'Helft mir Gott's Güte preisen' to a melody (1569) of secular origin.

THE CIRCUMCISION OF CHRIST (NEW YEAR'S DAY)

Epistle: Gal. III. 23–29 (We all are one in Christ).
Gospel: Luke II. 21 (His name shall be called Jesus).

Singet dem Herrn ein neues Lied (Sing to the Lord a new song).
Cantata BWV 190. Leipzig, 1724.

1 CHORUS
(As above)
SATB. Tr i, ii, iii, Timp, Ob i, ii, iii, Vln i, ii, Vla, Cont

In the Bach Gesellschaft score the first two numbers of this cantata present a strange appearance; the voice parts are there, and the parts for first and second violins, but the staves ruled for the other parts, as noted above, are blank.

The reason for this is, of course, that Bach left the autograph score incomplete, but the performance of the cantata was made possible by the reconstruction of the missing parts by W. Reinhardt in 1948. The actual scoring he adopts for No. 1 is not merely conjecture but based on Bach's constant practice of using the same instruments for concluding chorale as for opening chorus. The cantata, revised for the Augsburg Confession Jubilee (25 June 1730), has a libretto by Picander. If he was also the author of the present libretto it would be the earliest example of his collaboration with Bach. The verse of Psalm CXLIX provides the text for the first four entries of the chorus. The composer makes a delightful use of a little dotted semiquaver figure at the ends of the chordal phrases. The next line is from Psalm CL, 'Praise him with the timbrel and dance: Praise him with stringed instruments and the pipe'. Luther's version of the plainsong hymn 'Te Deum laudamus', is sung in octaves to the words 'Herr Gott, dich loben wir' ('Lord God, Thee do we praise'). This is enormously effective. The words of the second fugal section come from Psalm CL. 6, 'Let everything that hath breath praise the Lord', to which Bach (or his librettist) adds 'Alleluia'.

2 CHORALE
'Herr Gott, dich loben wir. Herr Gott, wir danken dir' ('Lord God, we give Thee praise, Lord God we thank Thee')
SATB. As at No. 1

32

The chorale melody consists only of the first two lines, as above, of Luther's version of the 'Te Deum' as in No. 1, but here punctuated with three passages of recitative for solo B.T.A. reflecting, as in Cantata BWV 28, on present blessings, New Year's Day, and favours to come for the preservation of 'our fair and dear' in the past year, and a final heartfelt expression of love, praise and thanks which leads into 'Herr Gott, wir danken dir'.

3 ARIA
'Lobe, Zion, deinen Gott' ('Praise, O Zion, praise Thy God!')
A. Vln i, ii, Vla, Cont

A straightforward aria without any special points of interest.

4 RECITATIVE
'Es wünsche sich die Welt, was Fleisch und Blut wohlgefällt' ('Let wish to itself the world, what flesh and blood well pleases')
B. Cont

The text goes on to beg the Lord that Jesus 'my joy, my faithful shepherd, my comfort and salvation and my soul's best part' may embrace and protect his 'lambkin'. A short arioso, with a firm bass in the continuo, asks for guidance to tread on an even path, 'So begin I in Jesu's name.'

5 DUET
'Jesus soll mein Alles sein, Jesus soll mein Anfang bleiben, Jesus ist mein Freudenschein' ('Jesus shall my all be, Jesus shall my beginning remain, Jesus is my joy light')
T.B. Ob d'am, Cont

The lovely melody for the oboe d'amore, heard six times in the course of the duet, is independent of the voices except for an allusion to its opening phrase at the first entry of the soloists. It is a perfect reflection of the tender sentiment of the words of the vocal parts in the first section, and of those of the second section, 'Jesus helps me through his blood . . . Jesus makes my end good'; but here the remembrance of the Passion clouds the music over until the last line. The gradual rise of the semiquavers, characteristic of all Bach's melodies, is very beautiful.

6 RECITATIVE
'Nun, Jesus gebe, dass mit dem neuen Jahr auch sein Gesalbter lebe' ('Now, Jesus grant, that with the New Year also His anointed may live')
T. Vln i, ii, Vla, Cont

D   33

The vocal part is formal and does not merit the sustained strings parts that halo it.

7 CHORALE

'Lass uns das Jahr vollbringen zu Lob dem Namen dein' ('Let us the year fulfil in the praise of Thy name')
SATB. As No. 1

The harmonization is plain and the trumpets are here confined to flourishes at various places. The remaining instruments double the voice parts.

Jesu, nun sei gepreiset (Jesu, now let us praise Thee).
Chorale Cantata BWV 41. Leipzig, 1725.

1 CHORUS

(As above)
SATB. Tr i, ii, iii, Timp, Ob i, ii, iii, Vln i, ii, Vla, Org and Cont

A tremendous chorus which begins with a fanfare for the three trumpets, a leaping figure for the upper strings and downward scales for the continuo. Two of the trumpets then have a joyous motif in thirds. This pattern is repeated four times between the lines of the chorale. At the ninth line 'that we in prosperous peace the old year have ended' there comes an unexpected and lovely *adagio*, a simple harmonization of the chorale accompanied only by violins and violas, and then a quick fugue, begun by the tenors and taken up by the other voices except the sopranos who enter at intervals with the melody of J. Herman's hymn (1591), verse i.

2 ARIA

'Lass uns, o höchster Gott, das Jahr vollbringen, damit das Ende so, wie dessen Anfang sei' ('Let us, oh Highest God, the year complete, that the end so, as its beginning may be')
S. Ob i, ii, iii, Org and Cont

This is one of Bach's enchanting pastoral movements in 6/8 time with the melody played by the three oboes in the introductory fifteen bars. A little rise of a fifth is its characteristic feature and is given particular charm when the soprano comes in with the melody.

In the middle section, related melodically to the first, the singer gives thanks for abundance of blessings, and has an ascending 'Hallelujah' which in the next section descends, but rises once more at the close before the *da capo*—a delightful example of Bach's musical logic.

3 RECITATIVE
'Herr, deine Hand, dein Segen muss allein das A und O, der Anfang und das Ende sein' ('Lord! Thine hand, Thy blessing must the A and O [Alpha and Omega] the beginning and end be')
A. Org and Cont

The text concludes with the acceptance of suffering or well-being as God wills.

4 ARIA
'Woferne du den edlen Frieden für unsern Leib und Stand beschieden, so lass der Seele doch dein selig machend Wort' ('So far as Thou the noble peace for our bodies and position hast allotted, so allow to the soul yet Thy blessed-making word')
T. V'cello picc solo, Org and Cont

Bach used the violoncello piccolo in nine cantatas only. It was a five-stringed instrument useful for its agility in the middle and upper compass at a time when ordinary violoncellists had not acquired the necessary technique to be secure in the upper range. The obbligato part, with leaps from string to string, and, in the first part of the aria, cascades of demisemiquavers down the scale, is the most attractive feature of this not very interesting aria.

5 RECITATIVE AND INTONATION
'Doch weil der Feind' ('What though the foe')
B. and SATB. Org and Cont

This recitative brings on to the scene Satan who night and day lies in watch for the unwary. The bass asks God for help when souls are in danger and the chorus reply with an intonation for the Lutheran plainsong litany, harmonized in emphatic chords, 'Satan under our feet tread'. Then the solo bass resumes his recitative ending with a prayer 'after suffering and sorrow we can depart hence to glory'.

6 CHORALE
'Dein ist allein die Ehre' ('Thine is alone the glory')
As at No. 1 but Tr i, ii, iii, Timp, Obb.

The sixth and last verse of the hymn in which the obbligato instruments play the fanfare motif of the instrumental prelude to No. 1.

35

Herr Gott, dich loben wir (Lord God, we do praise Thee).
Chorale Cantata BWV 16. Leipzig, 1726.

1 CHORUS
(As above)
SATB. Ob i, ii, with Vln i, ii, Vla, Cor da cacc with S. Cont

The first four lines of Luther's verse translation of the Te Deum set to his free version of the plainsong melody (as in Cantata BWV 190) are sung by the sopranos; basses, tenors and altos enter in close imitation. It is a lively chorus but, as we shall see, something more distinctive is to come in No. 3.

2 RECITATIVE
'So stimmen wir bei dieser frohen Zeit mit heisser Andacht' ('So sing we in this glad time with warm devotion')
B. Cont

A routine *secco* recitative.

3 CHORUS AND ARIOSO
'Lasst uns jauchzen, lasst uns freuen: Gottes Güt und Treu bleibet alle Morgen neu' ('Let us exult, let us rejoice, God's goodness and faithfulness remains every morning new')
SATB. and B. As at No. 1

The basses begin with a rousing fanfare phrase in which all join. In a short ritornello before the repetition of the words, violins i add two phrases of what one might call whoops of joy! These are later woven into the independent orchestral part. The middle section is the solo bass arioso—'Krönt und segnet seine Hand, ach so glaubt, dass unser Stand ewig glücklich sei' ('Crowns and blesses His hand, ah, so believe that our state eternally fortunate is').

4 RECITATIVE
'Ach treuer Hort, beschütz auch ferner hin dein wertes Wort' ('Ah! faithful refuge, protect even further Thy worthy word')
A. Cont

The prayer asks for church and school also to be protected, Satan's cunning disturbed, for peace and rest, water for the improvement of the land, and concludes 'Well for us, when we Thee ever and ever, my Jesus and Salvation, trust'.

In contrast with the perfunctory declamation of No. 2, this recitative has obviously engaged Bach's close attention.

5 ARIA
'Geliebter Jesu, du allein sollst meiner Seelen Reichtum sein'
('Beloved Jesus, Thou alone shalt my soul's wealth be')
T. Ob da cacc or Violetta, Cont

This aria has neither the tender beauty nor the fervour of its
counterpart in Cantata BWV 190.

6 CHORALE
'All solch dein Güt wir preisen, Vater in's Himmels Thron' ('All
such Thy goodness we praise, Father on Heaven's throne')
SATB. As at No. 1, all with voices. Cont

This is a plain harmonization of the sixth verse of Paul Eber's
hymn 'Helft mir Gott's Güte preisen' (1580) to its associated
melody (1569).

Gott, wie dein Name, so ist auch dein Ruhm (According
to Thy name, O God, so is also Thy praise).
Cantata BWV 171. 1729. Libretto by Picander.

1 CHORUS
(As above)
SATB. Tr i, ii, iii, Timp, Ob i, ii, Vln i, ii, Vla, Cont

The text is v. 10 of Psalm XLVIII. Bach adapted this fugal movement with the same orchestration but elaborated vocal parts for
'Patrem omnipotentem' of the B Minor Mass.

2 ARIA
'Herr, so weit die Wolken gehen, gehet deines Namens Ruhm'
('Lord, as far as the clouds go, so goes Thy name's renown')
T. Vln i, ii, Cont

The particular charm of this aria lies in the way the violins,
in the introduction, intertwine as they gradually rise and fall as
if in illustration, as Schweitzer suggests, of white clouds sailing in
the sky.

3 RECITATIVE
'Du süsser Jesus-Name du, in dir ist meine Ruh' ('Thou sweet
Jesus-Name Thou, in Thee is my rest')
A. Cont

A typical decorative figure on 'sweet'. The text speaks of
absolute confidence in the Saviour and ends '[Thee] my Gift for
the New Year'.

4 ARIA

'Jesus soll mein erstes Wort in dem neuen Jahre heissen' ('Jesus shall my first word in the New Year be')

S. Vln Solo, Cont

The music of this aria is not, however, Bach's 'first word', but an adaptation of the soprano aria beginning 'Angenehmer Zephyrus' ('Pleasant Zephyr') from the secular cantata 'Der zufriedengestellte Aeolus' ('The pacified Aeolus') performed in 1725 for the birthday of August Friedrich Müller, one of the professors at Leipzig University, and reproduced, with a remodelled libretto, in 1734 in honour of the Coronation of Augustus III, as King of Poland. The enchanting rising and falling phrases of the solo violin obbligato depict the 'pleasant Zephyr'. It is in the last section of the aria as adapted, repeating the opening words, that the semiquaver runs to 'Jesus' and 'year', seem misplaced. One can only guess that it was the lovely violin obbligato that led Bach to adapt the secular aria, deciding that the name of Jesus was like 'a refreshing Zephyr' to the soul.

5 RECITATIVE

'Und da du, Herr, gesagt, bittet in meinen Namen, so ist alles Ja, und Amen' ('And as Thou, Lord, [hast] said "Ask [only] in my name so is all Yea and Amen"'

B. Ob i, ii, Cont

The opening words are in recitative, the quotation from St John (XIV. 14) is an arioso. The oboes come in with the rest of the text which prays for protection from pestilence, fire and war, for wise ruling and the prosperity of the Church. Then, in another arioso the bass invokes the name of the Lord to grant this boon, ending with three 'Amens', the last one on long notes.

6 CHORALE

'Dein ist allein die Ehre' ('Thine is alone the honour')

SATB. Ob i, ii, Vln i, ii, iii and Vla, all with voices; Tr i, ii, iii, Timp, Cont

This is the third verse of Johann Heermann's 'Jesu, nun sei gepreiset' (1591), the same setting that Bach used to conclude Cantata BWV 41 and with the same fanfares for trumpets punctuating the lines, but the whole movement here raised a tone.

Lobe den Herrn, meine Seele (Praise the Lord, O my soul).
Cantata BWV 143. Leipzig.

1 CHORUS
(As above)
SATB. Cor da cacc i, ii, iii, Timp, Fag, Vln i, ii, Vla, Cont

In this notably concise cantata the libretto, possibly by Bach, makes three quotations from Psalm CXLVI of which the title, verse 1, is the first. Six festive introductory bars lead to the joyous outburst of the chorus, from sopranos to basses, on the word 'Praise', effectively followed by the same word sung to two sustained chords and 'the Lord' to detached chords, and finally to a combination of both underlined by fanfares from the horns and bassoons. This is the only known instance of Bach's use of three 'hunting horns' in a score, and in this chorus they alone, with the timpani, play the concluding cadence. This is a most brilliant little movement.

2 CHORALE
'Du Friedefürst, Herr Jesu Christ, wahr'r Mensch und wahrer Gott' ('Thou Prince of Peace, Lord Jesus Christ, true man and true God')
S. Vlns, Cont

The first verse of Jakob Ebert's chorale with the above title and the melody by Bartholomäus Gesius (1601). Bach places the melody in a lovely setting of rising figures for the violins.

3 RECITATIVE
'Wohl dem, des Hilfe der Gott Jakobs ist' ('Well for him, whose help the God of Jacob is')
T. Cont

Verse 5 of Psalm CXLVI.

4 ARIA
'Tausendfaches Unglück, Schrecken, Trübsal, Angst und schneller Tod' ('Thousandfold misfortune, horror, trouble, anxiety and sudden death')
T. Vln i, ii, Vla, Cont and Fag

This, the first of three arias in succession, is a direful description, painted by the tenor, of nations who are not experiencing the 'blessings-year' spoken of in the second section of the aria. The layout is interesting. The triplet theme played almost throughout by violins i represents the nations who put their

39

trust in the God of Jacob, the detached notes for the lower strings and continuo the disturbed state of those who do not.

5 ARIA

'Der Herr ist König ewiglich, dein Gott, Zion, für und für' ('The Lord is King everlastingly, thy God, Zion, for ever and ever')

B. Cor da caccia i, ii, iii, Timp, Fag, Cont

Brass, drums, bassoon and continuo herald the great proclamation of verse 10 of Psalm CXLVI, but without the 'Halleluia', which Bach holds in reserve for the final chorus.

The brief aria is a splendid piece of declamation with majestic phrases at 'everlastingly' and a most dramatic accompaniment ending with a two-bar trill for horns i and ii.

6 ARIA

'Jesus, Retter deiner Heerde, bleibe ferner unser Hort' ('Jesu, Saviour of Thy flock, remain still our refuge')

T. Fag, Vln i, ii, Vla, Cont

The bassoon and continuo in duet, one imitating the descending semiquaver groups of the other, enfold the voice part in this tender aria in which the strings play the melody of No. 2.

7 CHORALE

'Hallelujah! Gedenk, Herr Jesu, an dein Amt, dass du ein Friedfürst bist' ('Hallelujah! Bethink, Lord Jesu, on thy ministry, that thou a Prince of Peace art')

SATB. As No. 1

Bach begins the chorus with the 'Hallelujah' he kept back from verse 10 of Psalm CXLVI, and as the three lower voices continue to sing it the sopranos come in with the chorale melody in long notes.

SUNDAY AFTER THE CIRCUMCISION

Epistle: Titus II. 11–14 (Salvation hath appeared to all men) or
Titus III. 4–7 (Justified by grace, we are heirs of eternal life).
Gospel: Matt. II. 13–15 (The flight into Egypt) or
Matt. III. 13–17 (Jesus baptized by John).

**Schau, lieber Gott, wie meine Feind; damit ich stets
muss kämpfen** (Behold, dear God, how enemies with
whom I must continually do battle).
Solo Cantata BWV 153. Leipzig, 1724.

1 CHORALE
(As above)
SATB. Vln i, ii, and Vla, with voices, Cont

In this cantata Nos. 1, 5 and 9 are plainly harmonized chorales
that were evidently planned for congregational participation.
The libretto, as in Cantata BWV 58 for this Sunday, centres on
St Matthew's account of the flight of the Holy Family into
Egypt, which is mentioned in No. 7, and applied there and all
through to the Christian soul grievously attacked by its enemies.

This first verse of David Denicke's hymn (1646) is sung to the
melody of Luther's hymn 'Ach Gott, vom Himmel sieh darein',
commonly associated with it.

2 RECITATIVE
'Mein liebster Gott, ach lass dich's erbarmen' ('My dearest God,
ah let Thee on it take pity')
A. Cont

A cry for help, in broken phrases, for one beset 'by raging lions
and dragons'.

3 ARIA
'Fürchte dich nicht, ich bin mit dir' ('Fear not, I am with thee')
B. Cont

The words of the first section of this aria come from Isaiah XLI
and are very familiar to us in the chorus 'Be not afraid' from
Mendelssohn's *Elijah*, and in Bach's splendid motet BWV 228.
They are set simply, but with subtle inflexions, in this brief aria.

THE CHURCH CANTATAS OF J. S. BACH

4 RECITATIVE
'Du sprichst zwar, lieber Gott, zu meiner Seelen Ruh, mir einen
Trost in meinem Leiden zu' ('Thou speakest even, dear God, for
my soul's rest to me a comfort in my sorrow')
T. Cont

The soul is, however, not long consoled, but breaks out in
anguish against its enemies who shoot at it with bows and arrows.
An arioso follows 'I shall die at their hands'. 'Die' is set to tortured
vocal intervals and dissonant harmonies in the continuo. The
movement ends with another and even more despairing arioso
'Help, Helper, help, save my soul', in which the voice rises an
octave to a high-pitched phrase at 'soul'.

5 CHORALE
'Und obgleich alle Teufel dir wollten widerstehn' ('And although
all devils Thee would withstand')
SATB. As No. 1

This is verse 5 of one of the best-known and loved of all chorales,
Paul Gerhardt's 'Befiehl du deine Wege' (1653), with its associated
melody by Hans Leo Hassler.

6 ARIA
'Stürmt nur, stürmt, ihr Trübsalswetter' ('Storm only, storm, ye
trouble-tempest')
T. Vln i, ii, Vla, Cont

The mood changes again to defiance. The score of the aria is
black with semi- and demisemiquavers in both voice and instrumental parts.

7 RECITATIVE
'Getrost, mein Herz, erdulde deinen Schmerz, lass dich dein
Kreuz nicht unterdrücken' ('Be comforted, my heart, bear thy
pain, let thee thy Cross not weigh down')
B. Cont

The following sentences draw attention to the much greater
affliction the child Jesus must undergo and even now He is
threatened with death by the tyrant Herod. Already He must
become a fugitive. Then comes a consoling arioso, 'Those who
with Christ suffer, will He the heavenly Kingdom award.'

8 ARIA
'Soll ich meinen Lebenslauf unter Kreuz und Trübsal führen,

hört es doch im Himmel auf' ('Shall I my life's path under Cross
and trouble lead, ceases it yet in Heaven')
A. Vln i, ii, Vla, Cont

After all the conflicting moods we have experienced this beautiful aria falls like balm upon the ear. The melody of the first
section is heart-easing indeed. It has the flavour of a popular song.

9 CHORALE
'Drum will ich, weil ich lebe noch, das Kreuz dir fröhlich tragen
nach' ('Therefore will I, because I live still, the Cross Thee
joyfully bear after')
SATB. As No. 1

The hymn is verses xvi–xviii of Martin Moller's 'Ach Gott,
wie manches Herzeleid' (1587) with its anonymous melody. We
shall meet it again in the following cantata.

Ach Gott, wie manches Herzeleid (Ah God, how many a heart-pang).
Solo Cantata BWV 58. Leipzig, 1727.

This is Bach's second composition with this title, the other (BWV
3) is a chorale cantata for the second Sunday after Epiphany. He
described the present one on the autograph score as 'Concerto in
Dialogo': the two participants represent two states of the soul, one
troubled (soprano) the other encouraging (bass). The hymn is the
one mentioned above.

1 DUET
S: (As above)
B: 'Nur Geduld, Geduld, mein Herze, es ist eine böse Zeit! Doch
der Gang zur Seligkeit, führt zur Freude nach dem Schmerze'
('Only patience, my heart, it is an evil time, but the way to
blessedness leads to the joy after the pain')
S.B. Ob i, ii, Te, Vln i, ii, Vla, Cont

The soprano sings verse 1 and associated melody of Martin
Moller's hymn in single lines, punctuated by the bass's comforting
words. Bach maintains dotted rhythm figures in the orchestra
throughout. The bass's words are inspired by the Epistle (Titus
III. 4–7) for the day which embodies the Lutheran doctrine,
'justification by faith'.

2 RECITATIVE

'Verfolgt dich gleich die arge Welt, so hast du dennoch Gott zum Freunde' ('Persecutes thee even now the evil world, so hast thou nevertheless God as friend')

B. Cont

The recitative goes on to speak of Herod's rage and the angel who appeared to warn the dreaming Joseph to flee to Egypt and ends with a quotation from Isaiah LIV. 10 'If mountain and hill down sink, if thou in waterfloods wilt drown, so will I thee not leave, nor delay'. It is a fine example of declamation and bold harmonization.

3 ARIA

'Ich bin vergnügt in meinem Leiden, denn Gott ist meine Zuversicht' ('I am content in my sorrow for God is my confidence')

S. Vln solo, Cont

A flowing melody, especially eloquent in the violin solo part.

4 RECITATIVE

'Kann es die Welt nicht lassen, mich zu verfolgen und zu hassen' ('Can the world not cease me to persecute and to hate')

S. Cont

God points to another land. 'Ah, might it even happen today, that I my Eden might see.' These last words are an arioso, with eager little rushes of semiquavers for the voice over the quiet, confident continuo bass.

5 DUET

S: 'Ich hab' vor mir ein' schwere Reis'' ('I have before me a heavy journey') B: 'Nur getrost, getrost, ihr Herzen, hier ist Angst, dort Herrlichkeit' ('Courage, ye hearts! here is anguish, there glory')

S.B. Ob i, ii, Te, Vln i, ii, Vla, Cont

The soprano sings verse ii of Martin Behm's hymn 'O Jesu Christ, mein's Lebens Licht' (1610) set to its associated melody (1625) while the bass has a fine C major melody with exhilarating runs on 'glory'.

EPIPHANY

Epistle: Isa. LX. 1–16 (The Gentiles shall come to Thy light).
Gospel: Matt. II. 1–12 (The Wise Men seek Christ).

Sie werden aus Saba alle kommen (They will from Sheba all come).
Cantata BWV 65. Leipzig, 1724.

1 CHORUS
(As above)
SATB. Cor i, ii, Fl i, ii, Ob da cacc i, ii, Vln i, ii, Vla, Cont

The Leipzig liturgy called Epiphany 'The Feast of the Three Holy Kings' and it is nice to think that tribute is thus paid to the charming legend of Balthazar, Melchior and Caspar kneeling down one after the other and presenting their gifts of gold, frankincense and myrrh. The text of the opening chorus, 'They will from Sheba come forth, gold and incense bringing and the Lord's praise proclaim', comes from the Epistle. The two horns in the first bar announce the march-like theme, which is at once taken up by the flutes and violins, in unison, over three octaves —a device unusual with Bach—after which the horns develop the theme. One pictures the great caravan of camels with the kings and their attendants passing across the desert. In the bar before the chorus enter with the theme, in succession of bass to treble, the orchestra again plays the theme. The basses begin a stately fugue in the next section at 'Gold and incense bringing' with a new version of the opening theme as counter-subject. At the end the *whole* of the forces join in the great octave passage noted above.

2 CHORALE
'Die Kön'ge aus Saba kamen dar' ('The Kings from Sheba came there')
SATB. Fl i, ii (unis.), Ob da cacc i, ii, Cont

This is the third verse of the traditional melody to 'Ein Kind geborn zu Bethlehem' (1543) which is found in Catholic and Lutheran hymnals with both Latin and German texts.

3 RECITATIVE
'Was dort Jesaias vorhergesehn das ist zu Bethlehem geschehn' ('What there Isaiah foresaw, that has at Bethlehem happened')
B. Cont

45

The recitative describes the arrival of the Wise Men, lit by the star, at the manger and the presentation of their offerings to the newborn child, ending, 'What can I bring to Thee . . . my heart's not worthy to be given—yet take it graciously, 'tis the most precious part of me'.

4 ARIA
'Gold aus Ophir ist zu schlecht, weg nur weg mit eitlen Gaben' ('Gold of Ophir is too base, away, only away with vain gifts')
B. Ob da cacc i, ii, Cont

There are long runs for the bass on 'Gaben' as if the gifts are to be despised, as explained below. The ritornello, after this, is a triple canon between the oboes and continuo obviously in illustration of the gold, incense and myrrh. 'Away, only away with vain gifts, which ye from the earth break.' Jesus wishes to have the heart: 'Give this O Christian flock to Jesus at the New Year.' This is a most ingeniously devised aria and worth a closer examination than can be given here.

5 RECITATIVE
'Verschmähe nicht, du, meiner Seelen Licht, mein Herz, dass ich in Demuth zu dir bringe' ('Disdain not, Thou, my soul's light, my heart that I bring in humility to Thee')
T. Cont

The tenor interprets the gifts as 'Faith's gold, incense of prayer, myrrh of patience' and ends, 'give but Thyself also'.

6 ARIA
'Nimm mich dir zu eigen hin' ('Take me to Thyself as Thine own')
T. Cor i, ii, Fl i, ii, Ob da cacc i, ii, Vln i, ii, Vla, Cont

The rich scoring of this aria depicts 'the wealth's abundance' spoken of in the recitative. At the end of the introduction on a full close the tenor comes in with only the continuo accompanying his first line, giving it a most touching appeal. The melody is one of Bach's loveliest, full of tender fervour. In the middle section at 'All that I am, what I say, do, think, shall to my Saviour be only dedicated'. There are enchanting upward runs for flutes, violins, followed by joyous thirds for flutes and oboes.

7 CHORALE
'Ei nun, mein Gott, so fall ich dir, getrost in deine Hände' ('Yea, now my God, so fall I to Thee, comforted into Thy hands')
SATB. Cont. Instrumentation not stated

This is verse x of Paul Gerhardt's, 'Ich hab in Gottes Herz und Sinn' (1647) set to a secular French melody (1529). Bach did not indicate the scoring for this chorale.

Liebster Immanuel, Herzog der Frommen (Beloved Emmanuel, Lord of the righteous).
Chorale Cantata BWV 123. Leipzig, 1725.

The libretto of this cantata is based on Ahasuerus Fritsch's hymn with the above title (1679). The melody in Nos. i and vi is derived from the *courante*, a French dance measure in triple time. The hymn, and so the libretto, has no connexion with the Gospel and Epistle of the Feast or with any of the hymns sung at it.

1 CHORUS
(As above)
SATB. Fl trav i, ii, Ob d'am i, ii, Vln i, ii, Vla, Cont

The words of verse i speak of Emmanuel as our Salvation's hope. 'Thou knowst my heart is wholly Thine . . . Farewell earth's treasures and trivial pleasures. The day comes when Jesus will appear.'

The construction of the chorus is original. The eleven lines of the chorale are divided into the order of 4-3-4, with ritornelli in between each. The prevailing theme, based on the melody of the first bars of the chorale to 'Liebster Immanuel', is at once heard on the oboe d'amore, then on the flutes and in the continuo. Bach dwells lovingly on this theme throughout, both in the voice parts and the ritornelli. The movement, with its beautiful dance-like accompaniment, makes an intimate and tender meditation on the 'beloved Emmanuel'.

2 RECITATIVE
'Die Himmelssüssigkeit, der Auserwählten Lust' ('The heaven's sweetness, the elects' desire')
A. Cont

A recitative expressive of the joy at pronouncing the name of Jesus which releases pain and sorrow from the heart.

3 ARIA
'Auch die harte Kreuzesreise und der Tränen bitt're Speise

47

schreckt mich nicht' ('Even the hard cross-journey and the tears' bitter food affright me not')
T. Ob d'am i, ii, Cont

The last words of the recitative above prepare one for the abrupt change in mood of the aria. Bach's vocal line at 'affright me not' contradicts the sense of the words. 'The wanderer is afraid despite his protestations.' The word 'cross' in the opening line is always placed on a high note, as also is 'tears'. The tempo then changes from *lento* to *allegro*, 'when the storms rage', and rage they do in a flurry of demisemiquavers in the voice part, but give place, with another change of tempo to *adagio*, to the peace and light Jesus sends.

4 RECITATIVE
'Kein Höllenfeind kann mich verschlingen, das schreiende Gewissen schweigt' ('No hell-foe can me devour, my crying conscience is silent')
B. Cont

'Victory is certain for Jesus is my friend, my helper.'

5 ARIA
'Lass', o Welt, mich aus Verachtung in betrübter Einsamkeit' ('Leave me, O world, out of contempt in troubled loneliness')
B. Fl trav, Cont

The drop of a seventh (B above the stave to C natural below) in this D major aria is explained when the bass sings it at 'contempt'. There is a moving bar at the end of the section where the bass sings of his loneliness.

The words of the middle section are 'Jesus, who in the flesh has come and my offering has accepted remains with me always'. These words are accompanied by the continuo only and 'remains' is set to a run that goes up to the *da capo*, which, of course, brings back the soul's misery!

6 CHORALE
'Drum fahrt nur immer hin, ihr Eitelkeiten! Du, Jesu, du bist mein und ich bin dein' ('Therefore go now away, ye vanities! Thou, Jesus, Thou art mine, and I am thine')
SATB. As No. 1 but with voices, Cont

Bach directs that the last lines of the hymn (v. iii) be sung a second time *piano*, a unique procedure, and so it ends quietly, 'My whole life be to Thee surrendered, till they sometime lay me in the grave.'

48

FIRST SUNDAY AFTER EPIPHANY

Epistle: Rom. xii. 1–6 (We are at one in Christ).
Gospel: Luke ii. 41–52 (Jesus in the temple).

Mein liebster Jesus ist verloren, o Wort das mir Verzweiflung bringt (My dearest Jesus is lost, O Word that brings despair to me).
Cantata BWV 154. Leipzig, 1724.

1 ARIA
(As above)
T. Vln i, ii, Vla, Cont

The libretto naturally centres on the finding of the child Jesus in the Temple and His reply (quoted in No. 5) to the reproaches of His mother, and applies the incident to the individual soul. The impassioned tenor solo, in this wonderful aria, expresses the anguish at being bereft of Jesus. It reaches a dramatic climax at 'O sword that through the soul pierces'—this recalls Simeon's prophecy to Mary, 'a sword shall pierce through thine own soul' (St Luke ii. 35)—'O thunder-word in my ears'. The arpeggio that separates the two sentences foreshadows the 'sword' motif in Wagner's *Ring*, and the rapid chords for the strings, marked *piano*, under the sustained note for the voice on the first syllable of 'Ohren' ('ears') depict the symbolical thunder.

2 RECITATIVE
'Wo treff ich meinen Jesum an, wer zeiget mir die Bahn' ('Where shall I find my Jesus, who will show me the road')
T. Cont

3 CHORALE
'Jesu, mein Hort und Erretter, Jesu, meine Zuversicht' ('Jesus my refuge and rescuer, Jesus my confidence')
SATB. Ob i, ii, Vln i, ii and Vla, all with voices, Cont

A straightforward harmonization of the second verse of Martin Jahn's 'Jesu, meiner Seelen Wonne' (1661) set to Johann Schop's 'Werde munter, mein Gemüte' (1642).

4 ARIA
'Jesu, lass dich finden, lass doch meine Sünden keine dicke

E

49

Wolken sein' ('Jesus, let me find Thee, let my sins not be as thick clouds')
A. Ob d'am i, ii; Vln i, ii, Vla, all unis; Cembalo

Bach did not provide parts for bass strings in this aria but specified the harpsichord (or organ) doubling the upper string parts an octave below. He repeats the opening words, 'Jesus let me find Thee', at the beginning of each clause of this most touching aria.

5 ARIOSO
'Wisset ihr nicht, dass ich sein muss in dem, das meines Vaters ist?' ('Know'st thou not, I must be about my Father's business?')
B. Cont

It would be pedantic to have expected Bach to give these words, spoken by a child of twelve, to a soprano. The setting, with a good deal of repetition of the text, conveys the authority with which Jesus spoke to the teachers in the Temple.

6 RECITATIVE
'Dies ist die Stimme meines Freundes, Gott Lob und Dank' ('This is the voice of my Friend, to God be praise and thanks')
T. Cont

A lengthy text which ends with a reference to the Real Presence of Jesus in the Sacrament of the Bread and Wine.

7 DUET
'Wohl mir, Jesus ist gefunden, nun bin ich nicht mehr betrübt' ('Well for me, Jesus is found, now I am no more troubled')
A.T. Instrumentation not stated, but presumed to have used all the available forces

This is an entrancing duet, more delightful even than the later one in No. 5 of Cantata BWV 32 (p. 54) which has a similar text. A very interesting point is that Bach uses precisely the same phrases in the first part of the duet as in the later No. 5, where they become the main motif. In the second half at 'I will never more leave Jesus'—which, in quickened tempo forms a coda— there is a lovely chain of sequences like those in the 'Gloria' of the old French carol, 'Les anges dans nos campagnes' used for J. Montgomery's well-known Epiphany hymn, 'Angels from the realms of glory' (1816).

8 CHORALE

'Meinen Jesum lass ich nicht, geh mit ihm ewig an der Seiten'
('My Jesus, I do not leave, I go with Him ever by His side')
SATB. As No. 3

The sixth verse of Christian Keimann's hymn with the above
title (1658) set to the melody published with it.

Meinen Jesum lass ich nicht (My Jesus leave I not).
Chorale Cantata BWV 124. Leipzig, 1725.

Cantata 154 ended with the sixth verse of Christian Keimann's
'Meinen Jesum lass ich nicht' and the present cantata ends with
that verse and begins with verse i. The other verses are paraphrased
in the remaining movements. In BWV 154 sorrow turned into
joy with the finding of Jesus in the temple and now joy and trust,
except for a momentary clouding over in No. 4, are the dominant
themes.

1 CHORUS

'Meinen Jesum lass ich nicht, weil er sich für mich gegeben, so
erfordert meine Pflicht, klettenweis' an ihm zu kleben' ('My Jesus,
leave I not, because He Himself for me [hath] given, so requires
my duty, burr-like to Him to cling')
SATB. Vln i, ii, Vla, Cor with S. Ob d'am concertante, Cont

The elaborate part for the oboe d'amore accounts for Bach
marking its part 'concertante'. It often plays with the rest of the
orchestra but its many semiquaver runs are never shared by them.
The chorale is sung by the sopranos, with simple independent parts
for the other voices.

This is a most appealing movement.

2 RECITATIVE

'So lange sich ein Tropfen Blut in Herz und Adern reget soll Jesus
nur allein mein Leben und mein Alles sein' ('So long as a drop of
blood in my heart and veins stirs, shall Jesus only alone my life
and my all be')
T. Cont

3 ARIA

'Und wenn der harte Todesschlag die Sinnen schwächt, die Glieder
rühret, wenn der dem Fleisch verhasste Tag nur Furcht und
Schrecken mit sich führet, doch tröstet mich die Zuversicht; ich

lasse meinen Jesum nicht' ('And when the hard death-stroke the senses weakens, the limbs touches, when the by-the-flesh-hated day only brings fear and shrinking, yet confidence comforts me; I leave my Jesus not')
T. Ob d'am, Vln i, ii, Vla, Cont

'Trembling' semiquaver figures on the strings illustrate 'the hard death-stroke', etc., and a most expressive melody on the oboe d'amore expresses love for Jesus in this lovely aria.

4 RECITATIVE
'Doch, ach! welch schweres Ungemach empfindet noch allhier die Seele?' ('Then, ah! what heavy calamity experiences yet here the soul?')
B. Cont

Here is the familiar note of woe, but it is not maintained for the words then turn to where faith and hope shine, to the meeting with Jesus after 'the complete course is run'. Bach illustrates that event in an upward rush of semiquavers for the voice.

5 DUET
'Entziehe dich eilends, mein Herze, der Welt, du findest im Himmel dein wahres Vergnügen' ('Retire thee quickly, my heart, from the world, thou findest in heaven thy true delight')
S.A. Cont

Joy is unconfined in this duet. It is at once sounded in the continuo part, with its upward leaps of tenths. Just before the soprano comes in Bach puts *piano* and then *forte* in all the continuo ritornellos, but *piano* each time the voices come in. He evidently wants the expressions of joy to be of a more interior character.

6 CHORALE
'Jesum lass ich nicht von mir, geh ihm ewig an der Seiten' ('My Jesus leave I not, go with Him ever by His side')
SATB. As at No. 1, Insts. with voices, Cont

Liebster Jesu, mein Verlangen (Beloved Jesus, my desire).
Solo Cantata BWV 32. Leipzig, 1726.

The autograph score is inscribed 'Dialogus', a dialogue between Jesus and the Soul and not, as one might expect, Mary and Joseph. The libretto is possibly by Picander.

1 ARIA

'Liebster Jesu, mein Verlangen, sage mir, wo find ich dich? Soll ich dich so bald verlieren, und nicht ferner bei mir führen?' ('Blessed Jesus, my desire, tell me, where find I Thee? Shall I Thee so soon lose and no farther with me lead?')
S. Ob, Vln i, ii, Vla, Cont

The oboe begins with the phrase sung by the soprano to 'Liebster Jesu' and thereafter is most of the time in duet with the voice. The lovely music has none of the anguish of the opening aria in Cantata BWV 154. This is no dark night of the soul but a momentary feeling of the Saviour's absence. The words of the second section of the aria are: 'Ah! my refuge, rejoice me, allow Thyself most happily to be embraced'. Voice and oboe burst out into joyous runs illustrative of 'rejoice'. All is well.

2 RECITATIVE

'Was ist's dass du mich gesuchet?' ('Why is it, that thou me sought?')
B. Cont

The words are a paraphrase of St Luke II. 49, elaborately set in Cantata BWV 154, but here with appropriate simplicity.

3 ARIA

'Hier, in meines Vaters Stätte find't mich ein betrübter Geist' ('Here, in my Father's abode, finds me a troubled spirit')
B. Vln solo, Cont

The dignified melody on the solo violin breaks out into a flood of triplets and trills which depict the words of the middle section of the aria, 'There canst thou surely find me and with thy heart bind me because this is called my dwelling'. There seems to be an anticipation of the main theme of the duet following at several points in this aria.

4 DIALOGUE–RECITATIVE

'Ach! heiliger und grosser Gott' ('Ah! holy and great God')
S.B. Vln i, ii, Vla, Cont

The Soul expresses her adoration of the Almighty and Jesus follows by telling her to forsake the vanities of the wicked world and to seek the eternal dwelling. She replies with the words of Psalm LXXXIV. 1, 2, beginning, 'How lovely is then Thy dwelling, Lord'. This is a beautiful arioso which passes into a recitative, with an assurance from Jesus of eternal happiness and the Soul's loving reply.

5 DUET
'Nun verschwinden alle Plagen, nun verschwindet Ach und Schmerz' ('Now disappear all troubles, now disappears groaning and pain')
S.B. Ob, Vln i, ii, Vla, Cont

This is one of Bach's most uninhibited expressions of joy in Christ. Together the voices sing in canon, reflecting the happiness of both. The oboe in the opening ritornello and subsequently positively chortles with joy, the violins rush up and down the scale. It is to be hoped the 'pop' boys do not get hold of this number: they would inevitably vulgarize it.

6 CHORALE
'Mein Gott, öffne mir die Pforten solcher Gnad' und Gütigkeit' ('My God, open for me the gates of grace and goodness')
SATB. As No. 5

This glorious cantata ends with a simple harmonization of verse xii of Paul Gerhardt's hymn, 'Weg, mein Herz, mit den Gedanken' (1647) set to Louis Bourgeois' 'Ainsi qu'on oit le Cerf' (1542).

SECOND SUNDAY AFTER EPIPHANY

Epistle: Rom. XII. 6–16 (Love and other duties are required of us).
Gospel: John II. 1–11 (Christ turns water into wine).

Mein Gott, wie lang', ach lange? (My God, how long, ah long?).

Solo Cantata BWV 155. Weimar, 1716. Libretto by Salomo Franck.

This is the only one of the cantatas Bach composed for this Sunday that takes note of the appointed Epistle and Gospel. The libretto centres on the answer Jesus gave to his mother at the marriage feast in Cana, when she said, 'They have no wine' and He replied, 'Woman, what have I to do with thee? Mine hour is not yet come.' St Augustine took this to mean the hour of His Passion, but other commentators understood it to be the hour of His public manifestation through the working of miracles. Franck takes the former view.

1 RECITATIVE

'Mein Gott, wie lang', ach lange?' ('My God, how long, ah long?')
S. Vln i, ii, Vla, Cont

It is typical that the libretto should speak not of sorrow at what is to befall Christ, but of the Soul's own sorrow. The text goes on, 'I find, what poor me daily ails, the tears-cup is continually filled'. The continuo has a pedal bass, groups of four quavers, throbbing throughout most of the length of the recitative with frequent dissonant chords above. Bach graphically illustrates 'the joy-wine fails' in both voice and strings, as also the despairing conclusion, 'In me sinks almost all confidence'.

2 DUET

'Du musst glauben, du musst hoffen, du musst Gott gelassen sein' ('Thou must believe, thou must hope, thou must to God resigned be')
A.T. Fag, Cont

The text reflects not only the Gospel here but also the Epistle. 'Rejoicing in hope; patient in tribulation; continuing steadfastly in prayer.' These consolatory words are expressed in a gentle melody often in sixths and thirds. A solo bassoon provides the ritornellos and also plays with the voices except at the start and before the middle section. It is, as Whittaker says, one of the

55

finest bassoon obbligati Bach ever wrote, exploiting a wide reach of its compass.

3 RECITATIVE
'So sei, o Seele, sei zufrieden' ('So, oh soul, be content')
B. Cont

Rather long, but its dryness is relieved by some illustrative passages for the continuo. The text bids the soul wait patiently and its 'dearest friend' will return bringing 'joy-wine and honey', not gall. The suffering endured has been to test love and faith.

4 ARIA
'Wirf, mein Herze, wirf dich noch, in des Höchsten Liebesarme' ('Throw, my heart, throw thyself still into the Highest's loving arms')
S. Vln i, ii, Vla, Cont

The melody of the aria vividly reproduces, on the violins, the gesture of abandonment in the opening words and, two bars before the voice comes in, its loving reception.

5 CHORALE
'Ob sich's anliess, als wollt er nicht, lass dich es nicht erschrecken' ('Though it appeared as he would not, let thee it not alarm')
SATB. Vln i, ii, Vla, with voices, Cont

The twelfth verse of Paul Speratus' 'Es ist das Heil uns kommen her' (1524) set to its original melody.

Ach Gott, wie manches Herzeleid (Ah God, how many pains of heart).
Chorale Cantata BWV 3. Leipzig, 1725.

This is Bach's first setting of Martin Moller's hymn (1587) in a remodelled version. Verses i, ii and xviii are unaltered in Nos. 1, 2, 6. The rest are paraphrased. The melody in Nos. 1, 2, and 6 is that of 'O Jesus Christ, mein's Lebens Licht' (1625), commonly associated with the hymn. The second setting (BWV 58) of this hymn was a dialogue-cantata, in a key of a very different character to this chorale fantasia (see p. 43).

1 CHORUS
(As above)
SATB. Ob d'am i, ii, Vin i, ii, Vla, Trb with B. Cont

The chorale melody is, exceptionally, given to the basses, doubled by the trombone and continuo. The Adagio movement begins with an expressive ritornello which develops throughout in the orchestral part. The first two lines are begun by the altos, the second two by the tenors. The sopranos, at the line 'The narrow way is one of suffering', climb up, in a radiant phrase, to the goal which is Heaven. The texture, with its chromatic harmonies, is extraordinarily rich.

2 RECITATIVE AND CHORALE
'Wie schwerlich lässt sich Fleisch und Blut' ('How hardly allows itself flesh and blood')
SATB. (Chorale). TASB. solo recitatives between lines. Cont

This is the second verse of the chorale 'How hardly allows itself flesh and blood which only after earthly things and vain things aspires and neither God nor heaven heeds'. It is set chordally, and in strong contrast to the previous number, to diatonic harmony which underlines the last and the key line, 'On Thee, Oh Jesus, stands my being.'

3 ARIA
'Empfind' ich Höllenangst und Pein' ('I feel hell's anguish and pain')
B. Cont

These grim words are contradicted by those that follow, 'Yet must constantly in the heart a true joy-heaven be', and here Bach duly illustrates 'joy-heaven' with a long run and also when the words are repeated.

4 RECITATIVE
'Es mag mir Leib und Geist verschmachten' ('May my body and spirit pine away')
T. Cont

A recitative of routine character. The singer relies on Jesus, in spite of all fears 'Jesus will my treasure and kingdom be'.

5 DUET
'Wenn Sorgen auf mich dringen' ('When cares on me press')
S.A. Ob d'am i, ii, and Vln i, ii (unis.) Cont

The two last uninspiring numbers now give place to a most beautiful duet which Whittaker considers perhaps the finest in the cantatas. I agree. The lovely melody foreshadowed in the richly scored introduction is sung in free canon by alto and soprano, in that order. In 'I will in joyfulness to my Jesus sing', the soprano has an enchanting new phrase at 'joyfulness'.

6 CHORALE
'Erhalt mein Herz im Glauben rein' ('Sustain my heart in faith pure')
SATB. Cor, Ob d'am i, ii, Vln i, ii, Vla, all with voices, Cont
The last verse of the hymn mentioned in No. 1.

Meine Seufzer, meine Tränen (My sighs, my tears).
Cantata BWV 13. Leipzig, 1726.

This third and last cantata for the Second Sunday after Epiphany is the gloomiest of all. Like the other two, it concentrates on personal suffering and virtually ignores the miracle of the wedding feast at Cana. As Spitta says 'the libretto deduces no lesson from the Gospel story in which a tone of noble cheerfulness is evidently predominant'. It endlessly reiterates the despondent sinner's need for Jesus's help. The writer was perhaps a teetotaller! There is, however, one reference to the miracle in No. 4.

1 ARIA
'Meine Seufzer, meine Tränen, können nicht zu zählen sein' ('My sighs, my tears cannot numbered be')
T. Fl i, ii, Ob da cacc, Cont

If there is no 'noble cheerfulness' in the libretto there is certainly noble grief in the music in this superb aria. Flutes, classically associated with grief, together with the oboe da caccia and the continuo form, with the voice, a quintet of deep anguish.

The words above are repeated in broken utterances, as are those of the last part of the middle section, 'Ah! so must the pain for us already the way to death prepare'.

2 RECITATIVE
'Mein liebster Gott lässt mich annoch vergebens rufen' ('My dearest God allows me still in vain to cry')
A. Cont

At the last line of the text 'alone I must till then weep' there are three poignant chromatic bars on the first syllable of 'weep'.

3 CHORALE
'Der Gott, der mir hat versprochen seinen Beistand jederzeit'
('God, who to me has promised His assistance at all times')
A. Fl i, ii and Ob da cacc with voices; Vln i, ii, Vla, Cont

This is the first verse of Johann Heerman's hymn 'Zion klagt
mit Angst und Schmerzen' (1636) set to Louis Bourgeois' 'Ainsi
qu'on oit le Cerf' (1542).

The promised assistance is not yet forthcoming though the
orchestral accompaniment, in the major key, breathes forth a
note of confidence. The melody of the chorale is unadorned.

4 RECITATIVE
'Mein Kummer nimmet zu und raubt mir alle Ruh', mein
Jammerkrug ist ganz mit Tränen angefüllet' ('My sorrow grows
greater and robs me of all rest, my lamentation-pitcher is com-
pletely with tears filled')
S. Cont

And so it continues, but it does conclude with a reference to the
Gospel, 'God can the wormwood right easily into joy-wine turn.'

5 ARIA
'Ächzen und erbärmlich Weinen hilft der Sorgen Krankheit
nicht' ('Groaning and miserable wailing does not help the
sorrows' sickness')
B. Vln solo, Fl i, ii, unis. Cont

The text of the aria takes up the sentiments of the last sentence
in the recitative. In the first section (the words as above) the
violin solo depicts the groaning and wailing in descending semitones taken up by the continuo as the violin launches into florid
phrases gradually rising to a point of climax. These semitones,
Whittaker interprets as the contrary state of confidence which,
indeed, is expressed in the text of the following section and with
which the aria ends. 'But whosoever towards heaven looks and
himself there for comfort seeks, to him can easily a joy-light in the
mourning breast appear.' The aria is a wonderful example of
Bach's power in depicting contrary states of mind.

6 CHORALE
'So sei nun, Seele, deine, und traue dem alleine' ('So be now, soul,
thine, and trust Him alone')
SATB. All as at No. 1 but with oboe instead of oboe da caccia. All with
voices. Cont

59

The change of oboes here shows Bach's feeling for instrumental colour. The oboe da caccia has been associated with grief and so is not used in this confident chorale. The words are verse 15 of Paul Flemming's hymn 'In allen meinen Taten' (1642), to the melody of Heinrich Isaak's 'O Welt, ich muss dich lassen' (1539).

THIRD SUNDAY AFTER EPIPHANY

Epistle: Rom. xii. 17–21 (Overcome evil with good).
Gospel: Matt. viii. 1–13 (The cleansing of the leper).

Herr, wie du willt, so schicks mit mir (Lord, as Thou wilt, so ordain it with me).
Chorale Cantata BWV 73. Leipzig, 1723.

The librettists of the three cantatas for this Sunday base their texts on the chorales that have as their theme obedience to God's will. This is in accord with the words of the leper 'Lord, if thou wilt, thou canst make me clean'.

1 CHORUS
'Herr, wie du willt, so schicks mit mir im Leben und im Sterben' ('Lord, as Thou wilt, so ordain it with me in living and in dying')
Solo TBS. SATB. Ob i, ii, Vln i, ii, Vla, Cor or Org obb., Cont

The reason for horn *or* organ obbligato may arise, Whittaker suggests, from a horn, at some later performance, not being available and so the composer gave the line to the organ. The melody for the oboes in the introduction, which runs throughout the movement, is enriched by the use, as a kind of cadence, of the first four notes of the chorale and this little motto occurs frequently, at different pitches and keys in the course of the movement, right up to the last bar. It serves to emphasize the opening words. Verse i of Caspar Bienemann's hymn (1582) to the melody 'Wo Gott der Herr nicht bei uns hält' (1535) is interrupted three times by solo accompanied recitatives. The first one for tenor bewails 'Ah, but ah, how much lets me Thy will suffer'. The motto is here given poignant harmonies, the second recitative, for bass, prays 'Thou art my helper, comfort and refuge . . . Thou speakest words of joy to me'. The third and last recitative, for soprano, speaks of God's will as a sealed book, its blessings appearing to us often as a curse. 'But Thy spirit frees us of this error and shows us how healing is Thy will.'

2 ARIA
'Ach, senke doch den Geist der Freuden dem Herzen ein' ('Ah, plant then the spirit of joy in the heart')
T. Ob i, Cont

61

The oboe announces a very attractive melody characterized by groups of flowing semiquavers. The middle section has the familiar temporary change of mood, sickness of soul, doubts, failure of hope. There is an imaginative passage at 'I long for Thee', a sighing descending chromatic scale in quavers for the voice.

3 RECITATIVE
'Ach, unser Wille bleibt verkehrt, bald trotzig, bald verzagt' ('Ah, our will remains perverted, now obstinate, now timid') B. Cont

This short recitative ends with the words 'But a Christian, in God's spirit instructed, learns to sink himself in God's will and says' (the aria at once follows).

4 ARIA
'Herr, so du willt' ('Lord, as Thou wilt')
B. Vln i, ii, Vla, Cont

This is one of Bach's most beautiful and deeply felt arias for the bass voice. The words describe the Soul's readiness for death. The tolling bells will not frighten him, his lamentation is stilled. 'Lord, as Thou wilt.' The music is cast in the form of a free rondo with constant repetitions of the motto phrase in the vocal part, thirteen in all, and ten of them in varied form within the prescribed two bars except the final one, which touches the highest note, to rest at last. The death pangs are graphically depicted in broken utterances echoed by the violins, the tolling bells equally so with the strings marked *pizzicato*. The aria embodies complete trust in what God has willed.

5 CHORALE
'Das ist des Vaters Wille, der uns erschaffen hat' ('That is the Father's will, who us created has')
SATB. Cor, Ob i, ii, Vln i, ii, Vla, all with voices, Cont

This is the ninth and last verse of Ludwig Helmbold's hymn 'Von Gott will ich nicht lassen' (1569) with its anonymous melody (1571). It pays tribute to Father, Son and Holy Spirit.

Was mein Gott will, das g'scheh allzeit (What my God wills, that happens always).
Chorale Cantata BWV 111. Leipzig, 1725.

The libretto is based on Markgraf Albrecht of Brandenburg-Culmbach's hymn (*c.* 1554) with the above title set to a melody of

French origin. Verses i and iv in their original form are in Nos. 1 and 6, the rest are paraphrased.

1 CHORUS
(As above)
SATB. Ob i, ii, Vln i, ii, Vla, Cont

On paper, as Whittaker points out, there does not seem to be enough variety in this chorus to sustain interest. The chorale melody is in almost invariable minims and semibreves, the lower voices predominantly in crotchets. There is also 'a stern economy of resource' in the orchestral score, yet the number is ablaze with life, with fiery animation, with a vivid flow of imagination, and one regrets its apparent brevity. Bach could truly work miracles with the smallest means. The emphatic gesture made by the two chords for oboes and strings at the start of the introductory ritornello is repeated no less than sixteen times in the course of the movement as if proclaiming that 'God's will is the best'.

2 ARIA
'Entsetze dich, mein Herze, nicht, Gott ist dein Trost und Zuversicht und deiner Seelen Leben' ('Affright not thyself, my heart, God is thy comfort and confidence and thy soul's life')
B. Cont

This is a very straightforward aria with a new setting of the opening words instead of the conventional *da capo*.

3 RECITATIVE
'O Törichter, der sich von Gott entzieht und wie ein Jonas dort vor Gottes Angesichte flieht' ('Oh foolish one! who himself from God withdraws and as a Jonah thence from God's countenance flees')
A. Cont

The reference is to Jonah 1. 3, which tells the story of Jonah and the whale.

4 DUET
'So geh' ich mit beherzten Schritten, auch wenn mich Gott zum Grabe führt' ('So go I with courageous steps, even when God to the grave leads me')
A.T. Vln i, ii, Vla, Cont

This is a fascinating duet. The 'courageous steps' are marked by a kind of pedal bass in the prevailing dotted rhythm. The tenor and alto sing in canon at the start of the duet, as also in the middle section where the text speaks of the day, written down by God, when His hand will touch the soul and drive death's bitterness away.

5 RECITATIVE
'Drum wenn der Tod zuletzt den Geist noch mit Gewalt aus seinem Körper reisst so nimm ihn, Gott, in treuer Vaterhände' ('Therefore when the death at last the spirit even with force from the body tears, so take it God, in faithful Father-hands')
S. Ob i, ii, Cont

The oboes are included perhaps to add to the expressiveness of the lovely *arioso-adagio* at the close, 'O blessed, wished-for end'.

6 CHORALE
'Noch eins, Herr, will ich bitten dich, du willst mir's nicht versagen' ('Yet one thing, Lord, will I beg Thee, Thou wilt to me it not deny')
SATB. Ob i, ii, Vln i, ii, Vla, all with voices, Cont

'The one thing' prayed for is the power to overcome the evil spirit. Confident that the prayer will be answered the hymn ends 'Thereupon say I joyfully: Amen.'

Alles nur nach Gottes Willen (All only according to God's will).
Cantata BWV 72. Leipzig, 1726. Libretto by Salomo Franck.

1 CHORUS
(As above)
SATB. Ob i, ii, Vln i, ii, Vla, Cont

The opening ritornello begins with two chords as emphatic as those at a similar place in BWV 73: but here they are used much less often. It is the octave drops heard in the first seven bars that here prevails, most of the time underlining the cries of 'all'. The second section brings a new melody to the words 'God's will shall quiet me in clouds and sunshine', evidently storm-clouds judging by the vivid phrases given to 'clouds' and the pounding octave motif below.

2 RECITATIVE, ARIOSO AND ARIA
'O sel'ger Christ der allzeit seinen Willen in Gottes Willen sinkt' ('O blessed Christ who always His will in God's will sinks')
A. Vln i, ii, Cont

In Cantata BWV 73 Bach put a wonderful variety of expression into repetitions of the first line of the beautiful aria for bass, 'Herr, so du willt' ('Lord, as thou wilt').

In the present instance Franck's libretto compels Bach to set the line nine times as if it were a litany beginning, 'Lord as Thou wilt, so must themselves all things dispose'. Bach lays out these lines in phrases of five bars each, thereby giving the music a monotonous symmetry, for there are no ritornellos dividing the repetitions as in the other aria.

In the nine phrases themselves there is as much variety of treatment as the rigid scheme allows. A second, and very brief, recitative prays that when death comes 'Thy spirit this word into the heart speaks',—which leads into the aria, marked *vivace*, 'With all that I have and am will I myself to Jesus leave'. These words are left to sink into the mind during the twelve bars for the orchestra that follows, after which the aria proper may be said to begin. The rhythm of the vocal part is attractive and attention should be paid to the splendid instrumental bass of the ritornellos with its characteristic repeated notes.

At the line 'He leadeth me by flowery paths where thorns are mixed with roses' Bach introduces a new melody with a fall to a sustained note each time 'thorns' is sung. The final section brings a new version of the opening melody but with the same words. It ends with a beautiful phrase at 'Jesu'.

3 RECITATIVE
'So glaube nun! Dein Heiland saget. Ich will's tun' ('So believe now! Thy Saviour says: I will it do')
B. Cont

An expression of faith that the Saviour will be present to help and sustain the soul in suffering and pain, knowing all its needs, and will make His dwelling in contrite hearts.

4 ARIA
'Mein Jesus will es tun, er will dein Kreuz versüssen' ('My Jesus will do it, He will Thy suffering sweeten')
S. Ob i, Vln i, ii, Vla, Cont

This aria exudes love and trust. After the first ritornello, when the text is repeated, the voice runs joyfully up the scale at 'Jesus'. The rich texture simplifies at the start of the second section 'Although thy heart lies in great afflictions, yet shall it soft and quiet in His arms rest' and, as we expected, Bach gives 'ruh'n' ('rest') a long sustained note, as the orchestra recalls the opening melody. At the end of the ritornello comes—and *this* is wholly un-expected—a repetition for the voice of the opening words to this exquisite phrase. Note the high-pitched note at 'will'.

5 CHORALE
'Was mein Gott will, das g'scheh allzeit' ('What my God wills, that happens always')
SATB. Ob i, ii, Vln i, ii, and Vla, all with voices, Cont
See p. 62.

Ich steh mit einem Fuss im Grabe (I stand with one foot in the grave).

Solo Cantata BWV 156. Leipzig, ?1729. Libretto by Picander.

1 SINFONIA
Ob, Vln i, ii, Vla, Cont

This little movement is an adaptation for solo oboe and strings of the slow movement of the F minor concerto for clavier (BWV 1056) which itself is thought to be a reconstruction of a movement of a lost violin concerto. The melody in this Sinfonia sheds the decoration necessarily given to it in the harpsichord version, and appears in its unadorned beauty. It is well known as 'Sinfonia in F major to Cantata 156', thereby evading a title many people might find depressing! The strings accompany the oboe solo throughout in detached chords and the descending notes in the continuo part could be taken to describe the opening words of the aria, with chorale, that follows.

2 ARIA WITH CHORALE
'Ich steh mit einem Fuss im Grabe, bald fällt der kranke Leib hinein' ('I stand with one foot in the grave, soon falls the sick body therein')
S.T. Vln i, ii and Vla, all unis. Cont

The words show the link with the Gospel for this Sunday, the leper's plea 'Lord, if thou wilt, thou canst make me clean,' but none of his trustfulness that he will be cured of his disease, in this case symbolic of his sinful state. That is supplied by the chorale sung by the soprano (or better still by the chorus sopranos), 'Do with me, God, according to Thy goodness' which comes in at the fourth bar after the tenor entry. It is the first verse of

J. H. Schein's chorale with this title and its own melody (1628). The sustained note for the strings at the start of the movement and the downward syncopated scale passages for the continuo, depict the gradually sinking into the grave, and this is poignantly stressed by the falling chromatic phrases that follow.

The words in the next section express acceptance and readiness to depart when it pleases God, and conclude 'Nur lass mein Ende selig sein' ('Only let my end blessed be') repeated five times, with long held notes on 'blessed'.

3 RECITATIVE
'Mein Angst und Noth' ('My anguish and need').
B. Cont

The soul prays that God will be merciful to the sinner 'Let Thy goodness be greater than Thy justice' and, in an expressive three bars of arioso after 'Let my distress not long endure, the longer here, the later there.'

4 ARIA
'Herr, was du willst, soll mir gefallen' ('Lord, what Thou wilt shall me please')
A. Ob, Vln, Cont

The sombre mood of the preceding numbers now gives place to a lively aria full of confidence, with the same varied settings of 'Herr, was du willst' we have already had in Cantatas BWV 73.

In the second section 'In the joy, in the sorrow, in the death, in the prayer and in the pleading let it be always, Lord, as Thou willst'.

5 RECITATIVE
'Und willst du, dass ich nicht soll kranken, so werd' ich dir von Herzen danken' ('And willst Thou, that I shall not be ill, so will I thank Thee from the heart')
B. Cont

A prayer hoping to be granted health but to accept illness in the proper spirit.

6 CHORALE
'Herr, wie du willt, so schicks mit mir' ('Lord, as Thou wilt, so ordain it with me')
SATB. As No. 1. Insts. with voices. Cont

Verse i of Caspar Bienemann's hymn (1582) with the above title set to the melody associated with it (1525).

FOURTH SUNDAY AFTER EPIPHANY

Epistle: Rom. xiii. 8–10 (Love is the fulfilling of the law).
Gospel: Matt. viii. 23–27 (Christ stills the tempest).

Jesus schläft, was soll ich hoffen? (Jesus sleeps, what hope is there for me?).

Solo Cantata BWV 81. Leipzig, 1724. Libretto by Erdmann Neumeister.

It would be interesting to know exactly what Bach's superiors had in mind in exhorting him, in his contract, not to be 'theatrical'. As has been said, Neumeister described his librettos as similar to theatre pieces. It may be they had the Passions of Richard Keiser in mind, but they could not have meant to exclude drama, so inherent in the Gospels themselves and so powerfully stressed in such a cantata as this, which contains a most vivid picture of the storm that Jesus quelled.

1 ARIA
(As above)
A. Fl i, ii, Vln i, ii, Vla, Cont

Bach's feeling for the right tone colour made him not only choose recorders rather than transverse flutes but also often score them an octave above the violins as in this picture of Jesus asleep in the boat, as a storm threatens. The sombre accompaniment, thus coloured, seems to isolate Jesus from his disciples. This the alto expresses in her first phrases with a long note at the repeat of the line on 'sleeps'.

The whole situation is, of course, applied to the individual soul who, storm-tossed with fear, draws near to Death's abyss.

2 RECITATIVE
'Herr! warum bleibest du so ferne?' ('Lord, why remainest Thou so distant?')
T. Cont

A recitative with many dissonant harmonies. The singer thinks of the star that guided the Wise Men to Bethlehem and prays now to be led 'through Thine eyes' light.'

3 ARIA
'Die schäumenden Wellen von Belials Bächen verdoppeln die Wuth doch suchet die stürmende Fluth die Kräfte des Glaubens

68

zu schwächen' ('The foaming waves of Belial's rivers redouble their fury, still seeks the stormy flood the strength of faith to weaken')

T. Vln i, ii, Vla, Cont

The violins in the introductory bars of what is a scena rather than an aria, rush up and down the scale, abating their fury only as the voice comes in in the three brief *adagio* sections— and followed by *forte* allegros—that bring a lull.

At the first of these adagios, the storm bursts and as the tenor sings 'A Christian shall indeed like waves stand'—a curious simile—the storm bursts out again. Its fury is also expressed in the rapid runs in the vocal part—a trying one as it is consistently pitched high, but most effective if well sung.

4 ARIOSO

'Ihr Kleingläubigen, warum seid ihr so furchtsam?' ('Ye of little faith, why are ye so fearful?')

B. Cont

A tender rebuke by the Lord to His special friends. Why, of all men, should they be afraid in His presence?

5 (ARIA)

'Schweig, schweig, aufgetürmtes Meer! Verstumme, Sturm und Wind' ('Be still, be still, towering ocean! Be dumb, storm and wind.')

B. Ob d'am i, ii, Vln i, ii, Vla, Cont

The raging waves, again depicted as in No. 3, are not silenced by the Saviour's imperious command—except at the opening bars of the middle section, 'To Thee be thy boundary set, so that my chosen child [presumably Peter] no mishap ever harms', which the continuo alone accompanies. Just as in Cantata BWV 19 in which St Michael the Archangel vanquishes the dragon in the middle section and then fights the battle again, at the *da capo*, so here the storm bursts out once more, not yet stilled; but the convention does not detract from the high drama of this grand aria.

6 RECITATIVE

'Wohl mir, mein Jesus spricht ein Wort' ('Well for me! My Jesus speaks a word')

A. Cont

The angry storm subsides and so do the cares of the Christian soul when Jesus speaks the word.

69

7 CHORALE

'Unter deinen Schirmen, bin ich vor den Stürmen aller Feinde frei' ('Under Thy shelters am I from the storms of all enemies free')

SATB. Ob d'am i, ii, Vln i, ii, Vla, all with voices; Cont

The second verse of Johann Franck's hymn 'Jesu, meine Freude' (1653) set to Johann Crüger's melody (1653).

Wär Gott nicht mit uns diese Zeit, so soll Israel sagen wir hätten müssen verzagen (Were God not with us in this time, so must Israel say, we should have been obliged to despair).

Chorale Cantata BWV 14. Leipzig, 1735.

1 CHORUS

(As above)

SATB. Cor da cacc, Ob i, ii, unis, Vln i, ii, Vla, Cont

The text is based on Luther's free translation of Psalm CXXIV (1524). Verses i and iii are in their original form in Nos. 1 and 5, verse ii is paraphrased in the intervening movements.

The reason why Bach gave a psalm of deliverance such a 'stern, gloomy and relentless' setting in this movement arose from the War of the Polish Succession which lasted from 1733 to 1738, and in 1735, when this cantata was composed, seemed to offer no hope but rather threatened to involve most of Europe. Hence the lines 'Were God not with us in this time we should have been obliged to despair, who are such a poor little group, despised by so many men's children who all set upon us.'

Oboes and corno da caccia have the melody associated with the hymn, the voices, doubled by the strings, quote only its first phrase.

There are no ritornellos, in this motet-like chorus the voices drive through from start to finish. It is impossible in these pages to give an analysis of Bach's masterly treatment of the material.

2 ARIA

'Unsre Stärke heisst zu schwach, unsern Feind zu widerstehen' ('Our strength proves too weak, our enemy to withstand')

S. Cor da cacc, Vln i, ii, Vla, Cont

A semiquaver motif on second violins and violas in the introductory ritornello will remind many of the theme of the D major

Organ Fugue and, poetically treated, of the lovely introduction to the chorale on oboe and oboe d'amore to No. 7 of the *Christmas Oratorio*. Three motifs come into the introduction to the aria, (a) defiant, (b) confident, and (c) one already mentioned which challenges. The voice, by no means weak, has them all at one time or another.

3 RECITATIVE
'Ja, hätt' es Gott nicht zugegeben, wir wären längst nicht mehr am Leben' ('Yea, had God not allowed it, we should long ago have been dead')
T. Cont

This is an almost hysterical outburst, battalions of demisemiquavers rushing up and down the scale in rapidly changing tonalities, as the tenor displays his vindictiveness.

4 ARIA
'Gott, bei deinem starken Schützen sind wir vor den Feinden frei' ('God, by Thy strong protection are we from the enemies free')
B. Ob i, ii, Cont

Considering the war had still three years to run this rejoicing seems rather premature. This is a strong and well-designed aria with some fine declamatory phrases in the last half of the first section at the words 'when they themselves as wild waves from anger oppose us'.

5 CHORALE
'Gott Lob und Dank' ('To God praise and thanks')
SATB. As No. 1. Insts. with voices. Cont

The third verse of the chorale, giving praise for victory.

PURIFICATION OF THE
BLESSED VIRGIN MARY

Epistle: Mal. III. 1–4 (The Lord shall suddenly come to His temple).
Gospel: Luke II. 22–32 (Simeon prophesies of Christ).

Erfreute Zeit im neuen Bunde, da unser Glaube Jesum hält (Joyful time in the new dispensation when our faith Jesus holds).
Solo Cantata BWV 83. Leipzig, 1724.

1 ARIA
(As above)
A. Cor i, ii, Ob i, ii, Vln solo, Vln i, ii, Vla, Cont

It does not need much perception to assign the violin solo and its accompaniment in this movement to a lost violin concerto— its speech betrays it, and nowhere more so than during the middle section where the figuration at one point is that of alternate open and stopped strings. The movement could be played without the voice part and make perfect musical sense. Bach, needless to say, has fitted in the voice part with great skill. There are the expected runs on 'joyful', four of them, and in the middle section 'How joyfully will be at the last hour the resting-place, the grave, prepared'. 'Resting-place' is given characteristic groups of quavers, but here the violin figuration noted above does not at all fit the sentiment of the words.

2 INTONATION AND RECITATIVE
'Herr, nun lässest du deinen Diener in Friede fahren wie du gesaget hast' ('Lord now lettest thou thy servant depart in peace, according to Thy word')
B. Vln i, ii, and Vla unis., Cont

It is the first plainsong psalm tone that Bach styles 'Intonazione' in this movement, and uses for two verses of the *Nunc Dimittis*. Ritornellos divide up the two halves of these verses. The theme of these, a rising scale in 6/8 time, conveys the idea of journeying and is treated in canon. The interpolated recitatives are, as always, in common time, and Bach also separates them with phrases of the ritornello. The words of the first recitative begin 'What to us as men terrible appears, is for us an entrance into life'; then, after three bars of the ritornello, 'It is death [that is] an end of this time and suffering, a pledge that to us the Lord has given as sign that He it means sincerely and us after completed struggling into peace will bring.' The recitative continues after another three bars of the ritornello 'And because the Saviour now the eyes comfort, the heart's refreshment is, what wonder that a heart the death-fear forgets. It can joyfully the declaration make.' The drop in pitch for the plainsong tone at the last verse may be taken as reflecting the peace and resignation of the 'joyful declaration' of the recitative.

The librettist is not here portraying Simeon but the individual soul taking his words to heart. The beautiful 'dying' close should be noted.

3 ARIA
'Eile, Herz, voll Freudigkeit vor den Gnadenstuhl zu treten.'
('Hasten, heart, full of joyfulness before the mercy-seat to step')
T. Vln solo, Vln i, ii, Vla, Cont

This lovely aria may be taken as an adaptation of the last movement of the lost violin concerto. Triplet figures abound in both violin solo and voice part, with long runs in the latter on 'step' each time the word is repeated.

4 RECITATIVE
'Ja, merkt dein Glaube noch viel Finsterniss' ('Yea, observes thy faith yet much darkness')
A. Cont

The Soul is encouraged to believe that the Saviour will dissipate all shadows in His bright light.

5 CHORALE
'Er ist das Heil und selig Licht für die Heiden' ('He is the Salvation and blessed light for the heathen')
SATB. Cor i, Ob i, ii, Vln i, ii and Vla, all with voices, Cont

Verse iv of Luther's version of the *Nunc Dimittis* with the title below, set to his own melody (1524).

Mit Fried und Freud ich fahr dahin (With peace and joy I journey thither).
Chorale Cantata BWV 125. Leipzig, 1725.

This cantata is a remodelled version of Luther's hymn with the above title, a very free rendering of the *Nunc Dimittis*. Verses i, ii

73

and iv are set in Nos. 1, 3 and 6. The rest are paraphrased. The melody used in Nos. 1, 3 and 6 is attributed to Luther (1524).

1 CHORUS
'Mit Fried und Freud ich fahr dahin, in Gottes Willen; getrost ist mir mein Herz und Sinn, sanft und stille' ('With peace and joy I journey thither in God's will; comforted is for me my heart and spirit, soft and still')
SATB. Fl trav, Ob, Vln i, ii, Vla, Cor with S. Cont

The first phrase of the melody given out by the flute has a certain resemblance to the chorale widely known as 'Jesu, joy of man's desiring' from Cantata BWV 147. The chorus, the sopranos excepted, take this up and above them, in long notes, the sopranos sing the melody of Luther's chorale. Bach cannot pass over the words 'soft and still' which he treats most poetically.

2 ARIA
'Ich will auch mit gebrochnen Augen nach dir, mein treuer Heiland, sehn' ('I will even with dimming eyes look to thee, my Saviour')
A. Fl trav, Ob d'am, Cont

In this remarkable aria the librettist does not, as one would expect, paraphrase Luther's hymn but inserts a verse of his own which completely contradicts the peace and joy expressed in Nos. 1, 4, 5 and 6 and in No. 3 so far as the chorale is concerned.

By means of discordant clashes brought about by the constant use of the appoggiaturas, as in the example below, and a relentless continuo bass, Bach strongly emphasizes the agonized mood of the words. The aria is of considerable length and light only breaks into the words, not the music, of the middle section. 'My Jesus looks on me in death', these words being repeated at a lower pitch with the voice falling to B below the stave, and clashing with C sharp on the flute above the stave, followed by a sudden silence of one bar—rightly called 'awesome' by Whittaker.

3 RECITATIVE AND CHORALE
'O Wunder, dass ein Herz vor der dem Fleisch verhassten Gruft und gar des Todes Schmerz sich nicht entsetzt' ('O Wonder, that a heart before the flesh-hated tomb and even the death's pain itself not affrights')
B. Vln i, ii, Vla, Cont

Bach, as in many other instances, alternates the recitative with the lines of the chorale, in this case the second verse, and though he does not allot the latter to the basses' chorus, it is much more effective if sung by them. The strings accompany, with solemn harmonies, the beautiful long phrase at 'dying'. The text can only be briefly summarized here. The recitative marvels that the spirit is not frightened by death, the chorale responds that this is Christ's doing. He is life and salvation.

4 DUET
'Ein unbegreiflich Licht erfüllt den ganzen Kreis der Erden' ('An inconceivable light fills the whole orbit of the earth')
T.B. Vln i, ii, Cont

The text is an obvious paraphrase of the line in Simeon's Canticle 'To be a light to lighten the Gentiles and to be the Glory of Thy people Israel'.

In this brilliant duet, the sun bursts through the clouds. The word 'light' is continually thrown into high relief.

5 RECITATIVE
'O unerschöpfter Schatz der Güte' ('O inexhaustible source of blessing')
A. Cont

6 CHORALE
'Er ist das Heil und selge Licht für alle Heiden' ('He is the salvation and the blessed light for the heathen')
SATB. As No. 1. Insts. with voices. Cont

The fourth and last verse of the chorale.

Ich habe genug (It is enough).
Solo Cantata BWV 82. Leipzig, 1727.

1 ARIA
'Ich habe genug, ich habe den Heiland, das Hoffen der Frommen, auf meine begierigen Arme genommen' ('It is enough. I have the Saviour, the hope of the pious, taken into my longing arms')
B. Ob Vln i, ii, Vla, Org and Cont

In the long introduction to the aria the violins have a murmuring figure very much like—though syncopated—the accompaniment for recorders to the tenor aria in the Easter Oratorio BWV 249, 'Sanfte soll mein Todeskummer' ('Soft will be my death's approach') and the gentle mourning figure, also for recorders, in the *Sinfonia* to the funeral cantata (BWV 106), 'Gottes Zeit ist die allerbeste Zeit' ('God's time is the best time').

The motif that characterizes the whole aria, one that Bach uses in many contexts, will at once call to mind the alto aria, 'Erbarme dich, mein Gott' ('Have mercy my God') in the St Matthew Passion. In the middle section 'joy', set to a rising scale of demisemiquavers, expresses the spiritual elation of Simeon. Simeon's words paraphrase various lines in the *Nunc Dimittis*. 'I have seen Him, I long with joy to depart, I have enough.'

The recitative makes it clear that the aria expresses the meditation of the individual soul in the canticle—but it is Simeon I prefer to keep in mind.

2 RECITATIVE
'Ich habe genug! Mein Trost ist nur allein, dass Jesus mein und ich sein eigen möchte sein' ('I have enough! My comfort is this solely, that Jesus mine and I His own might be')
B. Org and Cont

Simeon is mentioned in the line that follows and the beautiful recitative ends with the opening words, 'I have enough'.

3 ARIA
'Schlummert ein, ihr matten Augen, fallet sanft und selig zu' ('Fall asleep, ye weary eyes, close softly and blissfully')
B. Vln i, ii, Vla, Org and Cont

Now begins the sublime melody of heavenly homesickness which combines the emotion of Simeon, detached from the things of this world and having had God's promise so gloriously fulfilled, with those of the aspiring believer who in his turn can share that bliss in the partaking of the holy Eucharist. Never were words more perfectly fitted to music than in this aria in which every bar is precious but none more beautiful than the quietly falling phrase to the words, 'close softly and blissfully', after the unexpected modulation, brought about by the sustained D flat, to A flat and then back to the home key of E flat.

4 RECITATIVE
'Mein Gott! Wann kommt das schöne Nun! da ich in Frieden fahren werde' ('My God! when comes the beautiful "Now" when I shall in peace journey')
B. Org and Cont

In the beautiful two bars of the arioso, at the end, the continuo descends two octaves down to C below the stave as the bass sings 'World, goodnight'.

5 ARIA

'Ich freue mich auf meinen Tod' ('I look forward to my death')
B. Ob, Vln i, ii, Vla, Org and Cont

The weariness in the 'slumber' aria has quite gone. Each section of the aria begins with a florid phrase on 'joy', three times repeated in the course of the aria. The words speak of the joy that death will bring after suffering in this world.

Ich lasse dich nicht, du segnest mich denn (I leave Thee not, Thou blessest me then).
Solo Cantata BWV 157. Leipzig, 1727. Libretto by Picander.

The libretto of this solo cantata was inscribed 'Funeral music at the grave of Herr J. C. von P. [Johann Christoph von Ponickau], October 31, 1726.' A memorial service for this distinguished man was held at Pomssen on 6 February 1727. Terry considers that the above cantata had already been sung four days before at Leipzig on the Feast of the Purification. Ponickau was Lord of Pomssen, and Spitta tells us that Picander had cause to be grateful to him 'and so gave expression to this feeling in his mournful Ode'. He suggests that Bach asked for personal allusions to be avoided so that the music could be used on the above Feast.

1 DUET

'Ich lasse dich nicht, du segnest mich denn' ('I leave thee not, except thou bless me')
T.B. Fl trav, Ob, Vln solo, Cont

These words, the only ones in the duet, come from Genesis XXXII. 24–30, which describes Jacob wrestling with a strange man till break of day, who only leaves him alone when he asks for a blessing. The stranger gives it but says Jacob shall henceforth be called 'striver with God', and so reveals His august name.

Flute, oboe and solo violin have three independent strands of melody and the voices are in canon—though hardly wrestling. As the duet proceeds the voices and instrumental parts become more florid as if to suggest the spiritual contest.

2 ARIA

'Ich halte meinen Jesum feste, ich lass ihn nun und ewig nicht' ('I hold my Jesus fast, I leave Him not now and evermore')
T. Ob d'am, Cont

77

The words continue, 'He alone is my sojourn therefore holds my faith with power his blessing-rich countenance, for this comfort is yet the best'. The decorative oboe d'amore part is the chief attraction of this aria. The vocal part keeps the singer cruelly high above the stave and gives him phrases of alternate sustained and quick notes with no chance to take a breath without breaking the line.

3 RECITATIVE

'Mein lieber Jesu du, wenn ich Verdruss und Kummer leide, so bist du meine Freude' ('My dear Jesus Thou, when I vexation and affliction suffer, then art Thou my joy')
T. Vln i, ii, Violetta, Cont

The tenor is again kept up high, though less often than in the aria above and again too it is the accompaniment that is the most attractive feature in the movement.

4 ARIA

'Ja, ja, ich halte Jesum feste, so geh' ich auch zum Himmel ein' ('Yes, yes, I hold Jesus fast, so go I also into heaven')
B. Fl trav, Vln, Cont

This splendid movement, built round the fine and confident theme the flute announces at the start, a kind of motto-refrain, is heard constantly in the course of the aria.

Now comes an arioso with the refrain, followed by an Adagio with an accompaniment of solemn repeated chords at the words, 'O beautiful place, come gentle death and lead me away', then another arioso and finally, in this varied section, another recitative. The coda to all this is marked 'arioso'; what we have here is, in fact, an adaptation of the operatic scena familiar in the operas of Monteverdi and Cavalli, and in Bach's time of Keiser and Handel. It is magnificent.

5 CHORALE

'Meinen Jesum lass' ich nicht, geh' ihm ewig an der Seiten' ('My Jesus leave I not. Go with Him, ever by His side')
SATB. Fl trav, Ob, Vln i, ii, Violetta, all with voices, Cont

Verse vi of Christian Keimann's hymn set to its associated melody (1658). The verse, according to C. S. Terry, should begin 'Jesum lass ich nicht von mir'.

Der Friede sei mit dir (My peace I give to you).
Solo Cantata BWV 158. Weimar.

1 RECITATIVE
(As above)
B. Cont

The opening words are from St Luke xxiv. 36, and have no
relation to the scene of the Purification. They are followed by
typical Lutheran comments: 'Thou fearful conscience! Thy
Mediator stands here, who has Thy guilt-book and the law's
curse annulled and torn up.' Luther always put the Law second
to the Gospel. The beauty of the recitative lies in the arioso
sections, associated with the opening words, the first at the start,
another a little further on, and five repetitions of 'der Friede'
at the end, preceded by a call to the troubled heart to realize
how much it is loved by God through Christ.

2 ARIA AND CHORALE
'Welt ade, ich bin dein müde' ('World, farewell, I am of thee
weary')
S.B. Vln solo, Ob. with S. Cont

The aria, combined with the first verse of J. G. Albinus's
hymn with the above title (1649) set to Johann Rosenmüller's
melody (1679), is an amazing outpouring of continuous melody,
contributed largely by the magnificent violin solo. An interesting
point is the similarity, not marked but present, of some of the
vocal phrases to the exquisite slumber song 'Schlummert ein' in
Cantata BWV 82 (see p. 76). The chorale, sung preferably—
in my opinion—by chorus sopranos rather than a solo soprano,
weaves its way through in even paced notes. The words of the
solo bass part are 'World, farewell, I am of thee weary, Salem's
dwellings stand for me open where I, in rest and peace, everlastingly blessed, regard God.'

3 RECITATIVE–ARIOSO
'Nun, Herr, regiere meinen Sinn, damit ich auf der Welt,
solang' es dir mich hier zu lassen noch gefällt, ein Kind des
Friedens bin' ('Now Lord, govern my mind, so that in the world,
so long as it pleases Thee still to leave me here, I am a child of
peace')
B. Cont

He begs to depart in peace like Simeon.

4 CHORALE
'Hier ist das rechte Osterlamm' ('Here is the true Easter lamb')
SATB. No instrumentation stated

This is the fifth verse of Luther's 'Christ lag in Todesbanden' (1524) ('Christ lay in death's bonds') which, if out of season, is here relevant.

SEPTUAGESIMA SUNDAY

Epistle: 1 Cor. IX. 24–27—X. 1–5 (Our life is like a race; only one receives the prize).
Gospel: Matt. XX. 1–16 (The labourers in the vineyard).

Nimm, was dein ist, und gehe hin (Take what is thine and go hence).
Cantata BWV 144. Leipzig, 1724.

The libretto of Cantata BWV 84 deals with the labourer who was contented with his lot although he had endured the heat and burden of the day and had to see the latecomers receive the same wage as he did. In the present cantata we meet the grumbler and the only words in the opening chorus are those of the rebuke administered to him by his master.

1 CHORUS
(As above)
SATB. Cont
    Bach sets the words in straightforward fugal style, placing 'thine' on the highest note of the subject, while the rhythm of the counter-subject at 'go hence' is equivalent to a curt dismissal. In the last four bars all parts sing together 'go hence'.

2 ARIA
'Murre nicht, lieber Christ, wenn was nicht nach Wunsch geschieht' ('Murmur not, beloved Christian, when anything not according to desire happens')
A. Vln i, ii, Vla, Cont
    The brusque 'go thy way' gives place, in this lovely aria, to gentle spiritual advice. The simplicity of the writing in the opening chorus is again present in the purely harmonic accompaniment to the melody, but into this Bach introduces from time to time full bars of repeated notes in the continuo. These could be taken as the murmurs; the soul has not yet succeeded in suppressing envy.

3 CHORALE
'Was Gott tut, das ist wohlgetan' ('What God does, that is well done')
SATB. Cont

G

A straightforward setting of verse i of Samuel Rodigast's hymn (1676) set to a melody possibly by Johann Pachelbel (1690).

4 RECITATIVE
'Wo die Genügsamkeit regiert und überall das Ruder führt' ('Where contentment reigns and everywhere the rudder guides') T. Cont

'There is the man contented with what God sends.' The discontented man reaps only grief and sorrow.

5 ARIA
'Genügsamkeit ist ein Schatz in diesem Leben' ('Contentment is a treasure in this life')
S. Ob d'am, Cont

The contentment spoken of in the recitative is praised as a treasure in both joys and sorrows. Bach repeats 'contentment' no less than fifteen times in this short aria, in the final bars five times in succession.

6 CHORALE
'Was mein Gott will, das g'scheh allzeit' ('What my God wills, may that always happen')
SATB. Cont

The first verse of the hymn by Markgraf Albrecht of Brandenburg-Culmbach, set to a melody of French origin (1529).

Ich hab in Gottes Herz und Sinn mein Herz und Sinn ergeben (I have into God's heart and being my heart and being delivered).
Chorale Cantata BWV 92. Leipzig, 1725.

The libretto of this cantata, possibly by Bach, is based on Paul Gerhardt's hymn (1647) with the above title. Verses i, ii, v, x and xii are set in their original form in Nos. 1, 2, 4, 7 and 9, with the melody set to the chorale with which Cantata BWV 144 ended (see above). The other verses of Gerhardt's hymn are paraphrased in the present cantata.

1 CHORUS
'Ich hab in Gottes Herz und Sinn mein Herz und Sinn ergeben' ('I have into God's heart and being my heart and being delivered')
SATB. Ob d'am i, ii, Vln i, ii, Vla, Cont

The chorale melody, sung by the sopranos, permeates all the other parts, vocal and instrumental.

2 RECITATIVE AND CHORALE
'Es kann mir fehlen nimmermehr' ('I can lack nevermore')
B. Cont

The chorale melody marked 'in varied manner' is continually interrupted by reflections by the bass in which the continuo part depicts the falling of the mountains and the hills at the end of the world, and the roaring of the sea, from which man will be saved by faith and stand firmly on the rock like Peter.

3 ARIA
'Seht, seht! wie bricht, wie reisst, wie fällt, was Gottes starker Arm nicht hält' ('See! See! how breaks, how tears, how falls, what God's strong arm not holds')
T. Vln i, ii, Vla, Cont

The continuo, in this powerful and apocalyptic aria, continually descends to the depths and there is a marvellous second section defying Satan, who rages and raves and finally crashes into the abyss.

4 CHORALE
'Zudem ist Weisheit und Verstand bei ihm ohn' alle Massen' ('Moreover wisdom and understanding is through Him without measure')
A. Ob d'am i, ii, Cont

The melody is sung straightforwardly to a curiously elaborate setting in which the unfortunate oboes d'amore have to play for fifty-eight bars with no more than a very occasional quaver rest of relief.

5 RECITATIVE
'Wir wollen nun nicht länger zagen' ('We shall now no longer hesitate')
T. Cont

'We are in God's care! Why then hesitate to trust Him?' The last two lines speak of Christ's sufferings on the Cross which brought us salvation, and ends, 'Trust God's favour and mark then what is necessary. Patience, patience!' This most expressive recitative ends with a bar of arioso at 'patience'.

6 ARIA
'Das Brausen von den rauhen Winden macht, dass wir volle

Ähren finden' ('The raging of the harsh winds ensures that we full ears [of corn] find')
B. Cont

This strange sentence is explained in the second half of the aria which speaks of 'the violence' of this Cross 'bearing fruit' in the Christian Soul. The bass is given long florid phrases at each repetition of 'raging', and the whirlwind of notes is three times checked at the end of the middle section as the bass sings, 'Kiss his Son's hand, respect the true discipline'.

7 CHORALE AND RECITATIVE
'Ei nun, mein Gott, so fall ich dir getrost in deine Hände' ('Indeed now, my God, thus fall I, comforted, into Thy hands!')
SATB. (Chorus). SATB. (Soloists). Cont

This has a much more satisfactory way of bringing reflections by soloists into a chorale movement than the scrappy manner of No. 2. Bach divides each line of the chorale in all voices in such a way that the rhythmic flow is not interrupted. The melody is richly harmonized. The words in general express gratitude to God and His Son, and the last line gives the cue for No 8. 'I can with subdued strings to the Peace-Prince a new song compose.'

8 ARIA
'Meinem Hirten bleib ich treu' ('To my Shepherd I remain faithful')
S. Ob d'am i, Vln i, ii, Vla, Cont

The oboe d'amore sings in duet with the solo soprano in this exquisite aria. The strings are pizzicato throughout. The short middle section ends, 'Jesus has sufficient done. Amen—Father receive me.'

9 CHORALE
'Soll ich denn auch des Todes Weg und finstre Strasse reisen?' ('Shall I then likewise Death's way and the dark road travel?')
SATB. Ob d'am i, ii, Vln i, ii, Vla, all with voices, Cont

**Ich bin vergnügt mit meinem Glücke, das mir der liebe
Gott beschert** (I am happy in my good fortune which to me
the dear Lord gives).
Solo Cantata BWV 84. Leipzig, 1727.

1 ARIA
(As above)
S. Ob, Vln i, ii, Vla, Cont

In the earlier cantata for this Sunday (BWV 144) the Christian
soul was gently rebuked for murmuring over his hard lot, like the
labourers who had endured the heat and burden of the day in the
parable of the labourers in the vineyard, but in this soprano solo
cantata the reverse is the case; this early labourer feels himself
unworthy of even the smallest reward.

In the introductory ritornello of this delightful aria in triple
time the oboe utters trills of quiet content which, of course, come
into the vocal part.

2 RECITATIVE
'Gott ist mir ja nichts schuldig' ('God owes nothing to me')
S. Cont

'God rewards man because He loves him. I can take no merit
for doing my duty, but man is so often impatient and grumbles
if he is not showered with gifts.' Then comes the charming ending,
simply but most expressively set: 'It is enough for me that I don't
go hungry to bed'.

3 ARIA
'Ich esse mit Freuden mein weniges Brot und gönne dem Nächsten
von Herzen das Seine' ('I eat with joy my scanty bread, and grant
my neighbour his from my heart')
S. Ob, Vln solo, Cont

In discussing Cantata BWV 41 (p. 34) I mentioned the rise of a
fifth as the chief characteristic of the soprano aria and here, in
a similar way, it is a sixth. The key, the triple rhythm are the
same.

4 RECITATIVE
'Im Schweisse meines Angesichts will ich indess mein Brot
geniessen' ('In the sweat of my brow I will meanwhile my bread
enjoy')
S. Vln i, ii, Vla, Cont

85

The closing lines look towards death when the soul will get its just reward of wages and no more.

5 CHORALE
'Ich leb' indess in dir vergnüget, und sterb' ohn Kümmerniss' ('I live meanwhile in Thee contented, and die without any anxiety')
SATB. Ob, Vln i, ii, Vla, all with voices; Cont

The last verse of the hymn 'Wer weiss wie nahe mir mein Ende' (1695), set to its associated melody, Georg Neumark's 'Wer nur den lieben Gott lässt walten' (1657).

SEXAGESIMA SUNDAY

Epistle: 2 Cor. xi. 19–xii. 9 (Paul justifieth himself).
Gospel: Luke viii. 4–15 (The parable of the sower).

Gleich wie der Regen und Schnee vom Himmel fällt
(Even as the rain and snow from Heaven fall).
Cantata BWV 18. Weimar, ?1714. Libretto by Erdmann Neumeister.

1 SINFONIA
Fl i, ii, Fag, Vla i, ii, iii, iv, V'cello, Cont

The scoring of this Sinfonia, with four violas but no violins, is remarkable but, Whittaker tells us, it was by no means uncommon among Bach's experimental predecessors. It may be taken as an illustration of the text, which is from Isaiah LV. 10–11, in the bass recitative that follows. It is in the style of a Chaconne but with a free bass part.

2 RECITATIVE
'Gleich wie der Regen und Schnee vom Himmel fällt und nicht wieder dahin kommet, sondern früchtet die Erde' ('Even as the rain and snow from Heaven falls and not again thither comes, but fructify the earth')
B. Fag, Cont

The biblical text is vividly illustrated by Bach.

3 RECITATIVE AND CHORUS
'Mein Gott, hier wird mein Herze sein, ich öffne dir's in meines Jesu Namen. So ströme deinen Saamen als in ein gutes Land' ('My God here will my heart be, I open it to Thee in my Jesu's name: so scatter Thy seed as into good soil')
T.B. and SATB. Fl i, ii, Fag, Vla i, ii, iii, iv, Cont

The tenor soloist prays that the seed may fall on good soil in his soul. Then the sopranos intone the first line of Luther's Litany praying for deliverance from hardness of heart, 'Satan's wiles and the assaults of the Turks and Papists', answered each time by the chorus, 'Hear us, good Lord'. The first bass recitative has a declamatory passage about the devil's attempt to rob the Christian of 'the Word' and in the following one, for tenor, which speaks of the 'persecution' of the faithful, Bach gives to that word ('Verfolgung') the most astonishing run in all his church music.

This is followed by the denunciation, in the litany, of the 'murderous' Turks and Papists. The last recitative, for bass, tilts at the gluttonous, the rich and the sensual, concluding with a tortuous phrase on 'going astray'.

4 ARIA
'Mein Seelenschatz ist Gottes Wort' ('My Soul's delight is God's Word')
S. Fl i, ii, Vla i, ii, iii, iv (all unis.), Cont

Bach holds to his four violas in the scoring of this delightful aria which, though it has a swipe at Satan, is very cheerful. It has a particularly charming phrase at 'Away with all, away' in the vein of a popular song, and very welcome after the grim No. 3.

5 CHORUS
'Ich bitt', O Herr, aus Herzensgrund, du wollst nicht von mir nehmen' ('I pray, O Lord, from heart's depth Thou wilt not from me take [Thy holy word from my mouth]')
SATB. Fl i, ii, Vla i, ii, iii, iv, Fag, all with voices, Cont

Verse viii of L. Spengler's 'Durch Adams Fall ist ganz verderbt' (1524), set to its melody (1535).

Leichtgesinnte Flattergeister (Scatterbrained and shallow people).
Solo Cantata BWV 181. Leipzig, 1724.

1 ARIA
'Leichtgesinnte Flattergeister rauben sich des Wortes Kraft' ('Light-minded, fickle persons rob themselves of the Word's strength')
B. Fl trav, Ob, Vln i, ii, Vla, Cont

The libretto is concerned with Jesus's interpretation of the parable of the sower, 'Those by the wayside are they that hear: then cometh the devil and taketh away the word out of their hearts lest they should believe and be saved.' The second half of the aria brings in the adversary. 'Belial with his brood seeks besides to prevent that it [the seed] any profit procures'. Bach is holding light-minded, fickle persons up to contempt.

2 RECITATIVE AND ARIOSO
'O unglücksel'ger Stand verkehrter Seelen, so gleichsam an dem

Wege sind' ('Oh, unfortunate condition of perverted souls which are by the wayside')
A. Cont

The text bears out the contention above, and at the start Bach quotes a phrase from the aria. In the arioso, which speaks of the rocky hearts of the second group of souls, the continuo has phrases almost identical with those of the subject of the G major Fugue (BWV 541). Two bars of recitative, 'There operates, yea, Christ's last word', are followed by a graphic illustration (*andante*) of the rocks bursting asunder as the angel's hand moves the grave-stone. This must be an allusion to St Matthew xxvii. 51. The last words are given poignant expression. 'Wilt thou, O heart, yet harder be?'

3 ARIA
'Der schädlichen Dornen unendliche Zahl, die Sorgen der Wollust, die Schätze zu mehren, die werden das Feuer der höllischen Qual in Ewigkeit nähren' ('The dangerous thorns' countless number, the cares of desire, the treasures to multiply, they will nourish the fire of hellish torment in eternity')
T. Cont

There is no warrant for this sadistic judgement in Christ's explanation of this parable. He said only that those who are choked with cares etc. 'bring to fruit no perfection', and Bach, in this lightly scored aria, does not attempt to reproduce in his charming melody the repellent imagery of the words.

4 RECITATIVE
'Von diesen wird die Kraft erstickt' ('By these is the strength choked')
S. Cont

5 CHORUS
'Lass, Höchster, uns zu allen Zeiten des Herzens Trost, dein heilig Wort' ('Grant, Highest, to us at all times the heart's comfort, Thy holy word')
SATB. Tr, Fl, Ob, Vln i, ii, Vla, Cont

The text is by the unknown librettist and is not a chorale.

Erhalt uns, Herr, bei deinem Wort (Uphold us, Lord, with Thy word).
Chorale Cantata BWV 126. Leipzig, 1725.

The first and third verses of Luther's hymn, with the above title (1542) are set to its anonymous melody in Nos. 1 and 3 in this cantata: the rest are paraphrased in Nos. 2, 4 and 5 respectively.

1 CHORUS

'Erhalt uns, Herr, bei deinem Wort und steur' des Papsts und Türken Mord' ('Uphold us, Lord, with Thy word and repress Papal and Turkish murder')
SATB. Tr, Ob i, ii, Vln i, ii, Vla, Cont

Luther on the war-path again! He called his hymn 'A children's song to sing against the two arch-enemies of Christ and His Holy Church, the Pope and the Turks', and Bach appropriately makes a battle-piece of the first verse. The trumpet sounds the alarm in the first bar of the introductory ritornello. The sopranos have the chorale melody. 'Murder' is given bloodcurdling runs. It is a stirring movement and one of its most thrilling moments comes in the penultimate reprise of the ritornello—when the trumpets shrill out above the stave.

2 ARIA

'Sende deine Macht von oben, Herr der Herren, starker Gott' ('Send Thy might from above, Lord of Lords, powerful God')
T. Ob i, ii, Cont

Two motifs run through the whole of this urgent prayer for the strong arm of God to come to the aid of the faithful. In the middle section of the aria the tenor voices the Church militant and is given a long, brilliant and florid phrase of patently instrumental character on the word '(zu)zerstreuen' ('to scatter').

3 RECITATIVE

'Der Menschen Gunst und Macht wird wenig nützen, wenn du nicht willst das arme Häuflein schützen' ('Man's favour and might will little avail, if Thou wilt not the poor little group protect')
A.T. Cont

The choral melody is introduced into the four *arioso/adagio* sections of this duet separated by passages of recitative for one or the other of the solo voices. They form a prayer for help against the false brethren in the persecuted City of God.

4 ARIA
'Stürze zu Boden, schwülstige Stolze, mache zu nichte, was sie
erdacht' ('Hurl to ground, arrogant proud ones, bring to naught
what they [have] devised')
B. Cont

These two lines suffice for the first section of this rapid tumult-
uous outpouring of rage against the foe. Bach uses the end chord
of each phrase on the continuo to underline 'stürze'—a fine piece
of dovetailing—in the first three vocal entries. The continuo part
is black with rushing demisemiquavers and in the middle section,
demanding that the abyss should suddenly engulf the enemy at
'Let their desires never succeed', angular vocal runs vividly depict
the abyss opening, the raging enemy, the extinction of his desires
which shall never ('nimmer' twice repeated, *staccato*, to rising
phrases) succeed. It is a superb piece of declamation, needing a
very accomplished bass to make its due effect.

5 RECITATIVE
'So wird dein Wort und Wahrheit offenbar und stehet auf in
höchstem Glanze dar' ('So becomes Thy word and truth manifest
and shows itself in highest splendour')
T. Cont

The battle is won—peace returns.

6 CHORALE
'Verleih uns Frieden gnädiglich, Herr Gott, zu unsern Zeiten'
('Grant us graciously, Lord God, peace in our time')
SATB. As No. 1, insts. with voices

This is Luther's version (1529) of the short plainsong antiphon
'Da pacem Domine in diebus nostris' to which he added a prayer
for peace and good government, 'a restful and quiet life, in all
godliness and fellowship to those under authority'. The chorale
concludes with a beautiful 'Amen'.

QUINQUAGESIMA SUNDAY

Epistle: 1 Cor. XIII. (The praises of charity).
Gospel: Luke XVIII. 31–43 (We go up to Jerusalem. The blind man receives sight).

Jesus nahm zu sich die Zwölfe (Jesus called to Him the Twelve).
Cantata BWV 22. Cöthen, 1723.

Librettists had a choice in writing for this Sunday, either of Christ's journeying to Jerusalem and His prophetic words about its significance, or the healing of the blind man on the way. The librettist's name is not known, but as this cantata was composed for Bach's 'Probe' or test-piece, in the competition for the post of Cantor of St Thomas, he may well have written it himself and chosen Jesus's journey to Jerusalem with His disciples as the most appealing subject.

1 ARIOSO AND CHORUS
'Jesus nahm zu sich die Zwölfe' ('Jesus called to Him the Twelve') T.B. and SATB. Ob, Vln i, ii, Vla, Cont

After the introductory ritornello the tenor soloist sings the first words of St Luke XVIII. 31 after which the bass soloist continues 'Behold, we go up to Jerusalem and all things are written by the prophets concerning the Son of Man shall be accomplished'.

The poignance of Jesus's words—for Bach would have had in mind what He goes on to tell the Twelve—is emphasized by one small two-bar motif first heard on the oboe in the introductory ritornello and repeated many times at various pitches. For the rest the oboe's melody suggests the start of the journey.

The aria is followed, without break, by a choral fugue, *allegro*, which vividly illustrates the disciples' inability to understand their Master's dire prophecies, 'the meaning was hidden from them and they knew not what He had spoken'. Bach brings in the oboe and strings to reinforce the climax and, when the voices cease, to depict the confusion left in the disciples' minds.

2 ARIA
'Mein Jesu, ziehe mich nach dir, ich bin bereit, ich will von hier und nach Jerusalem zu deinen Leiden gehn' ('My Jesus,

draw me after you, I am ready, I will go from here and to Jerusalem, to Thy Passion')

A. Ob. solo, Cont

The spiritual journey with the Saviour to Jerusalem, as if traversing the *via dolorosa*, is poignantly expressed in the melody of this aria. Bach uses a motif which he frequently employed to express sorrowful emotion.

The words of the middle section pray that the full meaning of Jesus's grief and death may be understood by the soul.

3 RECITATIVE

'Mein Jesu, ziehe mich, so werd ich laufen' ('My Jesus, draw me, so shall I run')

B. Vln i, ii, Vla, Cont

The text dwells on the soul's shame in recognizing, as the disciples did, the transfigured Jesus on Mount Tabor but not the crucified Jesus at Golgotha, and praying, as in the aria above, to be enlightened by having worldly desires crucified and to go joyfully then on the road to Jerusalem. A brief arioso illustrates these last words, the strings carrying the vocal phrase of joy up to a high peak of emotion.

4 ARIA

'Mein Alles in Allem, mein ewiges Gut' ('My all in all, my everlasting good')

T. Vln i, ii, Vla, Cont

The soul prays to be wholly converted and to become spiritually dead to worldly desires. The burden of the beautiful middle section is 'So draw me in peace after you in peace thither'. There are two wonderful moments, the long sustained note on 'peace' and the exultant eleven-bar phrase at 'eternal good'.

5 CHORALE

'Ertöt uns durch dein Güte, erweck uns durch dein Gnad' ('Mortify us by Thy goodness, awaken us by Thy grace')

SATB. As No. 1

This is the fifth verse of E. Kreutziger's Christmas hymn 'Herr Christ, der einig Gott's Sohn', with the melody given an exquisitely consoling instrumental accompaniment.

This is one of the most admirable librettos among the church cantatas, a true meditation consistently worked out, and unless the congregation were as stupid as the disciples it must have made a deep impression on those who first heard it.

Du wahrer Gott und Davids Sohn (Thou very God and David's Son)
Cantata BWV 23. Leipzig, 1724.

This libretto, taken from St Matthew xx. 30–34, is the account of *two* blind men, thereby giving Bach the chance of writing a duet.

1 DUET
'Du wahrer Gott und Davids Sohn, der du von Ewigkeit, in der Entfernung schon, mein Herzeleid und meine Liebespein umständlich angesehen, erbarm' dich mein' ('Thou very God and David's Son, Thou who from eternity, has, in the distance, already seen minutely my heart's grief and my body's pain, pity Thou me')
S.A. Ob i, ii, Cont

The text and the choice of voices show that Bach is treating the healing of blind men as related to the healing of the Christian soul.

2 RECITATIVE
'Ach, gehe nicht vorüber' ('Ah, do not pass by me')
T. Ob i, ii (both with Vln i), Vln ii, Vla, Cont

Oboes and first violins accompany the singer with a phrase of the plain-song 'Agnus Dei' as it appears in the Litany of Loretto, and it is interesting that Bach uses it in the chorale at the close of the cantata. The text of the last line is '[I] leave Thee not without Thy blessing' (Genesis xxxII. 26).

3 CHORUS
'Aller Augen warten, Herr, du allmächtiger Gott, auf dich' ('All eyes wait, Lord, thou almighty God, on Thee') (Psalm cxLv. 15)
SATB. Ob i, ii, Vln i, ii, Vla, Cont

The first line is repeated by the chorus no less than seven times in the course of this attractive movement, after the manner of a rondo, with four interpolations of added text for tenor and bass.

4 CHORALE
'Christe, du Lamm Gottes' ('Christ, Thou Lamb of God')
SATB. Cornetto, Trb i, ii, iii, all with voices, Ob i, ii, Vln i, ii, Vla, Cont

This fine chorale divides each petition into three lines, 'Christ, Thou Lamb of God'—'Thou that bearest the sins of men'—'Have mercy on us'—with brief instrumental passages between. The melody is in the soprano line throughout. Each petition is treated differently; the last one ends with a beautiful 'Amen' to the first phrase of the melody over expressive harmonies. It was with this that Bach ended his St John Passion in its second version (1725).

Herr Jesu Christ, wahr'r Mensch und Gott (Lord Jesus Christ, true man and God).
Chorale Cantata BWV 127. Leipzig, 1725.

The libretto has verses i and viii of Paul Eber's hymn with the above title in Nos. 1 and 5; the rest are paraphrased. The melody in Nos. 1, 4 and 5 is Louis Bourgeois' 'On a beau sa maison bastir' (1551).

1 CHORUS
(As above)
SATB. Fl i, ii, Ob i, ii, Vln i, ii, Vla, Cont

A remarkable feature of this movement is Bach's simultaneous use of the opening phrases of the chorale and the Lutheran version of the plainsong *Agnus Dei* which comes at the end of the Litany of Loretto and which Bach also uses in Cantata BWV 23. These are heard in the first four bars, over a pedal bass, on oboes, violins and violas respectively, with a dotted rhythmic figure on the flutes above.

The words of the chorale, which concentrate on the sufferings of Christ, mocked, spat on, scourged and at last crucified, explain Bach's use of these motifs.

No sermon on the Passion could be as moving, as eloquent as this wonderful movement.

2 RECITATIVE
'Wenn alles sich zur letzten Zeit entsetzet, und wenn ein kalter Todesschweiss die schon erstarrten Glieder netzet' ('When all at the last hour shudders, and when a cold death-sweat moistens the already stiffened limbs')
T. Cont

'The contemplation of Christ's agony breaks my heart, but faith tells me that Jesus is with me and His sufferings prepare for my rest'.

3 ARIA
'Die Seele ruht in Jesu Händen, wenn Erde diesen Leib bedeckt' ('The soul rests in Jesu's hands when earth this body covers')
S. Fl i, ii, Ob i, Vln i, ii, Vla, Cont

95

Below the slow procession of quavers, *staccato* on the flutes, the oboe sings the beautiful melody of rest, the string basses having pizzicato quavers. The middle section has broken phrases for the voice with the orchestra illustrating the line 'Ah, call me soon ye death-bells'. The singer continually repeats the words 'I am at death unaffrighted because my Jesus me awakens'. Whittaker suggests the opposite is the case, which may be so. I am reminded of Orestes's aria in Gluck's *Iphigenia* when the orchestra—in this case—contradicts his assertion, 'My heart is calm within my breast'.

4 RECITATIVE AND ARIA
'Wenn einstens die Posaunen schallen' ('When one day the trumpet sounds')
B. Tr, Vln i, ii, Vla, Cont

This dramatic movement is divided into seven sections, the third of which is a vivid picture of the Last Judgement. The trumpets ring out in Nos. 1, 3 and 7. No. 2 quotes St Matthew XXIV. 34. 'Beware I say unto you', to quiet music, quoting the first line of the chorale. After No. 3, 'when heaven and earth in fire disappear, yet shall a believer eternally endure'. No. 4 quietens again to reassure the soul that it will not die eternally, No. 5 adds to this, in powerful phrases, that Christ will break death's enclosing hand. Nos. 2 and 3 are then repeated.

5 CHORALE
'Ach Herr, vergieb all unsre Schuld, hilf, dass wir warten mit Geduld' ('Ah, Lord, forgive all our guilt, help that we wait in patience')
SATB. As No. 1, with voices, Cont

The sixth verse of the chorale.

Sehet, wir gehen hinauf gen Jerusalem (Come let us go up to Jerusalem).
Solo Cantata BWV 159. Leipzig, ?1729. Libretto by Picander.

Pascal wrote in an unforgettable phrase 'Jesu Christ will be in agony until the end of the world', suffering with man in his trials, and from man's sins. Alto, tenor, and bass soloists, in the four numbers of this beautiful cantata all give expression, in varying ways, to this poignant saying, from the setting out of the Saviour to His death on the Cross. They represent the Christian soul.

1 RECITATIVE AND ARIOSO
'Sehet, wir gehen hinauf gen Jerusalem' ('Come let us go up to Jerusalem')
A.B. Vln i, ii, Vla, Cont

The bass utters the first word 'Come' to a long-drawn phrase (arioso) after which the alto sings in recitative 'Come, then, my heart, behold whither goes Thy Jesus.' The second arioso covers the succeeding words 'Let us go up', with the alto again breaking in, and the sentence is then completed in the third arioso 'to Jerusalem' followed by the repetition of the whole of it.

The voices, therefore, move on two planes, the past and the present, with the soul living the journey in imagination, picturing the road as steep, rough, and thorny to the feet. Jesus passes out of sight and in the concluding recitative the soul is haunted by the sight of the instruments of the Passion and cries 'Ah! do not go, yet if Thou goest now, and I with Thee, then hell will be my lot.' The music continually modulates from key to key in this vivid declamation.

2 ARIA AND CHORALE
'Ich folge dir nach durch Speichel und Schmach am Kreuz will ich dich noch umfangen' ('I follow after Thee through spittle and shame: on the Cross I will Thee yet embrace')
A.S. Ob with S. Fag i, ii with Cont

After the dire prediction at the end of the recitative above, the soul recovers faith and courage to follow in the Saviour's footsteps. With his usual perception, Bach leaves the alto's first phrase unaccompanied. The melody has the expected 'walking' rhythm and above it the soprano (or, better, the choral sopranos) softly sing the sixth verse of Paul Gerhardt's hymn 'O Haupt voll Blut und Wunden': 'I will here with Thee stand, despise me then not! From Thee I will not go, even till Thy heart breaks. When Thy head becomes pale, in the last death stroke, then will I Thee hold in my arm and bosom.' The remaining words for the alto paraphrase those of the chorale. Bach achieves a perfect union between the melodies of the two parts in this most lovely movement.

3 RECITATIVE
'Nun will ich mich, mein Jesu, über dich in meinem Winkel grämen' ('Now will I, myself, my Jesu, over Thee in my hiding place grieve')
T. Cont

H   97

The soul looks forward, through tears, to the joy of the Resurrection.

4 ARIA

'Es ist vollbracht, das Leid ist alle' ('It is fulfilled, the sorrow is over')

B. Ob, Vln i, ii, Vla, Cont

This aria will at once call to mind the alto aria with the same opening words in the St John Passion. It moves on the same high plane of inspiration.

There are three motifs: (1) the oboe melody, with its answering phrase at once inverted, (2) the florid phrases in the middle section expressing 'Now will I hasten to give Jesus my thanks' followed by (3) 'World, goodnight' ('farewell'), a phrase falling from C above the stave to the octave below. 'It is finished, it is finished' is sung to the opening melody, the oboe then bringing this most poignant movement to a close.

5 CHORALE

'Jesu, deine Passion ist mir laute Freude' ('Jesus, Thy Passion is for me pure joy')

SATB. As No. 4. Insts. with voices

This is verse xxxiii of Paul Stockmann's 'Jesu Leiden, Pein und Tod' (1633) set to Melchior Vulpius' melody (1609), praying that, little though we deserve to share in His sufferings 'My soul on roses walks as I think that you prepare an abode for us in Heaven'.

THE ANNUNCIATION OF THE BLESSED VIRGIN MARY

Epistle: Isa. vii. 10–15 (Behold, a virgin shall conceive).
Gospel: Luke i. 26–38 (Gabriel salutes Mary).

Wie schön leuchtet der Morgenstern (How brightly shines yon morning star).

Chorale Cantata BWV 1. Leipzig, 1725.

It was a happy thought of the editors of the *Bach Gesellschaft* to choose this cantata to open its first volume, for it is not only one of the most beautiful but one of the happiest. Verses i and vii of the medieval hymn are in their original form in Nos. 1 and 6, the rest are paraphrased. Bach used the chorale melody in six of his cantatas and two of the organ chorale preludes.

1 CHORUS
(As above)
SATB. Cor i, ii, Ob da cacc i, ii, Vln concertante i, ii, Vln ripieno i, ii, Vla, Cont

In the introductory ritornello the horns' theme is preceded by one for the concertante violins. Sopranos have the chorale melody in long notes of shorter value, to one or other of the lower voices. This is most effective.

The Morning Star is, of course, Jesus, 'Son of David from Jacob's stem, my King and my Bridegroom'. There is a touching moment when the chorus sing, in chords, 'Gracious lovely' ('priceless treasure'). Vocal and orchestral basses have a splendid series of sequences in the last part of the chorus.

2 RECITATIVE
'Du wahrer Gottes und Marien Sohn' ('Thou true son of God and Mary')
T. Cont

The Angel Gabriel's message is here recalled.

3 ARIA
'Erfüllet, ihr himmlischen göttlichen Flammen die nach euch verlangende, gläubige Brust' ('Fill, ye heavenly divine flames the after-you-longing, believing breast')
S. Ob da cacc, Cont

99

A lightly scored and delightfully melodious aria with a most infectious rhythm.

4 RECITATIVE
'Ein irdscher Glanz' ('An earthly ray')
B. Cont

The text relates a far greater joy than earth's light or worldly happiness can give, the gift of the Saviour's body and food for a perfect possession and spiritual refreshment.

5 ARIA
'Unser Mund und Ton der Saiten sollen dir für und für Dank und Opfer bereiten' ('Our mouth and sound of the strings shall to Thee ever thanks and offering prepare')
T. Vln concertante i, ii, Vln ripieno i, ii, Vla, Cont

The scoring provides the sound of two solo violins, as well as the orchestral strings, to fit the words above. This is an aria as delightfully melodious as No. 3.

6 CHORALE
'Wie bin ich doch so herzlich froh' ('How am I so heartily happy')
SATB. All as No. 1. Insts. with voices; Cor ii with Cont

(NO CANTATAS WERE PERFORMED DURING LENT.)

PALM SUNDAY

Epistle: Phil. II. 5–11 (Christ humbleth Himself even unto death).
The Passion according to St Matthew is read in place of the Gospel.

Himmelskönig, sei willkommen (King of Heaven, be Thou welcome).
Cantata BWV 182. Weimar, 1714.

The score of this cantata is inscribed 'Tempore Passionis aut Festo Mariae Annunciationis'. When Palm Sunday and the Marian feast day coincided, as happened twice (in 1725 and 1736) in Bach's cantorate, either this cantata or No. 1 could be sung in place of the St Matthew Passion, and presumably that was the case at Weimar.

The form of the cantata is unusual as the body of it consists of three arias in succession, the first preceded by a recitative, the last followed by a chorale and a concluding chorus.

1 SONATA
Fl, Vln concertante, Vln ripieno, Vla i, ii, V'cello, Cont

In this processional movement, marked *Grave. Adagio*, the solo violin and the flute in duet have the solemn dotted rhythm Bach so often associates with God or Christ. The other instruments play chords *pizzicato*. It is a beautiful little movement.

2 CHORUS
'Himmelskönig, sei willkommen' ('King of Heaven, be Thou welcome')
SATB. Fl, Vln, Vla i, ii, V'cello, Cont

This is not an exuberant welcome. It begins with a fugato which leads to another of a picturesque character, with four entries in close order.

3 RECITATIVE
'Siehe, siehe, ich komme' ('Behold, behold I come')
B. V'cello, Cont

The quotation is from Psalm XL. 7–8, an arioso in which the continuo takes over the first phrase of the recitative and repeats it ten times with a drop of a seventh between the end of one bar and the next. In this way Bach underlines the submission of Christ's will to that of His Father.

4 ARIA

'Starkes Lieben, das dich, grosser Gottessohn von dem Thron deiner Herrlichkeit getrieben' ('Mighty love, that Thee, great son of God, has driven from the throne of Thy glory')
B. Vln, Vla i, ii, V'cello, Cont

The music, though dignified, is oddly neutral and does not reflect the lofty sentiment of the text.

5 ARIA

'Leget euch dem Heiland unter, Herzen die ihr christlich seid' ('Put yourselves the Saviour under, hearts, ye who Christian are')
A. Fl solo, V'cello, Cont

This also is an aria in slow time but with a quicker middle section and now some warmth of expression.

6 ARIA

'Jesu, lass durch Wohl und Weh mich auch mit dir ziehen' ('Jesus, through weal and woe, let me with Thee go')
T. V'cello, Cont

In each of the two preceding arias Bach reduces the scoring and now uses the continuo only. This is one of the most poignant arias Bach ever composed. Five times the vocal phrases break off and there is a silent beat. It is as if Bach had in mind the Saviour's falling to the ground as He bore the Cross to Calvary. There is a cry of anguish—'the weal and the woe'—near the end leaving the voice on a high G, the continuo bass on a low C sharp, and there is a more astonishing discord at 'crucify' ('cries the world') in the first half of the aria.

The loneliness this superb aria, which speaks of 'cross-crown and palms', conveys is heartbreaking.

7 CHORALE

'Jesu, deine Passion ist mir laute Freude' ('Jesus, Thy Passion is for me pure joy')
SATB. As No. 2

Verse xxxiii of Paul Stockmann's 'Jesu Leiden, Pein und Tod' (1633) set to Melchior Vulpius's melody (1609), a fugal treatment in the Pachelbel style, quite elaborate, and with the melody in the soprano line doubled by flute and violin.

8 CHORUS

'So lasset uns gehen in Salem der Freuden' ('So let us go in the Salem of joy')
SATB. As No. 2

The melody of this mainly light-hearted processional chorus has an outline and rhythm similar to the opening chorus of *The Sages of Sheba* (BWV 65).

The line 'accompany the King in love and sorrow' alone reminds the listener of the price paid for 'the Salem of joy'.

EASTER SUNDAY

Epistle: 1 Cor. v. 7–8 (Christ our Passover is sacrificed for us).
Gospel: Mark xvi. 1–8 (Christ is risen).

Der Himmel lacht, die Erde jubilieret (The heavens laugh, the earth rejoices).
Cantata BWV 31. Weimar, 1715. Libretto by Salomo Franck.

The Easter Alleluia, prominent in the Roman rite throughout the Easter Liturgy, comes only into the succeeding cantata (No. 4) and not at all into the present one for the Sunday, though it does do so in one of those for Easter Monday and Tuesday and the following Sunday. Bach, however, conveys all that 'Alleluia' stands for in the present cantata.

1 SONATA
Tr i, ii, iii, Timp, Ob i, ii, iii, Te, Fag, Vln i, ii, Vla i, ii, V'cello i, V'cello ii, Cont

Bach draws on all the forces available at Weimar for this sonata and the chorus that follows. The sonata begins and ends with a unison outburst to illustrate the laughter of the heavens and the rejoicing of the earth. The movement points continually heavenwards.

2 CHORUS
(As above)
SSATB. As No. 1

This is a rare instance of Bach's use of a five-part chorus. The laughter and the rejoicing are expressed in realistically florid phrases passing from part to part until all are engaged, vocal and instrumental, and the music shakes with mirth, spiritual and physical. The joyous onrush is then checked by an expressive *adagio* at the words 'Who for Himself the grave for rest hast chosen, the Holiest cannot decay'. Here, needless to say, brass and percussion are silent.

3 RECITATIVE
'Erwünschter Tag! sei, Seele, wieder froh' ('Desired day! Be, soul, again glad')
B. V'cello ii, Cont

The greater part of this recitative is, in fact, arioso. The

104

tempo continually changes from *allegro* to *adagio* and *andante*. The words speak of 'our heavy guilt' in imprisoning the Saviour now 'risen out of distress' and in most lovely and lyrical phrases speak of His living again 'Head and limbs'.

4 ARIA

'Fürst des Lebens, starker Streiter, hochgelobter Gottessohn' ('Prince of Life, strong champion, highly-praised God's Son')
B. V'cello ii and Cont

The cross raised God's highly praised Son to the highest throne of honour. The rhythm of solemnity, as Whittaker always calls this dotted note pattern, dominates this austere aria in both vocal and instrumental parts.

5 RECITATIVE

'So stehe denn, du gottergebne Seele, mit Christo geistlich auf' ('So arise then, thou God-devoted Soul, with Christ spiritually')
T. V'cello and Cont

The Christian is exhorted to show forth his Saviour in his life. He runs quickly from the grave, leaving the cloth of sins behind, to live with Christ.

6 ARIA

'Adam muss in uns verwesen, soll der neue Mensch genesen, der nach Gott geschaffen ist' ('Adam must in us decay, the new man shall recover, who is created in the image of God')
T. Vln i, ii, Vla i, ii, V'cello i, V'cello ii and Cont

A short and more melodious aria than No. 4 and much more richly accompanied.

7 RECITATIVE

'Weil denn das Haupt sein Glied natürlich nach sich zieht, so kann mich nichts von Jesu scheiden' ('Because then the head its limb naturally after itself draws, so can nothing separate me from Jesus')
S. V'cello ii and Cont

The recitative ends with a very familiar quotation from Job XIX. 26, 'So in my flesh shall I see God'.

8 ARIA

'Letzte Stunde, brich herein, mir die Augen zuzudrücken' ('Last hour, break herein, to me the eyes to close')
S. Ob i, Vln i, ii (unis.), Vla i, ii (unis.), V'cello ii and Cont

It is a relief to get away from anatomical details of head and limb even if to a death-wish so curiously dwelt on this festival day. The tender melody is in Bach's loveliest vein and at 'Let me Jesu's joys-glory and His bright light descry' its beauty is heightened as the violins and violas in unison play the melody of the chorale with which the cantata ends, 'When my last hour at hand is', in each of the three sections of the aria.

9 CHORALE
'So fahr ich hin zu Jesu Christ' ('So journey I thither to Jesus Christ')
S.S. (unis.) A.T.B. Tr i, Ob i, ii, iii, Te, Fag, Vln i, ii, Vla i, ii, V'cello i, ii and Cont

Verse v, added posthumously to the original of Nikolaus Hermann's 'Wenn mein Stündlein vorhanden ist' (1560) set to his own melody (1569). The cantata, as this final verse emphasizes, deals with mortal man's resurrection rather than with present joy after the rigours of Lent and the sorrows of the Passion and death of Christ.

Christ lag in Todesbanden (Christ lay in Death's dark prison).
Chorale Cantata BWV 4. Leipzig, 1724.

For the libretto of this cantata Bach took the entire text of Luther's hymn with the above title. The melody is derived from one of the oldest German hymns 'Christ ist erstanden' which in turn is a version of the ancient plainsong sequence 'Victimae Paschali laudes' sung in the Easter Sunday Mass. Bach scholars believe the cantata to have been composed at Weimar and revised at Leipzig because the composer has reverted to the past for the form of the work, basing it on chorale variations for organ in the manner of Böhm and Pachelbel.

1 SINFONIA
Vln i, ii, Vla i, ii, Cont

In fourteen bars Bach depicts Christ in the dark tomb, using the descending semitone of the first two notes of the melody (vln i; G–F sharp) and in the last five bars, the ascending phrase of the 'Alleluia'. Luther appended it at the end of each verse.

2 CHORUS

'Christ lag in Todesbanden für unser Sünd gegeben' ('Christ lay in the bonds of death for our sins')

SATB. Strings as at No. 1 but the voices doubled respectively by Cornetto, Trb i, ii, iii, Cont

The sopranos sing the melody in long notes, altos and basses a diminution of the first five notes of the melody, otherwise proceeding independently as do the strings, with the violins continually stressing the semitonal motif. The music soon reflects with joy Christ's rising out of the tomb and the 'Alleluias' burst forth. The last section, in quicker tempo, and in syncopated rhythm, expresses uninhibited joy, with the sopranos in the penultimate bar singing 'Alleluia' all by themselves.

3 DUET

'Den Tod niemand zwingen kunnt, bei allen Menschenkindern' ('O'er Death no one could prevail among all men's children')

S.A. Cornetto with S., Trb i with A. Cont

The falling semiquaver of the chorale melody is stressed in the continuo part, for the verse speaks of man unable of himself to escape the imprisonment of death. The 'Alleluias' here should be muted in performance.

4 CHORALE

'Jesus Christus, Gottes Sohn an unser Statt ist kommen' ('Jesus Christ, God's Son, in our stead has come')

T. Vln i, ii, Cont

This verse speaks of Christ taking away our sins and death's claim on us. The tenors sing the melody unaltered, to a forceful violin counter-melody, up to a sudden *adagio* preceded by quadruple and double stopping on the violins and a violent descent of the continuo part as Satan falls into Hell. Brilliant 'Alleluias' triumph in his fall.

5 CHORALE

'Es war ein wunderlicher Krieg, da Tod und Leben rungen' ('It was a strange fight when death and life struggled')

SATB. Cont

A free fantasia on the melody ending with a shout of 'Alleluia' after the taunt of 'O death, where is now thy victory?'

6 CHORALE

'Hier ist das rechte Osterlamm' ('Here is the true Easter Lamb')

B. As No. 1

107

It is possible that Bach wrote this wonderful aria, which takes the bass down to low E at one point and E sharp at another—followed by a high D!—for the Hofcantor Wolfgang Christoph Alt, the chief bass singer in the Weimar choir.

7 DUET
'So feiern wir das hohe Fest mit Herzens Freud' und Wonne' ('So keep we this High Festival with heart's joy and bliss')
S.T. Cont

The singers break out into joyful triplet phrases on such words as 'bliss' and 'joy' and, of course, 'Alleluia'. Christ is hailed as the 'sun' who banishes the darkness of sin and enlightens the heart. The continuo part dances along in an unbroken rhythm of dotted quavers.

8 CHORALE
'Wir essen und leben wohl in rechten Osterfladen' ('We eat and live well in the true Passover')
SATB. As No. 2

A straightforward presentation of the chorale.

EASTER MONDAY

Epistle: Acts x. 34–41 (Peter preaches Christ to Cornelius).
Gospel: Luke xxiv. 13–35 (Christ appears on the road to Emmaus).

Erfreut euch, ihr Herzen, entweichet ihr Schmerzen, es lebet der Heiland und herrschet in euch (Rejoice ye hearts, yield ye pains, lives the Saviour and governs in you). Cantata BWV 66. Leipzig, ?1724.

1 CHORUS
   (As above)
   SATB. Tr, Ob i, ii, Vln i, ii, Vla, Fag, Cont

   The text of the first section of the chorus is a general rejoicing in the glorious event of the Resurrection. It is preceded by a brilliant orchestral prelude in which one joyous little figure leaps out of the score and is prominent in the accompaniment to the chorus and, of course, in the ritornellos.

   Altos and tenors give out the opening line, then altos and basses and the latter again after the first ritornello. This makes for effective entries of the full chorus but does rather reduce the tension. After the second ritornello the second section, of some length, is confined to a duet for altos and basses in which the words are 'You can drive away the mourning, the fear, the anxious trembling'. These words, set to chromatic descending phrases, seem to contradict the sentiment of the opening words.

2 RECITATIVE
   'Es bricht das Grab und damit unsre Not, der Mund verkündigt Gottes Taten, der Heiland lebt' ('Broken is the grave and therewith our need, the mouth proclaims God's doings, the Saviour lives')
   B. Vln i, ii, Vla, Cont

3 ARIA
   'Lasset dem Höchsten ein Danklied erschallen für sein Erbarmen und ewige Treu' ('Let thanks to the Highest resound for His pity and everlasting faithfulness')
   B. Ob i, ii, Fag, Vln i, ii, Vla, Cont

   A fine aria in which Bach dwells on 'everlasting' in its first section. The second section begins with the words 'Jesus appears to us peace to give, Jesus calls us with Him to live'.

4 RECITATIVE DIALOGUE
'Bei Jesu Leben freudig sein, ist in unsrer Brust ein heller Sonnen-
schein' ('To rejoice in Jesu's life is in our breast a bright sunshine')
A. 'Fear', T. 'Hope' Cont

The first clear allusion to the Gospel account of Jesus appearing
to the two disciples as they walked to Emmaus is clumsily handled
in the libretto. Both men were sick at heart, because the prophet
they had trusted in as 'mighty in deed and word' had been put to
death and had not risen on the third day after. 'Hope' apparently
represents one of these men and 'Fear' the other. There is an
expressive moment in Hope's recitative where he quotes the
Saviour's words 'My grave and death brings you life, my Resurrection is your comfort'. A duet follows in which Hope sings
'My eye sees the Saviour arise' and Fear 'No eye sees the Saviour
arise'. Both sing the same music in canon. Bach made this same
mistake in the Hope-Fear duet in Cantata BWV 60, 'O Ewigkeit,
du Donnerwort'.

5 DUET
'Ich fürchte zwar des Grabes Finsternissen' ('I fear indeed the
grave's darkness')
A.T. Vln solo, Cont

Once again the singers have the same text—except that one
sings 'indeed', the other 'not' and later 'mourned' and 'hoped'.
In the middle section Fear is at last converted and both sing 'Now
is my heart full of comfort, I will know how to conquer through
God'.

This is a long duet but the music is continuously interesting and
exultant so that one can forget Fear's timorousness.

6 CHORALE
'Alleluja! des soll'n wir alle froh sein: Christus will unser Trost
sein, Kyrie eleis!' ('Alleluia, of this shall we all glad be: Christ
will our comfort be, Kyrie eleison')
SATB. Cont. No instrumentation stated

This is the third verse of 'Christ ist erstanden' (1529), a twelfth-
century German folksong derived from the Easter Sequence
Victimae paschali laudes.

Bleib bei uns, denn es will Abend werden (Stay with us, for it will evening become).
Cantata BWV 6. Leipzig, 1725.

The libretto concentrates on verses 28–9 of the Gospel 'And they drew nigh unto the village, whither they were going: and he made as though he would go further. And they constrained him, saying, Abide with us: for it is toward evening, and the day is now far spent. And he went in to abide with them.'

1 CHORUS
(As above)
Ob i, ii, Ob da cacc, Vln i, ii, Vla, Cont

Bach begins this lovely chorus with a gently falling theme on the wind instruments, accompanied by the strings low down in their compass, which at once brings to mind the opening strains of the concluding chorus, before the chorale, of the *St John Passion*. The relationship is beautifully apposite as Cleophas, one of the two disciples whom the mysterious stranger has joined on the road, after expressing astonishment at his request to know what was the subject of their earnest conversation recalls the crucifixion and death of Jesus and their bitter sorrow that he has disappointed their hopes of his redeeming Israel. It is his reply that, later, they said caused their hearts to burn within them.

The orchestral part paints a picture of the twilight as the choral voices together or in separate strands of melody repeat their plea 'Stay with us'. There is a wonderful moment, not to be missed, in the ritornello between the choral entries when the woodwind suddenly rise from a low note to a high one and again as this first section ends.

In the second section of the chorus the disciples press their plea more urgently. Bach here writes a double-fugue in the course of which, on instruments and voices, the plea 'Stay with us' is re-iterated seven times in long notes. As the chorus ends abruptly at 'Stay with us', Bach puts a rest of one beat, an urgent question mark. No reply comes. The first section is then repeated in shortened form with the sopranos given a high-pitched cry to a new phrase. The final chord in the major suggests the plea is answered.

2 ARIA
'Hochgelobter Gottessohn' ('Highly-praised Son of God')
A. Ob da cacc, Cont

111

This alto aria with an elaborate oboe da caccia obbligato, prays that the 'Son of God, enthroned on High' may be 'Our shining light through the darkness of the night'. The *pizzicato* continuo bass relieves the rather sombre atmosphere of the aria.

3 CHORALE
'Ach bleib bei uns, Herr Jesu Christ' ('Ah remain with us, Lord Jesus Christ')
S. V'cello piccolo, Cont

Light breaks into the soprano's singing of the above chorale. Verses i and ii of the hymn by Nikolaus Selnecker (1611) are set to its associated melody of 1589. The movement is the fifth of the Schübler Organ Preludes, but in that transcription the violoncello piccolo obbligato part loses much of its scintillating charm.

4 RECITATIVE
'Es hat die Dunkelheit an vielen Orten überhand genommen' ('There has the darkness on many sides prevailed')
B. Cont

Thus we are plunged into gloom after the joyous chorale movement.

5 ARIA
'Jesu, lass uns auf dich sehen' ('Jesus, let us Thee see')
T. Vln i, ii, Vla, Cont

The dark mood is shaken off in the strongly moulded phrases of this aria. The prayer concludes, 'Let the light of Thy word on us more brightly shine', during which the violins' triplets hearten the traveller with light from above.

6 CHORALE
'Beweis dein Macht, Herr Jesu Christ' ('Prove thy might, Lord Jesus Christ')
SATB. As No. 1

This has the second stanza of Luther's 'Erhalt uns, Herr, bei deinem Wort' (1542) set to an anonymous melody. It is a prayer that Christ will manifest His might and protect His 'poor Christendom'.

EASTER TUESDAY

Epistle: Acts XIII. 26–33 (Paul, at Antioch, preaches Christ risen).
Gospel: Luke XXIV. 36–47 (Jesus appears to the Twelve).

Ein Herz, das seinen Jesum lebend weiss (A heart that its Jesus living knows).
Cantata BWV 134. Leipzig, 1724.

Bach adapted three of the numbers in this cantata from a congratulatory ode to the Prince of Anhalt-Cöthen, adding three recitatives. The libretto, naturally enough, has little connection with the Gospel, but Bach did manage to work in a reference to the risen Christ in a lengthy duet (No. 4).

1 RECITATIVE
'Ein Herz, das seinen Jesum lebend weiss, empfindet Jesu neue Güte und dichtet nur auf seines Heilands Preis' ('A heart that its living Jesus knows, feels Jesu's new goodness, and meditates only on its Saviour's worth')
T.A. Cont
The tenor's recitative is followed by a charming arioso for alto, 'How joys itself a believing mind'.

2 ARIA
'Auf, Gläubige, singet die lieblichen Lieder' ('Up, believers, sing the glad songs')
T. Ob i, ii, Vln i, ii, Vla, Cont
The exhortation is expressed at the start by the rising notes of the tonic chord of B flat (F to F[1]) and, as in 'Jauchzet Gott in allen Landen' (BWV 51), it is carried up to B flat above the stave in the vocal fanfare that ends the first section of this very melodious aria.

3 RECITATIVE
'Wohl dir, Gott hat an dich gedacht' ('Well for thee, God has on thee thought')
T.A. Cont
This continues the dialogue in No. 1, but there are no arioso passages and it is rather dull. The text speaks of Satan trembling at the conquering might of the Saviour. The alto alludes to the

merits of the Passion and the tenor concludes that God takes away the distress of 'the last enemy' (the grave and death).

4 DUET
'Wir danken, wir preisen dein brünstiges Lieben und bringen ein Opfer der Lippen für dich' ('We thank, we praise Thy burning love and bring an offering of the lips for Thee')
A.T. Vln i, ii, Vla, Cont

The first two lines do duty for six pages of the vocal score, which includes a fairly long instrumental prelude and one extended ritornello. Bach's delightful music disguises the repetitiveness of the text.

5 RECITATIVE
'Doch wirke selbst den Dank in unser Munde' ('Then bring forth Thyself thanks in our mouth')
T.A. Cont

6 CHORUS
'Erschallet ihr Himmel, erfreue dich Erde' ('Resound ye heavens, rejoice thee earth')
SATB. Ob i, ii, Vln i, ii, Vla, Cont

A brilliant chorus. There is a good deal of chordal writing for the full chorus in the first section, several fugatos and, in the closing bars, a splendid chordal passage to the line, 'He comforts and places himself as victor there'.

So du mit deinem Munde bekennest Jesum das ist der Herr (If thou shalt confess with thy mouth the Lord Jesus). Cantata BWV 145. Leipzig, ?1729. Libretto: 3–7 Picander; 1–2 Bach's additions.

1 CHORALE
'Auf, mein Herz! Des Herren Tag hat die Nacht der Furcht vertrieben' ('Up my heart! The Lord's day has the night of fear dispersed')
SATB. No instrumentation given

Verse i of Caspar Neumann's hymn (1700) with the above title set to the melody of Johann Crüger's 'Jesu meine Zuversicht'.

2 CHORUS
'So du mit deinem Munde bekennest Jesum das ist der Herr'
SATB. Tr, Vln i, ii, Vla, Cont

Bach turned to the Epistle of St Paul to the Romans (x. 9) for the text of this chorus. 'If thou shalt confess with thy mouth Jesus as Lord; and shalt believe in thy heart that God raised him from the dead, thou shalt be saved.' The whole of the first section is for sopranos and altos only in canon with continuo accompaniment. There are long runs on 'raised'. When the sopranos, with first violins, begin the fugue, at 'so becomest thou blessed' one feels in true Bach country; the long notes he gives to 'blessed' are typical. Joy now invades all parts of the score and in the closing bars the trumpet sounds brief fanfares.

3 Duet
'Ich lebe, mein Herze, zu deinem Ergötzen' ('I live my heart, for thy glorification')
S.T. Vln, Cont

The words which the tenor sings are obviously those of Jesus. The soprano replies with the same words in the second person, but Bach departs here from his invariable habit of allotting Jesus's words to a bass. This is a very melodious duet and one wonders at first what is the meaning of the constant up-rushing scale passages for the violin.

4 Recitative
'Nun fordre, Moses, wie du willt' ('Now claim, Moses, what thou wilt')
T. Cont

The decree Moses claimed was the Old Law, of which St Paul, in the Epistle to the Colossians, II. 14, described as 'having blotted out the bond written in ordinances that was against us'. The words of the recitative continue, 'I have my receipt here with Jesu's blood and wounds signed . . . I am redeemed, I am freed'. At the end there is a moving little arioso, 'My heart, that mark to thee'. These words lead into the following aria.

5 Aria
'Merke, mein Herze, beständig nur dies' ('Mark, my heart, constantly only this')
B. Tr, Fl trav, Ob d'am i, ii, Vln i, ii, Cont

Bach brings in the additional instruments to give full force to the resounding octaves with which he presents his main theme, and which 'marks' that 'thy Saviour living is'.

6 RECITATIVE

'Mein Jesus lebt, das soll mir niemand nehmen, drum sterb' ich
sonder grämen' ('My Jesus lives, that shall no one from me take,
therefore I die without sorrow')
S. Cont

The music is full of confidence and imagination, the soul rises
to heaven to behold the risen Saviour.

7 CHORALE

'Drum wir auch billig fröhlich sein: singen das Halleluia fein'
('Therefore we also justly joyful are and sing Hallelujah well')
SATB. Cont. No instrumentation given

This is the fourteenth verse of Nicolaus Hermann's hymn and
melody 'Erschienen ist der herrlich Tag' (1560), fittingly in
triple time. Bach would surely have brought in all his instrumental
forces here.

FIRST SUNDAY AFTER EASTER

Epistle: 1 John v. 4–10 (Faith overcomes the world).
Gospel: John xx. 19–31 (Christ appears to the Twelve).

Halt im Gedächtnis Jesum Christ, der auferstanden ist von der Todten (Hold in remembrance Jesus Christ who was raised from the dead).
Cantata BWV 67. Leipzig, 1724.

1 CHORUS
(As above)
SATB. Cor, Fl Trav, Ob d'am i, ii, Vln i, ii, Vla, Org and Cont

The one sentence of the text comes from the Second Epistle of St Paul to Timothy, ii. 8.

The sustained note on the horn at the start of the brief instrumental prelude is associated with the word 'halt' which Bach emphasizes continually in all the vocal parts: but in the instrumental ones he gives this sustained note always to the horn. The florid quaver theme, illustrative of Christ's rising, first comes into the vocal parts as a fugato, during which Bach silences all the instruments except the continuo.

The exultant climb of the horn to the top of its compass as the magnificent music ends expresses the full tide of Easter joy.

2 ARIA
'Mein Jesus ist erstanden, allein, was schreckt mich noch?' ('My Jesus has risen, but what affrights me still?')
T. Ob d'am i, Vln i, ii, Vla, Org and Cont

The aria is a fine example of Bach's power of expressing contrary emotions, one affirming the resurrection, the other doubting it, as St Thomas did when Christ appeared in the Upper Room for the second time and called those blessed who 'have not seen but who have believed'.

The middle section is a most poignant appeal for comfort by one whose faith tells him of the Saviour's victory but whose heart feels full of 'strife and war'.

3 RECITATIVE
'Mein Jesu, heissest du des Todes Gift und eine Pestilenz der Hölle' ('My Jesus, Thou art called death's poison and a pestilence of Hell')
A. Org and Cont

The text is based on Hosea xiii. 14, in which the anthropo-
morphic God of the Old Testament speaks in the harshest terms
to Israel. It is odd for this frightened and doubting soul to apply
these words to Jesus. But the closing words speak of a 'hymn of
praise we have sung' and this is immediately followed by No. 4.

4 CHORALE
'Erschienen ist der herrlich Tag' ('Appeared is the glorious day')
SATB. As No. 1. Insts. with voices. Org and Cont

The first verse of Nicolaus Hermann's joyous hymn 'Erschienen
ist der herrlich Tag' (1560) straightforwardly sung.

5 RECITATIVE
'Doch scheinet fast, dass mich der Feinde Rest . . . nicht ruhig
bleiben lässt' ('Yet appears almost that me the enemies' dregs
. . . . do not peacefully leave me alone')
A. Org and Cont

The fears and doubts are still present but, as the last words of
the text show, they are about to vanish. 'Thou, O Prince of peace,
Thy word and work in us will fulfil'.

6 ARIA AND CHORUS
'Friede sei mit euch' ('Peace be unto you')
B. SAT. Fl trav, Ob d'am i, ii, Vln i, ii, Vla, Org and Cont

The cantata reaches its climax in this movement, which in fact
is an exquisite remembrance of Christ's appearance in the Upper
Room to bless, with peace, all troubled and fearful souls. The
orchestral introduction portrays the raging of the enemies of the
soul without and returns at each entry of the chorus. At the close
of the introduction there is a sudden hush, the tempo changes
from common to triple time, and the solo bass sings Christ's words,
with a sustained note on 'Peace be unto you' to the accompaniment of the wind instruments only. This pattern is repeated
throughout.

After the fourth and last (extended) blessing, and the quiet
choral response, the cantata ends with the following chorale.

7 CHORALE
'Du Friedefürst, Herr Jesu Christ, wahr Mensch und wahrer Gott'
('Thou Prince of Peace, Lord Jesus Christ, true man and true God')
SATB. As No. 4

This is the first verse of Jakob Ebert's hymn (1601) to Bartholomäus Gesius's melody (1601).

Am Abend aber desselbigen Sabbaths (Then the same day at evening, being the first day of the week).
Solo Cantata BWV 42. Leipzig, 1725.

1 SINFONIA
Ob i, ii, Fag, Vln i, ii, Vla, Org and Cont

This is a splendid and most enjoyable movement, cast in the three-part form of an aria da capo and with the unique feature that the violins play most of the passage work in unison.

2 RECITATIVE
(As above)
T. Cont, Org and Fag

By the simplest of means the astonishing event of the Resurrection is solemnly depicted by the throbbing of the continuo over a sustained note on organ and bassoon. The continuo moves up under the words 'came Jesus and stood in the midst'.

3 ARIA
'Wo zwei und drei versammelt sind in Jesu teurem Namen, da stellt sich Jesus mitten ein und spricht dazu das Amen' ('Where two or three gathered are in Jesu's dear name there Jesus places Himself in their midst and speaks thereto Amen')
A. Ob i, ii, Fag, Vln i, ii, Vla, Org and Cont

The text of this aria is a gloss on St Matthew xviii. 20. This is a slow-moving and lengthy aria with an elaborate accompaniment to a vocal line that sounds contrived. The oboes' solo parts are the best part of it.

4 DUET
'Verzage nicht, o Häuflein klein, obgleich die Feinde willens sein, dich gänzlich zu verstören' ('Tremble not, O little flock, altho' the enemies are disposed wholly to destroy thee')
S.T. Fag and V'cello, Org and Cont

This movement is headed 'chorale' but in fact it quotes the first verse of the chorale by J. M. Altenburg but not the melody. Terry says this is contrary to Bach's practice and finds traces of the melody, especially at the closing cadence, in the duet. Almost throughout the continuo part drops an octave. The impression given is that the 'little flock' do fear but manage to hold out as the enemy will be defeated.

119

5 RECITATIVE
'Man kann hiervon ein schön Exempel sehen' ('One can see here
a good example')
B. Fag, Org and Cont

A good example of how the Saviour, while the Disciples went in
fear of the Jews, came in their midst as a token of His protection
of His church.

6 ARIA
'Jesus ist ein Schild der Seinen, wenn sie die Verfolgung trifft'
('Jesus is a shield of His own when persecution strikes them')
B. Vln i, ii, Fag, Org and Cont

The strong continuo part underlines the words of this confident
aria in which 'persecution' is given dramatic treatment.

7 CHORALE
'Verleih uns Frieden gnädiglich, Herr Gott, in unsern Zeiten'
('Grant us peace graciously, Lord God, in our time')
SATB. As No. 1. Insts. with voices. Fag, Org, Cont

This is Luther's version of the words of the antiphon 'Da pacem
Domine in diebus nostris' but the melody is his adaptation of the
plainsong hymn 'Veni redemptor gentium'.

SECOND SUNDAY AFTER EASTER

Epistle: 1 Pet. II. 21–25 (You were as sheep, gone astray).
Gospel: John x. 11–16 (I am the good shepherd).

Du Hirte Israel, höre (Thou shepherd of Israel, hear).
Cantata BWV 104. Leipzig, 1724.

The picture of Christ as the Good Shepherd clearly made a great appeal to Bach for his three cantatas on this theme are among the loveliest he composed. Each of them takes an individual course. The libretto of the present one concentrates on the first verse of Psalm LXXX in the opening chorus.

1 CHORUS
'Du Hirte Israel, höre der du Joseph hütest wie der Schafe, erscheine der du sitzest über Cherubim' ('Thou shepherd of Israel, hear us, thou who guardest Joseph like a flock, appear [from Thy throne] Thou who sittest above the Cherubim')
SATB. Ob i, ii, Te, Vln i, ii, Vla, Cont

The oboes are marked *staccato* on all single notes, as if a shepherd's pipe, and in the course of the orchestral introduction all parts come to share in the pastoral motif.

A fugue begins at the repetition of 'Thou who leads Joseph like a shepherd' with long phrases on the last word punctuated with cries of 'appear'. This is repeated towards the end with all the voices crying out as if the Cherubim were joining in.

2 RECITATIVE
'Der höchste Hirte sorgt für mich was nützen meine Sorgen?' ('The highest herdsman cares for me, what avail my cares?')
T. Cont

Here is a hint of the disquiet so familiar in Lutheran librettos; it becomes more explicit in the aria that follows.

3 ARIA
'Verbirgt mein Hirte sich zu lange' ('Conceals my Shepherd Himself too long')
T. Ob d'am i, ii, Cont

The soul feels lost in the wilderness in this aria in the minor key, his distress emphasized by drawn-out phrases at 'long'. He cries out to the good Shepherd 'O Good Shepherd teach me to know

thee as "Abba, Father" '. The reference here is to Romans
VIII. 15 (also Galatians IV. 6) 'Ye received the spirit of adoption,
whereby we cry Abba, Father.' The music vividly describes the
'wandering' of this disturbed soul.

4 RECITATIVE
'Ja, dieses Wort ist meiner Seelen Speise, ein Labsal meiner
Brust' ('Yes, this word is my soul's food, a refreshment of my
breast')
B. Cont

The words go on to pray that all living sheep may be brought
into the sheepfold (this recalls verse 16 of the Gospel text 'other
sheep I have which are not of this fold: them also I must bring').

5 ARIA
'Beglückte Heerde, Jesu Schafe, die Welt ist euch ein Himmelreich' ('Fortunate flock, Jesu's sheep, the world to you is a
heavenly kingdom')
B. Vln i, ii, Ob d'am i, Vla, Cont

This aria, in the tempo of a gigue, perfectly sums up the soul's
joy in having such a shepherd. In the middle section the words
speak of faith's reward after death. The enchanting pastoral motif
persists in the orchestra.

6 CHORALE
'Der Herr ist mein getreuer Hirt' ('The Lord is my true Shep-
herd')
SATB. As No. 1. Insts. with voices, Cont

The chorale is the first verse of Cornelius Becker's hymn with
the above title (1598) set to Nikolaus Decius's 'Allein Gott in der
Höh sei Ehr' (1539). And so with the promise of the green
meadows and the fresh pastures this beautiful cantata ends.

Ich bin ein guter Hirt (I am the good Shepherd).
Cantata BWV 85. Leipzig, 1725.

This second cantata on the theme of the Good Shepherd does
not take its text from Psalm LXXX. 1, as No. 104 did, but from the
first verse of St John's Gospel for the Sunday: and in place of the
happy pastoral character in the earlier cantata the opening movement reflects the price the Good Shepherd has to pay.

1 ARIA

'Ich bin ein guter Hirt, ein guter Hirt lässt sein Leben für die Schafe' ('I am a good shepherd and a good shepherd giveth his life for the sheep')

B. Ob, Vln i, ii, Vla, Cont

The key is minor, the tempo, unmarked, slow, on the evidence of the music. There are two themes, a beautifully moulded oboe melody tinged with sadness, and a counter-melody for the strings, pastoral in feeling. These themes are marvellously developed in the course of the movement which ends with a repetition of the instrumental introduction.

2 ARIA

'Jesus ist ein guter Hirt' ('Jesus is a good shepherd')

A. V'cello picc, Cont

The text speaks again of Jesus readily giving His life for His sheep of whom no one can rob him.

3 CHORALE

'Der Herr ist mein getreuer Hirt' ('The Lord is my true Shepherd')

S. Ob i, ii, Cont

This is the first verse of Cornelius Becker's hymn set to Nikolaus Decius's 'Allein Gott in der Höh sei Ehr' (1539).

4 RECITATIVE

'Wenn die Mietlinge schlafen, da wachet dieser Hirt bei seinen Schafen' ('When the hirelings sleep this shepherd watches over his flock')

T. Vln i, ii, Vla, Cont

5 ARIA

'Seht, was die Liebe tut' ('See, what love does')

T. Vln i, ii, with Vla, Cont

This is one of Bach's most beautiful arias. The vocal part is independent of the flowing orchestral accompaniment in which the strings are in unison. The opening words are repeated at the close, followed by the lovely opening bars of the aria.

6 CHORALE

'Ist Gott mein Schutz und treuer Hirt' ('If God is my shield and shepherd true')

SATB. Ob i, ii, Vln i, ii, Vla, all with voices, Cont

123

The fourth verse of Ernst Christoph Homburg's 'Ist Gott mein Schild und Helfersmann' (1658) set to an anonymous melody.

Der Herr ist mein getreuer Hirt (The Lord is my faithful shepherd).
Chorale Cantata BWV 112. Leipzig, 1731.

This cantata, the last and perhaps the most beautiful of the three on the theme of the Good Shepherd, is a setting of Wolfgang Meusslin's metrical version of Psalm XXIII (1530) to the melody in Nos. 1 and 5 of N. Decius's 'Allein Gott in der Höh sei Ehr' (1539).

1 CHORUS

'Der Herr ist mein getreuer Hirt, hält mich in seiner Hute' ('The Lord is my faithful shepherd, He holds me in His keeping')
SATB. Cor i, ii, Ob d'am i, ii, Vln i, ii, Vla, Cont

The metrical version (verses i–ii) keeps closely to the words of the much-loved psalm.

The first horn doubles the sopranos' line with the chorale melody but the second has repeated calls suggestive of a shepherd's pipe. The other instruments are given a happy pastoral theme. I cannot do better than quote Whittaker's verdict on the movement: 'The fantasia is one of the most miraculously beautiful things Bach ever wrote.'

2 ARIA

'Zum reinen Wasser er mich weist, das mich erquicken tue' ('To pure water He directs me that it may refresh me')
A. Ob d'am solo, Cont

The refreshing waters (verse iii) are pictured in the phrases of semiquaver runs principally in the oboe d'amore and voice parts, but occasionally in the continuo part. The movement has a quiet charm.

3 RECITATIVE

'Und ob ich wandert im finstern Tal fürcht ich kein Unglück' ('And though I wander in the dark valley, I fear no misfortune')
B. Vln i, ii, Vla, Cont

The bass sings the words three times, beginning each line with much the same notes but otherwise with varied music. There is a suggestion of a pilgrim chanting as he walks through the dark valley. The strings, silent till now, enter with poignant effect in the arioso (*adagio*) that follows, in which the pilgrim speaks of 'Persecution, sorrow, and trouble', but it ends with the certainty that the Good Shepherd is near with His rod and staff, His comforting words.

4 DUET

'Du bereitest für mich einen Tisch vor mein'n Feinden allenthalben' ('Thou preparest for me a table before my enemies everywhere')

S.T. Vln i, ii, Vla, Cont

This is a joyous duet with delightfully varied figuration in the long opening and succeeding ritornellos. The triplet figures of the ritornello come into the voice parts in the middle section, which tells of the anointing of the soul with the spiritual oil of joy.

5 CHORALE

'Gutes und die Barmherzigkeit folgen mir nach im Leben' ('Goodness and mercy follow after me in life')

SATB. Ob d'am i, ii, Vln i, ii, Vla, all with voices; Cor i, ii, Cont

THIRD SUNDAY AFTER EASTER
(JUBILATE)

Epistle: 1 Pet. II. 11–20 (Suffer patiently for well-doing).
Gospel: John XVI. 16–23 (Ye now have sorrow, but your heart shall rejoice).

Weinen, Klagen, Sorgen, Zagen (Weeping, complaining, sorrowing, fearing).
Cantata BWV 12. Weimar, 1714.

Verses 20–22 of the Gospel provide the clue to the progression from sorrow to joy found in the three cantatas Bach composed for 'Jubilate' Sunday—so named after the Motet 'Jubilate Deo omnes terra' (Psalm LXVI. 1–3) sung earlier in the service: in the present one and in the third the joy is not exuberant, for Jesus is not only telling his disciples that He must leave them but that during 'the little time' before they see Him again, great trials await them.

1 SINFONIA
Ob, Vln i, ii, Vla i, ii, Fag and Cont

The eloquent arabesques of the oboe solo, the tearful detached phrases for the violins, growing in the closing bars into one long phrase that brings the music to a halt, as if Jesus and His disciples were overcome by emotion, form a most poignant introduction to the chorus that follows.

2 CHORUS
'Weinen, Klagen, Sorgen, Zagen' ('Weeping, complaining, sorrowing, fearing')
SATB. Ob, Vln i, ii, Vla i, ii, Fag and Cont

It is inevitable that we should compare the music of this chorus to Bach's adaptation of it in the 'Crucifixus' of the B minor Mass, composed many years later, and find the latter superior. One example of this must suffice. The ground bass in the cantata is written in minims, in the 'Crucifixus', to express greater poignancy and pain, in crotchets: the marvellous modulation at 'sepultus est' is also absent here. It is only fair to say that the words of the cantata present a different picture. Here 'Anxiety and need are the Christian's tears-bread'. The tempo changes to *un poco allegro* for the second half of the chorus, 'who the mark of Jesus bear', accompanied only by the continuo. The tempo slows to *andante* for the last repetition of the words. This section is certainly on a lower level of inspiration compared with what has gone before.

3 RECITATIVE
'Wir müssen durch viel Trübsal in das Reich Gottes eingehen' ('We must through much tribulation into the Kingdom of God enter')
A. Vln i, ii, Vla i, ii, Fag and Cont

The words come from Acts XIV. 22. Bach repeats the first clause three times as the violins rise up the scale, to depict the entry into the Kingdom of God.

4 ARIA
'Kreuz und Krone sind verbunden, Kampf und Kleinod sind vereint' ('Cross and crown are bound together, conflict and treasure are united')
A. Ob, Cont

Not an outstanding aria.

5 ARIA
'Ich folge Christo nach' ('I follow after Christ')
B. Vln i, ii, Cont

A rather attractive aria with Bach's familiar 'step' motif prominent and a feeling of joy in the music.

6 ARIA
'Sei getreu, alle Pein, wird doch nur ein Kleines sein' ('Be faithful, all pain will be a little thing')
T. Tr, Cont

This is a more original movement. The trumpet plays Johann Crüger's melody 'Jesu, meine Freude' (1653), the continuo, with a repeated figure like a ground bass but at different pitches, underlines, as the soloist does, the strength of faith.

7 CHORALE
'Was Gott tut, das ist wohlgetan' ('What God does is well done')
SATB. Ob or Tr, voices with the strings, Fag and Cont

This is the sixth verse of Samuel Rodigast's hymn (1676) set to its own melody (1690) perhaps by Johann Pachelbel. Oboe (or trumpet) have a counter-melody above the soprano line.

Ihr werdet weinen und heulen, aber die Welt wird sich freuen (Ye shall weep and lament but the world will rejoice). Cantata BWV 103. Leipzig, 1725.

1 CHORUS
(As above)
SATB. Fl piccolo, with Vln concertante or Fl trav, Ob. d'am i, ii, Vln i, Vln ii, Vla, Cont

The text of this chorus stays so close to verse 20 of the Gospel for this Sunday that it is best to quote the relevant words from the New Testament . . . 'Ye shall weep and lament, but the world shall rejoice: ye shall be sorrowful, but your sorrow shall be turned into joy.'

Where the Authorized and Revised Versions have 'lament' the Lutheran Bible has 'howl' ('heulen') and this accounts for Bach's use of the shrill piccolo on the top line of the orchestral introduction. This is the voice of an unbelieving world maliciously mocking the Christians apparently deserted by their leader.

Bach gives another theme to the two oboes d'amore and the violins to illustrate the rejoicing of the world. When the chorus comes in he plays off their lamenting fugal theme against the orchestral themes. After a huge outburst of ribald laughter, there is a sudden change of tempo to *adagio* as these mocking voices die away and the basses sing 'Ye shall be sorrowful' to beautiful and sustained harmonies. At 'be turned into joy' the fugue subject returns for a moment but is followed by the rejoicings of the faithful. The worldly and spiritual rejoicings as we now hear share the same material. In this way Bach makes a subtle point worth thinking about.

2 RECITATIVE
'Wer sollte nicht in Klagen untergehn, wenn uns der Liebe wird entrissen?' ('Who should not in mourning sink, when from us the Beloved is snatched away?')
T. Cont

The remaining lines of this brief movement lament that the Saviour is not present to heal the soul's afflictions.

3 ARIA
'Kein Arzt ist ausser dir zu finden' ('No physician except Thee is to be found')
A. Vln concertante or Fl trav, Cont

The text of the aria, carrying on the train of thought in the recitative, is based on Jeremiah VIII. 22, 'Is there no balm in Gilead; is there no physician there?'

The continuo part, marked at the start *staccato* and *piano*, is expressive of the anxious search for the healer of sins, without whom the soul will die.

4 RECITATIVE
'Du wirst mich nach der Angst auch wiederum erquicken' ('Thou wilt me after the anguish ever afresh revive')
A. Cont

At last the doubts and fears and anguish disappear, sadness shall be turned into joy.

5 ARIA
Erholet euch, betrübte Stimmen, ihr tut euch selber allzu weh' ('Recover yourselves, troubled voices, you make yourselves all too sorrowful')
T. Tr, Ob d'am i, ii, with Vln i, ii, Vla, Cont

The clouds dissolve, the sky is clear and the trumpet part proclaims new health and happiness, reflected in all the other parts, vocal and instrumental. At 'My Jesus lets Himself be seen again' Bach expands the two-bar florid phrases at 'Oh, joy' to one of five ecstatic bars, showing how intensely he had lived through this fine libretto.

6 CHORALE
'Ich hab dich einen Augenblick, o liebes Kind verlassen' ('I have left thee a moment, O dear child')
SATB. Tr, Fl trav, Ob d'am i, ii, Vln i, ii, Vla, all with voices, Cont

This is the ninth verse of Paul Gerhardt's hymn 'Barmherz'ger Vater, höchster Gott' (1653) set to the melody 'Was mein Gott will' (1571).

Wir müssen durch viel Trübsal in das Reich Gottes eingehen (We must through much tribulation enter into the Kingdom of God).
Cantata BWV 146. Leipzig.

1 SINFONIA
Ob i, ii, Te, Vln i, ii, Vla, Org, Cont

Why did Bach transcribe the first movement of his piano concerto in D minor (BWV 1052A) for organ solo and orchestra for the first movement of this cantata? Two reasons have been put forward. He liked the transcription—which had been made in 1728 as a prelude to BWV 188 'Ich habe meine Zuversicht'—and wanted to hear it again or, in both cases, he needed an orchestral introduction to lengthen the cantatas. This latter suggestion will not do for No. 146, which already has two long da capo arias among its five numbers. The D minor's first movement is far too long for its purpose and has no more relevance to this cantata than to No. 188, but, needless to say, the transcription makes delightful hearing.

2 CHORUS
(As above)
SATB. Vln i, ii, Vla, Org, Cont

The words of the chorus come from Acts XIV. 22. Bach continues with the second movement of the D minor piano concerto, superimposing the four voice parts on it with extraordinary skill by adapting the solo part to the organ, but leaving the string parts as they were.

3 ARIA
'Ich will nach dem Himmel zu, schnödes Sodom ich und du sind nunmehr geschieden' ('I will towards the heavens [go], evil Sodom, I and thou are henceforth separated')
A. Vln, Cont

Sodom is dismissed summarily in this delightfully melodious aria, with its constant use of a little motif in rising and descending passages, on violin and voice, always aspiring to heaven. Bach's placing of the rests in the dismissive phrases—particularly after the third ritornello at the repeats of 'I and thou'—is wonderfully effective.

4 RECITATIVE
'Ach! wer doch schon im Himmel wär' ('Ah! who then already in Heaven would be')
S. Vln i, ii, Vla, Cont

This is a long and poignant complaint comparing the lot of the soul at war with an evil world, with the lot of the souls who are with Jesus in Heaven, going on to wish herself with them there. The many modulations are remarkable.

5 ARIA
'Ich säe meine Zähren mit bangem Herzen' ('I scatter my tears with anxious heart')
S. Fl trav, Ob d'am i, ii, Cont

A long aria that passes, as in verse 20 of the Gospel, from tears to joy. The section which describes how 'heart-sorrow will turn into glory in the blessed harvest time in heaven', draws some very attractive music from the composer, and there is much to admire of melodic inventiveness in the first section.

6 RECITATIVE
'Ich bin bereit, mein Kreuz geduldig zu ertragen' ('I am ready my cross patiently to bear')
T. Cont

The words of the recitative are based on Romans VIII. 18, 'For I reckon that the sufferings of this present time are not worthy to be compared with the glory which shall be revealed to us-ward'.

7 DUET
'Wie will ich mich freuen, wie will ich mich laben, wenn alle vergängliche Trübsal vorbei' ('How I shall myself rejoice, how shall I myself refresh, when all transient afflictions [are] past')
T.B. Ob i, ii, Vln i, ii, Vla, Cont

'Joy cometh in the morning' might be the text of this joyous duet which so melodiously illustrates rejoicing and refreshment in its vocal and instrumental parts. The middle section brings a new theme to the words 'Then shine I like stars and gleam like the sun, then no mourning, howling and crying disturb the heavenly rapture'.

8 CHORALE
SATB.

Bach provided no text for this chorale but only the notes of the vocal parts. The melody is that of Johann Schop's 'Werde munter, mein Gemüte' (1642).

Epistle: Jas. I. 17–21 (Every good gift is from above).
Gospel: John XVI. 5–15 (It is expedient that I go away).

Wo gehest du hin? (Where goest Thou?).
Cantata BWV 166. Leipzig, 1724.

1 ARIA
(As above)
B. Ob, Vln i, ii, Vla, Cont

The text of this brief aria consists of only a few words in verse 5 of the Gospel for the day, spoken soon after Jesus's wonderful discourse at the Last Supper.

The lovely sequential phrases at the end of the prelude, extended in the middle of the aria and repeated at the end, seem to suggest the gentleness of Jesus.

2 ARIA
'Ich will an den Himmel denken und der Welt mein Herz nicht schenken' ('I will on Heaven think and on the world my heart not bestow')
T. Ob, Cont

The material of the aria is adapted from a Trio in G minor for Organ (BWV 584) published by G. W. Körner in 1842 in a collection of pieces by various composers. He attributed it to Bach.

The text is, of course, a meditation on Jesus's discourse and, as if to stress the difficulty in ignoring worldliness, Bach separates, each time the words come, 'I' from 'will' by a semiquaver rest. The words of the middle section underline the question in the mind, 'Man, ah man, whither goest thou?' The end is most poignant, 'So lies to me the question in the mind' being sung on one note except for the last word, and then an impassioned final appeal, 'Man, ah man, whither goest thou?'

3 CHORALE
'Ich bitte dich, Herr Jesu Christ, halt mich bei dein Gedanken' ('I pray Thee, Lord Jesus Christ, hold me in Thy thoughts')
S. Vln i, ii, and Vla (unis.), Cont

A setting in long notes of the third verse of Bartholomäus Ringwaldt's 'Herr Jesu Christ, ich weiss gar wohl' (1582) set to the melody 'Herr Jesu Christ, du höchstes Gut' (1593) with a beautifully devised accompaniment.

4 RECITATIVE
'Gleichwie die Regenwasser bald verfliessen' ('Even as the rainwaters soon flow away')
B. Cont

A warning that worldly joy, so sought after by man, can vanish, maybe unexpectedly with the striking of the last hour. A fine piece of declamation.

5 ARIA
'Man nehme sich in Acht wenn das Gelücke lacht' ('One should take care when fortune laughs')
A. Ob, Vln i, ii, Vla, Cont

The aria carries on the warning in the recitative but Bach evidently thought that his listeners needed cheering up. He, himself, as we know, relished the pleasures of the world, good food and drink, and jolly company, and so laughter is depicted at once in the orchestral prelude and in the florid phrases given to 'laughs' in the vocal part. The middle section, more lightly scored, warns that before the evening trouble may come, but the music continues on its hilarious course.

6 CHORALE
'Wer weiss, wie nahe mir mein Ende, hin geht die Zeit, hier kommt der Tod' ('Who knows how near to me mine end, away goes time, hither comes death')
SATB. Ob, Vln i with S. A. with Vln ii, T. with Vla, B. with Cont

Sobriety returns. This is the first verse of Countess Ämilia Juliana of Schwarzburg-Rudolstadt's hymn (1695) as above set to Georg Neumark's melody, 'Wer nur den lieben Gott lässt walten' (1657).

Es ist euch gut, dass ich hingehe (It is for your good that I go away).
Cantata BWV 108. Leipzig, 1725. Libretto by Marianne von Ziegler.

1 (ARIA)
(As above)
B. Ob d'am i, Vln i .ii, Vla, Cont

The text is practically the same as in St John's Gospel XVI. 7, 'It is expedient for you that I go away: for if I go not away the comforter will not come to you; but if I depart, I will send him unto you.'

Bach omitted the designation of 'aria' whenever, as here, our Lord speaks in person.

Staccato phrases for the strings hover about the main melody on the oboe d'amore heralding the promised comforter.

Bach has here imagined the consoling tones of the Saviour's voice, alleviating the sorrow that filled the disciples' hearts at the thought of His leaving them.

2 ARIA
'Mich kann kein Zweifel stören, auf dein Wort, Herr, zu hören' ('No doubt can disturb me, listening, Lord, to Thy word')
T. Vln solo, Cont

Another beautiful aria beginning in the minor but going into major in the middle section at the words 'I believe, goest Thou forth'. The last words are set, after the long note on 'believe', to a rising scale passage twice repeated with magical effect. The believer consoles himself with the belief that he will come to the wished-for haven.

3 RECITATIVE
'Dein Geist wird mich also regieren, dass ich auf rechter Bahne geh' ('Thy Spirit will me so govern, that I go on the right path')
T. Cont

This brief recitative ends 'I ask anxiously, ah! is He [the Comforter] not already here?' The question is touchingly repeated.

4 CHORUS
'Wenn aber jener, der Geist der Wahrheit, kommen wird' ('But when he, the Spirit of truth, is come')
SATB. Ob d'am i, Vln i, Ob d'am ii, Vln ii, Vla, Cont

This is a superb fugal setting of verse 13 of the Gospel of the day 'When he, the Spirit of truth, is come, he shall guide you into all the truth: for he shall not speak from himself; but what things soever he shall hear, *these* shall he speak; and he shall declare unto you the things that are to come.'

The subject of the first fugue is declamatory, with the repeated notes that Bach so often uses to drive home a fact of faith; the counter-subject resounds with joy. The second fugue begins at

'For He will not of Himself speak' and has two counter-subjects, the first using the joyous one in the opening fugue; the third, and the longest, fugue begins at 'And what to come is He will proclaim' with a varied version of the subject of the first fugue. This great and brilliant fugal chorus ends with a blazing proclamation of 'what is to come'.

5 ARIA
'Was mein Herz von dir begehrt, ach, das wird mir wohl gewährt' ('What my heart from Thee desires, ah, that is to me well granted')
A. Vln i, ii, Vla, Cont

An aria, after that mighty chorus, could have been a sorry anticlimax but this one turns out to be beautiful. A particularly lovely feature of the aria is a group of three motifs, for the first violin, in the introduction and repeated throughout with the alto sharing the first two. In the second half Bach twice repeats the words of the prayer 'Cover me with blessing, guide me on Thy way, that I in eternity may behold Thy glory', giving at the close a sustained note to 'eternity' and a joyous run up the scale to 'behold'.

6 CHORALE
'Dein Geist, den Gott vom Himmel gibt' ('Thy spirit, which God from Heaven gives')
SATB. As No. 4. Insts. with voices

Verse x of Paul Gerhardt's hymn, 'Gott Vater, sende deinen Geist' (1653) set to the melody of 'Kommt her zu mir, spricht Gottes Sohn' (1530).

FIFTH SUNDAY AFTER EASTER
(ROGATION SUNDAY)

Epistle: Jas. i. 22–27 (Be ye doers of the Word, not hearers only).
Gospel: John xvi. 23–30 (What ye ask in My name, the Father will give).

Wahrlich, wahrlich, ich sage euch (Truly, truly, I say unto you).
Cantata BWV 86. Leipzig, 1724.

1 (ARIA)
(As above)
B. Vln i, ii, Vla, Cont

As was said in discussing the first number of Cantata BWV 108, Bach never gives the title 'Aria' to a setting of Christ's words sung in the first person.

This fine libretto explores the implications of Christ's promise to His disciples. Bach begins the bass aria as a triple fugue. It is in the same key as the E major Fugue in the second book of The 48 (No. 9) and is filled with the same spiritual and melodic beauty. The three motifs, that are presented simultaneously in the first six bars, are thereafter successively allotted to Christ's words. The interweaving of these themes between voice, strings, and continuo, the lovely sequential passages, make this a movement of outstanding beauty.

2 ARIA
'Ich will doch wohl Rosen brechen, wenn mich gleich die Dornen stechen' ('I shall then forsooth gather roses even if the thorns prick me')
A. Vln solo, Cont

The words warn that the liberal promise made must be rightly interpreted. The violin solo charmingly suggests the blossoming roses in this very melodious aria. The words of the middle section express confidence that the prayer of petition will be answered.

3 CHORALE
'Und was der ewig gütge Gott, in seinem Wort versprochen hat' ('And what the everlastingly good God in His word has promised')
S. Ob d'am i, ii, Cont

The sixteenth verse of Georg Grünwald's hymn 'Kommt her zu mir, spricht Gottes Sohn' (1530). The text ends with the lines,

'He helps us to the angel host through Jesus Christ, Amen'. Whittaker considers the 'waving counterpoint' of the oboes is meant to suggest the 'swaying of throngs of angels'. They move predominantly in thirds and sixths and are given a chance to take a breath, at a rest, three times only in the course of the aria, none at all in its last twenty-seven bars!

4 RECITATIVE
'Gott macht es nicht gleichwie die Welt' ('God does not even as the world')
T. Cont

The world promises much but fulfils little. How different is God.

5 ARIA
'Gott hilft gewiss' ('God helps certainly')
T. Vln i, ii, Vla, Cont

The repetition of the opening words at the start of each clause of the text in the first section and woven into the words of the second are a moving declaration of faith expressed in a joyous melody that knows that God will give His help, even if not immediately or necessarily in the way expected.

6 CHORALE
'Die Hoffnung wart' der rechten Zeit' ('The hope awaits the right time')
SATB. Instruments not stated

The words point the moral. God knows what is best for us so let us trust in Him. The text is the eleventh verse of Paul Speratus's 'Er ist das Heil uns kommen her' (1524) set to its original melody.

Bisher habt ihr nichts gebeten in meinem Namen

(Hitherto have you nothing asked in my Name).
Cantata BWV 87. Leipzig, 1725. Libretto by Marianne von Ziegler.

1 ARIA
(As above)
B. Ob i, ii, with Vln i, ii, Ob da cacc, with Vla, Cont

This libretto is based on Chapter XVI of St John's Gospel, verse 24. Bach sets the text contrapuntally, but not as a fugue, and in the minor. The reason for the rather stern tone—which is completely absent from Christ's words in the Gospel—emerges in the two succeeding numbers of the cantata.

2 RECITATIVE
'O Wort, das Geist und Seel erschreckt' ('O Word, that spirit and soul affrights')
A. Cont

The librettist is here, and in the aria, clearly thinking of the Epistle for this Sunday (James I. 22–27) which exhorts Christians to be doers of the Word and not hearers only.

3 ARIA
'Vergib, o Vater, unsre Schuld und habe noch mit uns Geduld' ('Forgive, O Father, our guilt and still with us have patience')
A. Ob da cacc i, ii, Cont

This is the lament of a guilt-ridden soul. Arpeggios continually rise in supplication in the continuo part.

Bach twice repeats the low-pitched phrase at 'and still with us have patience' which paints a picture of true humility. The words of the middle section, 'Lord, at Thy bidding, ah, speak not more in parables, help us rather to intercede', are based on St John XVI. 25 'the hour cometh when I shall no more speak to you in proverbs'. This has an even greater intensity of emotion than the first section.

4 RECITATIVE
'Wenn unsre Schuld bis an den Himmel steigt' ('When our guilt to Heaven ascends')
T. Vln i, ii, Vla, Cont

Bach interpolated this recitative to prevent three arias following in succession. It ends with a brief arioso, 'Seek me to comfort'.

5 (ARIA)
'In der Welt habt ihr Angst, aber seid getrost, ich habe die Welt überwunden' ('In the world ye have tribulation but be of good cheer, I have overcome the world')
B. Cont

These are Christ's last words in Chapter XVI. The sixfold repetition of the first clause and the rather close-knit vocal writing make this number a little disappointing. Its most expressive moments are the first nineteen bars and the last nine of the final ritornello.

6 ARIA
'Ich will leiden, ich will schweigen, Jesus wird mir Hilf' erzeigen' ('I will suffer, I will be silent, Jesus will to me help render')
T. Vln i, ii, Vla, Cont

Heartfelt sorrow and contrition are poured out in this beautiful aria, in the tempo of a Sicilienne. The first violin breathes out sympathy for and comfort to the soul and in the middle section he lifts up his troubled heart and casts away despair.

7 CHORALE

'Muss ich sein betrübet? So mich Jesus liebet, ist mir aller Schmerz über Honig süsse' ('Must I be troubled? Because me Jesus loves is for me all sorrow sweeter than honey')

SATB. Ob i, Ob da cacc i, ii, Vln i, ii, Vla, all with voices, Cont

Verse 9 of Heinrich Müller's 'Selig ist die Seele' (1659) set to Johann Crüger's 'Jesu, meine Freude' (1653).

THE ASCENSION

Epistle: Acts I. 1–11 (Christ prepares His disciples for the Ascension).
Gospel: Mark XVI. 14–20 (Christ ascends into heaven).

Wer da glaubet (He who believeth).
Cantata BWV 37. Leipzig, 1724.

1 CHORUS
'Wer da glaubet und getauft wird, der wird selig werden' ('He
who believeth and is baptized, he will blessed become')
SATB. Ob d'am i, ii, Vln i, ii, Vla, Cont

This libretto is strangely planned to celebrate one of the greatest Feasts of the Church. The only allusion to Christ's Ascension
comes in No. 5, an aria for bass.

Verse 16 of the Gospel provides the text for the opening chorus
and the general tone of the libretto, which is an exposition of the
Lutheran doctrine that faith is more important than works.

In the orchestral introduction Bach assembles a complex of
motifs. Those motifs in minims proclaim steadfastness in faith.
It is one of those complex choruses that can be better appreciated
if one has the miniature full score at hand.

2 ARIA
'Der Glaube ist das Pfand der Liebe, die Jesus für die Seinen hegt'
('The faith is the pledge of the love which Jesus bears his own')
T. Cont

The rather angular continuo part is not in accord with the
emphasis Bach gives to 'belief', 'love', and 'Jesus', each time these
words occur.

3 DUET, CHORALE
'Herr Gott Vater, mein starker Held, du hast mich ewig vor der
Welt in deinem Sohn geliebet' ('Lord God Father, my strong
hero, Thou hast me ever before the world in Thy Son loved')
S.A. Cont

Bach's inspiration, not evident in the tenor aria, is fully present
in this fine duet. The chorale is the fifth verse of Philipp Nicolai's
hymn 'Wie schön leuchtet der Morgenstern' (1599) (see Cantata
BWV 1), with its original melody. The melody is ornamented by
both the soloists to accord with the text. 'Thy Son is my treasure, I
am his bride, very highly I am in Him rejoicing.' This rejoicing

bursts out exuberantly in the 'eya! eya!' phrases, rising to a climax in the last line of the text 'ewig soll mein Herz ihn loben' ('ever shall my heart Him praise').

4 RECITATIVE
'Ihr Sterblichen, verlanget ihr mit mir das Antlitz Gottes anzu-schauen?' ('Ye mortals, desire you with me the countenance of God to contemplate?')
B. Vln i, ii, Vla, Cont

Dogma returns, in this accompanied recitative, to remind the Lutheran that he must not forget the uselessness of good works without faith.

5 ARIA
'Der Glaube schafft der Seele Flügel, dass sie sich in den Himmel schwingt' ('Faith creates the Soul's wings, that it into heaven soars')
B. Ob d'am i, Vln i, ii, Vla, Cont

Perhaps there is a remote reference to the Ascension here in the sense that Christians can share by analogy with it until the last day. The repeated chords on second violins, violas and continuo joined, when the voice comes in, by the other instruments may be meant to suggest the stirring of wings.

6 CHORALE
'Den Glauben mir verleihe an dein' Sohn, Jesus Christ' ('The faith lend me in Thy Son, Jesus Christ')
SATB. As No. 1. Insts. with voices

This is the fourth verse of J. Kolross's hymn 'Ich dank dir, lieber Herre' (1535) set to a secular melody (1662).

Auf Christi Himmelfahrt allein ich meine Nachfahrt gründe (On Christ's ascension alone I base my after-journeying).
Chorale Cantata BWV 128. Leipzig, 1725. Libretto by Marianne von Ziegler.

1 CHORALE
(As above)
SATB. Cor i, ii, Ob i with Vln i, Ob ii with Vln ii, Ob da cacc, Vla, Cont

Marianne von Ziegler, authoress of this libretto, leaves us in no doubt as to what Feast is being celebrated—in contrast to the libretto of Cantata BWV 37—and the inclusion of two horns lends brilliance to the instrumental part. The chorale is the first verse of Josua Wegelin's hymn (1636) set to Nikolaus Decius's 'Allein Gott in der Höh sei Ehr' (1539).

The main motifs in the orchestral introduction which are taken up by the lower vocal parts—the chorale melody being in the top one—are all 'pointed to the skies'. One has a picture of the disciples 'looking steadfastly toward heaven' as Christ vanished in a cloud out of their sight (Acts 1. 9–10).

With his love for pictorial illustration Bach might well have had St Paul's account of the Ascension in mind. He certainly ignored the doubt, anxiety, and pain mentioned in line three, overcome by the joy of this supreme event.

2 RECITATIVE

'Ich bin bereit, komm hole mich! Hier in der Welt ist Jammer, Angst, und Pein' ('I am ready, come, fetch me! Here in the world is lamentation, anxiety and pain')
T. Cont

Here are the emotions Bach ignored, but the text continues in tune with St Paul's words 'For now we see through a glass darkly; but then face to face' and ends 'as to me His holy word promises'.

3 ARIA

'Auf, auf, mit hellem Schall verkündigt überall, mein Jesus sitzt zur Rechten' ('Up, up, with clear sound proclaim everywhere; my Jesus sits at the right hand')
B. Tr, Vln i, ii, Vla

The trumpet does proclaim with no uncertain sound that the Son sits in glory at the right hand of the Father. In this splendid bass aria the long sustained notes at 'sits', as the trumpet fanfares blaze out, help one to picture the majestic vision. But it fades in the words of the second section of the aria 'Who seeks me to attack' repeated four times and followed by the unaccompanied words 'is He even from me taken?', a rush up the scale by the strings, and another after 'I shall one day thither come'. This runs into a recitative accompanied by the strings with all parts marked *piano* as the soul contemplates in hushed tones the vision of the Redeemer who dwells both in Heaven and earth, an unfathomable mystery to our finite minds.

4 DUET

'Sein' Allmacht zu ergründen, wird sich kein Mensche finden, mein Mund verstummt und schweigt' ('His omnipotence to fathom, no man will be found, my mouth grows dumb and is silent')

A.T. Ob d'am i, Cont

The thought expressed at the end of the recitative is dwelt on in this amiable but not very interesting duet.

5 CHORALE

'Alsdann so wirst du mich in deiner Rechten stellen' ('Then so wilt Thou me at Thy right hand place')

SATB. Ob i, ii, Ob da cacc, Vln i, ii, Vla, all with voices; Cor i, ii, Cont

This is the fourth verse of Matthäus Avenarius's 'O Jesu, meine Lust' (1673) set to 'Die Wollust dieser Welt' (1679). The horns have independent parts in this chorale. The rest of the text prays for a merciful judgement—an odd thing to ask by one who seems to consider his position assured—and for the joy of contemplating Christ's glory for all eternity.

Gott fähret auf mit Jauchzen, und der Herr mit heller Posaune (God goeth up with exultation and the Lord with the ringing trumpet).
Cantata BWV 43. Leipzig, 1726.

The construction of this cantata is strange. It begins with a chorus (Psalm XLVII. 5), followed by a recitative and aria, and this is followed by another such sequence; but the text of the second aria is the first of the six verses of an anonymous hymn, the remainder of which are set in a succession of recitatives and arias, all this covering Nos. 5–10. The cantata ends with two verses of another hymn. Bach, evidently aware of the monotony that might ensue, sets all the arias without *da capo*. With a really good team of soloists this curious mixture works, for the arias are of good quality.

PART I

1 CHORUS

(As above)

SATB. Tr i, ii, iii, Timp, Ob i, ii with Vln i, ii, Vla, Cont

After a brief Adagio for the oboes and strings, the first trumpet sounds the C major theme of the splendid fugue the basses begin

143

to the opening words, declaimed also by the upper voices, with fanfares from the trumpets, to a rising motif. Tenors, altos and sopranos complete the exposition. 'And the Lord with the ringing' is set to repeated notes and 'trumpet' to a resounding long phrase. The brilliant exposition ends on a dominant pedal note for timpani and continuo. In the second section, 'Sing praise to God . . . our mighty King', the last word is strongly emphasized by long notes. The final cadence, with the first trumpet trilling up to high C, is thrilling.

2 RECITATIVE
'Es will der Höchste sich ein Siegsgepräng bereiten, da die Gefängnisse er selbst gefangen führt' ('There will the Highest prepare a victory-pomp, when He leads captivity captive')
T. Cont

The exultant text speaks of the heavenly host singing of 'God's glory, salvation, praise, kingdom, power and might . . . Hallelujah'.

3 ARIA
'Ja tausendmal Tausend begleiten den Wagen, dem König der Kön'ge lobsingend zu sagen' ('Yea, thousand times thousand accompany the chariot praise-singing to declare to the King of Kings')
T. Vln i, ii unis., Cont

A delightful feature of this tuneful aria is the repeated notes in the melody on the violins (e.g. GG, DD, BB) suggested by the opening words.

4 RECITATIVE
'Und der Herr, nachdem er mit ihnen geredet hatte' ('And the Lord, as soon as He had spoken to them')
S. Cont

This is St Mark's description of the Ascension (XVI. 19).

5 ARIA
'Mein Jesu hat nunmehr das Heiland-Werk vollendet' ('My Jesus has by now the salvation-work completed')
S. Ob i with Vln i, Ob ii with Vln ii, Vla, Cont

The first verse of the anonymous hymn mentioned above. It does not appear in the great collection of Bach's four-part chorales and nothing is known of the melody that must have been associated with it. Pomp and circumstance are absent here. As Whittaker, with his unfailing sympathy, says, 'the image is of Christ, Bach's Friend and Companion, in the arms of His Father'.

PART II

6 RECITATIVE
'Es kommt der Helden Held, des Satans Fürst und Schrecken'
('There comes the heroes' "Hero", Lord and terror of Satan')
B. Vln i, ii, Vla, Cont

He is heralded by arpeggios rushing up on the strings, down on the continuo, and a thudding of repeated notes at a low pitch to depict 'Satan's terror' and the defeat of his troop. The Victor is carried up to heaven, in a whirl of demisemiquavers in the final bars, leaving Satan, depicted, in the instrumental parts below, as trembling.

7 ARIA
'Er ist's, der ganz allein die Kelter hat getreten' ('He it is, who quite alone the winepress has trodden')
B. Tr, Cont

A majestic start, quietening at mention of the price paid for the victory 'full of affliction, torture and pain', but ending triumphantly.

8 RECITATIVE
'Der Vater hat ihm ja ein ewig Reich bestimmet: nun ist die Stunde nah' ('The Father has for Him yea an eternal kingdom appointed: now is the hour nigh')
A. Cont

The Father crowns His Son.

9 ARIA
'Ich sehe schon im Geist, wie er zu Gottes Rechten auf seine Feinde schmeisst' ('I see, already in spirit, how He at God's right hand smites His enemies')
A. Ob i, ii, Cont

This is the longest and the most beautiful aria. The oboes move frequently in thirds up to and in the second section. This speaks of 'lamentation, distress and shame' which the Christian recalls as he gazes yearningly after his Saviour.

L

145

10 RECITATIVE
'Er will mir neben sich die Wohnung zubereiten' ('He will for me, near Himself, prepare the dwelling')
S. Cont

11 CHORALE
'Du Lebensfürst, Herr Jesu Christ, der du bist aufgenommen gen Himmel' ('Thou Life's Prince, Lord Jesus Christ, Thou who art taken up to heaven')
SATB. Tr i, ii, iii, Ob i, ii, Vln i, ii, Vla, all with voices, Cont

The first and thirteenth verses of Johann Rist's hymn with the above title set to Johann Schop's 'Ermuntre dich, mein schwacher Geist' (1641).

SUNDAY AFTER ASCENSION

Epistle: 1 Pet. IV. 7–11 (Be charitable to one another).
Gospel: John XV. 26–XVI. 2 (They shall put you out of the synagogues).

Sie werden euch in den Bann tun (They will put you under
the ban).
Cantata BWV 183. Leipzig, 1725. Libretto by Marianne von Ziegler.

1 RECITATIVE
(As above)
B. Ob d'am i, ii, Ob da cacc i, ii, Cont

It is evident from first to last in this short and beautiful cantata
that Bach was even more inspired by Marianne von Ziegler's
well-planned libretto than by the one, based on the same verse of
the Gospel, in Cantata BWV 44 (p. 148). The harsh text is the
more effective for being tersely proclaimed in this recitative,
strikingly accompanied by the orchestral reeds, than in the
canonic duet of No. 44.

2 ARIA
'Ich fürchte nicht des Todes Schrecken, ich scheue ganz kein
Ungemach' ('I fear not death's terror, I shun altogether no
adversity')
T. V'cello piccolo, Cont

In this death-defying aria the continuo part is in the composer's most relentless manner, playing in every one of the seventy-
seven bars, punctuated only by some quaver rests. It seems to
express, in the cello's aspiring arpeggios, the generosity of a willing
sacrifice of life if that is demanded. The words of the middle
section speak of Jesus's protecting arm while (in a reference to
verse 2 of the Gospel) 'those that think to kill you, and boast of
doing a service to God, have no conception of the heavenly
rewards of constancy'.

3 RECITATIVE
'Ich bin bereit, mein Blut und armes Leben vor dich, mein
Heiland, hinangeben' ('I am ready, my blood and poor life
for Thee, my Saviour, to give up')
A. Ob d'am i, ii, Ob da cacc i, ii, Vln i, ii, Vla, Cont

The two groups of oboes tenderly echo the first phrase the

soloist sings, 'I am ready', one group responding to the other throughout this recitative.

4 ARIA
'Höchster Tröster, heilger Geist, der du mir die Wege weis'st, darauf ich wandeln soll' ('Highest Comforter, Holy Ghost, who show me the ways whereon I shall walk')
S. Ob da cacc i, ii, Vln i, ii, Vla, Cont

The words are suggested by St John xv. 26. 'But when the Comforter is come, whom I will send unto you from the Father, *even* the Spirit of truth, which proceedeth from the Father, he shall bear witness of me'.

In this gloriously melodic aria, which has a lengthy orchestral introduction, it is as if Bach wanted to let the instruments fully express the joy of the coming of the Holy Spirit in anticipation of Whitsunday.

5 CHORALE
'Du bist ein Geist, der lehret, wie man recht beten soll' ('Thou art a Spirit who teaches how to pray aright')
SATB. Ob d'am i, ii, Vln i with S. Ob da cacc i, Vln ii with A. Ob da cacc ii with T.

The fifth verse of Paul Gerhardt's Whitsuntide hymn, 'Zeuch ein zu deinen Toren' (1653) set to 'Helft mir Gott's Güte preisen' (1569).

Sie werden euch in den Bann tun (They shall put you out of the synagogues).
Cantata BWV 44. Leipzig, 1724.

1 DUET
(As above)
T.B. Ob i, ii, Fag, Cont

The two cantatas Bach composed for this Sunday share only verse 2 of St John, chapter xvi. Christ prophesied, during his discourse at the Last Supper, that His disciples would be cast out of the synagogues and that the time would come when 'whoever kills you will think that he does God a service'.

In Cantata BWV 183 the first two numbers are a recitative and an aria (see p. 147) but are here a duet for solo tenor and bass followed, without pause, by the full chorus.

The forbidding words are graphically depicted in the orchestral prelude to the duet by a terse motif in canon on the oboes—with the voices following suit—and by a figure on the continuo that suggests contemptuous expulsion.

2 CHORUS
'Es kommt aber die Zeit' ('But there will come a time')
SATB. Ob i, ii with Vln i, ii, Vla, Fag and Cont

The chorus agitatedly bursts in with the dire words of Christ's prophecy, and the continuo part rages furiously throughout with the hate that will be shown by the persecutors to the disciples.

3 ARIA
'Christen müssen auf der Erden Christi wahre Jünger sein' ('Christians must on earth Christ's true disciples be')
A. Ob i, Fag and Cont

The aria expresses some comfort but, musically, is overloaded with triplet figures unsuited to accompany thoughts of martyrdom and pain.

4 CHORALE
'Ach Gott, wie manches Herzeleid begegnet mir zu dieser Zeit' ('Ah, God, how many pains of heart trouble me at this time')
T. Fag and Cont

A brief and touching setting of the first verse of Martin Moller's hymn (1587) set to the melody of 'O Jesu Christ, mein's Lebens Licht' (1625).

The last bars speak of the narrow way that leads to Heaven.

5 RECITATIVE
'Es sucht der Antichrist, das grosse Ungeheuer, mit Schwert und Feuer die Glieder Christi zu verfolgen' ('There seeks the anti-Christ, the great monster, with sword and fire the members of Christ to persecute')
B. Fag and Cont

A curiously routine setting of words that one would have expected to stir Bach to better music.

6 ARIA
'Es ist und bleibt der Christen Trost, dass Gott für seine Kirche wacht' ('It is and continues [to be] the Christian's consolation that God watches over His church')
S. Ob i with Vln i, Ob ii with Vln ii, Vla, Fag and Cont

The lively measures that break forth at once in the orchestral prelude anticipate the words of the second section of the aria in which the Christian laughs with the 'joyous sun' at a storm that cannot touch him. The aria, plentifully adorned with joyful triplets, is full of melodic and harmonic interest and is altogether delightful.

7 CHORALE
'So sei nun, Seele, deine und traue dem alleine, der dich erschaffen hat' ('So be now, my Soul, thine and trust Him alone who has created thee')
SATB. As No. 2. Insts. with voices. Cont

Verse 15 of Paul Flemming's 'In allen meinen Taten' (1642) set to its associated melody, Heinrich Isaak's 'O Welt, ich muss dich lassen' (1539).

WHITSUNDAY

Epistle: Acts II. 1–13 (The descent of the Holy Spirit).
Gospel: John XIV. 23–31 (If a man love Me, he will keep my word).

Erschallet, ihr Lieder, erklinget, ihr Saiten! (Ring out, ye songs, resound, ye strings!).
Cantata BWV 172. Weimar, 1714.

1 CHORUS
(As above)
SATB. Tr i, ii, iii, Timp, Vln i, ii, Vla i, ii, Fag, Cont

It is strange that not one of the four librettos Bach set for Pentecost makes any allusion to the awe-inspiring descent of the Holy Spirit as related in Acts II. 1–13, appointed to be read on this Sunday, and so we are deprived of the stirring picture Bach would have made of the mighty rushing wind and the tongues of fire.

The present chorus certainly rejoices in the blessedness of the times, the songs ring out, the strings and the trumpets resound. The brass are silent during the splendid fugal middle section in which the text is 'God will prepare for himself souls as temples'.

2 RECITATIVE
'Wer mich liebet, der wird mein Wort halten' ('Whosoever loves me he will my word keep')
B. Cont

We will encounter these words and what follows them set as a duet in Cantata BWV 59 and as a chorus in Cantata BWV 74. In this brief recitative there is in the last part, 'und Wohnung bei ihm machen' ('and dwelling with him make'), a long-drawn-out phrase on the final word.

3 ARIA
'Heiligste Dreieinigkeit, grosser Gott der Ehren, komm doch in der Gnadenzeit bei uns einzukehren' ('Most Holy Trinity, Great God of honours, come to dwell with us then in the mercy time')
B. Tr i, ii, iii, Timp, Fag with Cont

The Holy Trinity is greeted by ringing fanfares on the brass, who have the field to themselves in the thirty bars of this aria. The brilliant writing, demisemiquaver roulades for the first trumpet part, could only have been played by a virtuoso, such as the principal 'town pipers' often were.

4 ARIA

'O Seelenparadies, das Gottes Geist durchwehet' ('O Soul's Paradise, which God's spirit breathes through')
T. Vln i, ii, Vla i, ii (all unis.), Cont

The tone of the strings in unison playing the gently ascending and descending legato phrases of the serene melody, the arpeggiated chords for the continuo, fall gratefully on the ear after the brilliant movement just heard, and delight in this aria is complete when the tenor begins to sing of the bliss of Paradise.

5 DUET

S: 'Komm, lass mich nicht länger warten, komm, du sanfter Himmelswind' A: 'Ich erquicke dich, mein Kind' ('Come let me no longer wait, come, Thou soft Heaven's wind') ('I refresh thee, my child')
S.A. Vln, Org or V'cello obb. Cont

This is one of the loveliest duets between Christ and the Soul in the cantatas. The violin intertwines with the voices in the melody, highly decorated, of Luther's version of the Whitsun hymn, 'Veni creator Spiritus'.

The exquisite music brings to mind Gerard Manley Hopkins' great lines, 'Because the Holy Ghost over the bent world broods with warm breast and with ah! bright wings'. At the close of the duet, with the soprano crying, 'Highest love, come within! Thou has from me the heart taken, be in faith to me welcome', and the Holy Spirit replying 'I am thine and thou art mine', the gently descending phrases for both seem to picture exactly what the words say.

6 CHORALE

'Von Gott kommt mir ein Freudenschein, wenn du mit deinen Äugelein mich freundlich tust anblicken' ('From God comes to me a joy-light when Thou with Thy dear eyes me friendly makes look')
SATB. Vln ii, Vla i, ii with voices, Vln i, Fag with Cont

The fourth verse of Philipp Nicolai's 'Wie schön leuchtet der Morgenstern' set to his own melody (1599).

The last two lines are 'Take me lovingly in Thine arms, that I warm shall be through grace, to Thy word come laden down'. The independent part for the first violin rises above the voices with beautiful effect—the 'joy-light' made manifest.

The opening chorus is here repeated.

Wer mich liebet, der wird mein Wort halten (Who loves
me, he will keep my word).
Solo Cantata BWV 59. Weimar, 1724. Libretto by Erdmann Neumeister.

1 DUET
(As above)
S.B. Tr i, ii, Timp, Vln i, ii, Vla, Cont

The words are those of verse 23 of the Gospel and continue,
'and my Father will love him, and we will come to him and make
our abode with him'.
This is a modest cantata for one of the chief festivals in the
Church's year. The trumpets and timpani give dignity to the
charming duet, in which the voices sing in canon, and freely.
The words 'Wer mich liebet' and its motif precede each of their
five entries and in the last one they sing together in sixths.

2 RECITATIVE
'O! was sind das für Ehren, wozu uns Jesus setzt' ('Oh! what are
these honours to which Jesus us calls')
S. Vln i, ii, Vla, Cont

There is now a mention of the Holy Spirit who with the Son
and the Father will enter the souls of the faithful.

3 CHORALE
'Komm, heilger Geist, Herre Gott, erfüll mit deiner Gnaden Gut
deiner Gläubigen Herz, Mut und Sinn' ('Come, Holy Ghost,
Lord God, fill with Thy mercy's fullness, Thy believers' heart,
mind and being')
SATB. Vln i, ii, Vla, Cont

Verse i of Luther's version of the plainsong sequence 'Veni
Sancte Spiritus', the melody of which is altered almost beyond
recognition.

4 ARIA
'Die Welt mit allen Königreichen, die Welt mit aller Herrlichkeit' ('The world with all its kingdoms, the world with all its
glory')
B. Vln i, Cont

A short bass aria contrasting material with spiritual values and
concluding 'how blessed become we then when after this time on
earth we with Thee in Heaven shall dwell'.
The only indication that a chorale is to follow is to be found

in the original bass part on which 'Chorale seque' is written by a copyist, but it is not known if it is Bach's direction.

Wer mich liebet, der wird mein Wort halten (Whosoever loves me he will keep my words).
Cantata BWV 74. Leipzig, 1725. Libretto by Marianne von Ziegler.

1 CHORUS
(As above)
SATB. Tr i, ii, iii, Timp, Ob i, ii, Ob da cacc, Vln i, ii, Vla, Cont

Bach delightfully gives the prevailing little motif (sung by bass and soprano soloists responding to one another in the previous cantata) to the violins, sometimes to the oboes and, of course, to the chorus. The first and second trumpet parts are little changed. In this adaptation the music is even more attractive than before.

2 ARIA
'Komm, komm, mein Herze steht dir offen, lass es deine Wohnung sein!' ('Come, come, my heart stands open, let it Thy dwelling be')
S. Ob da cacc, Cont

This is an adaptation of the bass aria in C in Cantata BWV 59, but now transposed to F major and with oboe da caccia obbligato, not violin. Bach pays no regard to the completely different sentiments of the words in the two librettos.

3 RECITATIVE
'Die Wohnung ist bereit, du findst ein Herz, das dir allein ergeben' ('The dwelling is ready, Thou findest a heart that to Thee alone [is] devoted')
A. Cont

The remainder of the text is a plea never to be deserted by the Holy Spirit.

4 ARIA
'Ich gehe hin und komme wieder zu euch. Hättet ihr mich lieb, so würdet ihr euch freuen' ('I go hence, and come again to you. Did you me love, then would you yourselves rejoice')
B. Cont

The text is taken from verse 28 of the Gospel. The chief feature of this aria is the ascending phrases at 'I go hence' and the descending ones at 'and come again to you'. The impression left is one of Christ's disappointment with the response of His disciples to His message.

5 ARIA

'Kommt! eilet! Stimmet Sait' und Lieder in muntern und erfreuten Ton' ('Come! hasten! tune strings and songs in merry and joyous tone')
T. Vln i, ii, Vla, Cont

A welcome note of joy, with the voice and strings vividly illustrating the words. In the middle section Satan, never far from the Lutheran consciousness, is contemptuously dismissed in his endeavours to curse the Trinity.

6 RECITATIVE

'Es ist nichts Verdammliches an denen, die in Christo Jesu sind' ('There is no condemnation to them who in Christ Jesus are')
B. Ob i, ii, Ob da cacc, Cont

The words are from the Epistle to the Romans, VIII. 1, and the scoring indicates the importance Bach attached to them.

7 ARIA

'Nichts kann mich erretten von höllischen Ketten, als, Jesu, dein Blut' ('Nothing can save me from hellish chains, but, Jesus, Thy blood')
A. Ob i, ii, Ob da cacc, Vln solo, Vln i, ii, Vla, Cont

In this dramatic aria Bach realistically depicts the rattling of the chains in the figures dominated by rapidly repeated notes. The tumult dies away in the last lines before the *da capo*, 'Thy suffering, Thy dying makes me indeed Thine heir'. 'I laugh at the raging', and laugh contemptuously the vocal part does.

8 CHORALE

'Kein Menschenkind hier auf der Erd, ist dieser edlen Gabe wert' ('No mortal child here upon the earth is worthy of this noble gift')
SATB. Tr i, Ob i, ii, Ob da cacc, Vln i, ii, Vla, all with voices, Cont

Verse ii of Paul Gerhardt's 'Gott Vater, sende deinen Geist' (1653), to the anonymous melody, 'Kommt her zu mir, spricht Gottes Sohn' (1530).

O ewiges Feuer, o Ursprung der Liebe (O eternal Fire, O source of love).
Cantata BWV 34. Leipzig, 1735.

In 1726 Bach composed a wedding cantata (BWV 36A) with this title, to a libretto possibly by Christian Weiss, Jnr. and, again, possibly for one of the Leipzig clergy. There are seven numbers in the libretto but in several numbers either some instrumental or vocal parts are missing. In need of a Whitsuntide cantata in 1735— if this is the correct date—mention of the 'tongues of fire' at the descent of the Holy Spirit may well have reminded Bach of how easily the libretto of his wedding cantata could be adapted for his purpose. The mystics, as Bach would have known, can use no other language for their union with Christ than that used of union between man and woman—little was needed in this cantata except for different recitatives.

1 CHORUS
(As above)
SATB. Tr i, ii, iii, Timp, Ob i, ii, Vln i, ii, Vla, Cont

The 'fire', as the text implies, is not that of the historic event but symbolic. Fire gives light and flames, and typical figures in all the instrumental parts are marked staccato to enhance the radiant effect. There is a fine homophonic passage at 'inflame the hearts and consecrate them', repeated—with the brass silent —at greater length and yet again with a thrilling re-entry of the brass.

2 RECITATIVE
'Herr! unsre Herzen halten dir dein Wort die Wahrheit für' ('Lord! our hearts hold Thy word for truth')
T. Cont

3 ARIA
'Wohl euch, ihr auserwählten Seelen, die Gott zur Wohnung ausersehen' ('Well for you, ye chosen souls, whom God [has] selected as his dwelling')
A. Fl trav i, ii, Vln i, ii, Vla (all muted), Cont

The original words spoke of 'chosen sheep loved by Jacob' and the remaining lines are altered accordingly, but the music is the same as in No. 5 of the wedding cantata except for the addition of the flutes—which would have been equally appropriate in the original.

This is arguably the most beautiful aria Bach ever composed. The syncopated melody begins with a lightly accented up-beat on the first note—a movement to repose on the succeeding beat. All the instrumental parts are marked *pp* when the voice enters. At the third repeat of the melody flutes and strings play in thirds and sixths with exquisite, almost intoxicating effect.

4 RECITATIVE
'Erwählt sich Gott die heilgen Hütten, die er mit Heil bewohnt' ('God chooses [for] Himself the holy dwellings which He with salvation inhabits')
B. Cont

5 CHORUS
'Friede über Israel' ('Peace over Israel')
SATB. As No. 1

The chorus at once sing the above words, verse 6 of Psalm CXXII to two massive choral bars. A lengthy ritornello (the signing of the register in the original work?) is followed by 'Ja, sein Segen wirkt mit Macht, Friede über Israel' ('Yes, His blessing works with might, peace over Israel').

WHIT MONDAY

Epistle: Acts x. 42–48 (Descent of the Holy Spirit upon Cornelius and his company).
Gospel: John iii. 16–21 (God so loved the world).

Erhöhtes Fleisch und Blut (Exalted flesh and blood).
Solo Cantata BWV 173. Leipzig, ?1724.

Bach adapted the six numbers of this cantata from the eight he had composed as a Serenata, in 1717, for the birthday of Prince Leopold of Anhalt-Cöthen (see p. 165).

1 RECITATIVE
(As above)
T. Vln i, ii, Vla, Cont

'Most serene Leopold, sings Anhalt's world' becomes, 'Exalted flesh and blood that God Himself on Him takes', the reference being, of course, to the Gospel: 'God so loved the world that He gave His only begotten Son that whosoever believeth on Him should not perish but have eternal life'.

2 ARIA
'Ein geheiligtes Gemüte sieht und schmecket Gottes Güte' ('A sanctified mind sees and tastes God's goodness')
T. Fl trav i, ii with Vln i, Vln ii, Vla, Cont

3 ARIA
'Gott will, o ihr Menschenkinder, an euch grosse Dinge tun' ('God will, O ye men's children, in you great things do')
A. Vln i, ii, Vla, Cont

An aria for high bass in the original here transposed to the alto with praise of God substituted for that of the Prince, with little alteration of the text. The music is pleasing, but little more.

4 ARIA
'So hat Gott die Welt geliebt' ('So has God loved the world')
S.B. Fl trav i, ii, Vln i, ii, Vla, Cont

This aria culminates in a duet, marked in the original *tempo di menuetto*, and composed in a popular style. However secular in tone it remains, this is a very attractive number.

5 RECITATIVE
'Unendlichster, den man doch Vater nennt, wir wollen dann das
Herz zum Opfer bringen' ('Most eternal, whom one yet Father
calls, we will then the heart as offering bring')
S.T. Cont
   The words, except at the start, are those of the Serenata with a
tenor substituted for the bass.

6 CHORUS
'Rühre, Höchster, unsern Geist, dass des höchsten Geistesgaben
ihre Wirkung in uns haben' ('Touch, Highest, our Spirit, that the
Spirit's highest gifts have their results in us')
SATB. Fl trav i, ii, Vln i, ii, Vla, Cont
   This was a duet in the Serenata in the form of a minuet. The
words refer to the Gospel.

Also hat Gott die Welt geliebt (Thus has God loved the
world).
Cantata BWV 68. Leipzig, 1725. Libretto by Marianne von Ziegler.

1 CHORUS
(As above)
SATB. Ob i, ii with Vln i, ii, Te with Vla, Cor with S. Cont
   The words of the chorus are those of the first verse of Salomo
Liscow's hymn with the above title (1675) set to a melody by
Gottfried Vopelius (1681). The setting, in 12/8 time, has the
rhythm of a Siciliano, established by the oboes and violins in the
instrumental introduction and introduced into the singing of the
chorale in delightfully varied ways. The first lines are plainly sung,
the second ones ornamented with the Sicilian rhythm, the third
plainly set again: and this pattern is then repeated in slightly
different form.

2 ARIA
'Mein gläubiges Herze frohlocke, sing', scherze' ('My believing
heart, be glad, sing, make merry')
S. Ob i, Vln i, V'cello piccolo, Cont
   This aria used to be, together with the Air from the D major
Suite (BWV 1068), the most popular of Bach's melodies. In
earlier days one heard it tricked out with an orchestral accom-
paniment that effectively blanketed the violoncello piccolo

obbligato. This latter Bach borrowed from the continuo part of a soprano aria in the hunting cantata, 'Was mir behagt', which he composed for the hunting festival on the birthday of Duke Ernst Wilhelm of Weimar, 23 February 1716.

If the hunting cantata had been lost we should have been at a loss to explain the instrumental movement with which this aria concludes. The fact is that at the end of the aria in the secular cantata Bach developed the material into a trio for oboe, violin and continuo and evidently could not resist including it here. It is scored for the same instruments but with the addition of the violoncello piccolo.

3 RECITATIVE
'Ich bin mit Petro nicht vermessen, was mich getrost und freudig macht, dass mich mein Jesus nicht vergessen' ('I am like Peter not presumptuous, what makes me comforted and joyful is that my Jesus has not forgotten me')
B. Cont

A reference to Cornelius and his company (Acts x. 25–26) addressed by Peter.

4 ARIA
'Du bist geboren mir zu Gute, das glaub ich, mir ist wohl zu Mute, weil du für mich genug getan' ('Thou art born for me as good, that believe I, and I am content, because Thou hast done for me sufficient')
B. Ob i, ii, Te, Cont

This number is also derived from the hunting cantata referred to but this time with very little alteration of the music.

5 CHORUS
'Wer an ihn glaubet, der wird nicht gerichtet' ('Who on Him believes, is not judged')
SATB. Ob i, Vln i, Ob ii, Vln ii, Te, Vla. Tr i, ii, iii, with B.T.A. Cornetto with S.

The words are from verse 18 of the Gospel. This is an austere, fugal movement with the bass announcing the subject in bar 1, followed by tenor, alto and soprano, each voice doubled as detailed above.

Ich liebe den Höchsten von ganzem Gemüte (I love the Highest with [my] whole mind).
Cantata BWV 174. Leipzig, 1729. Libretto by Picander.

1 SINFONIA
Cor da cacc i, ii, Ob i, ii, Te, Vln i, ii, iii, Vla i, ii, iii, V'cello i, ii, iii; Fag, Violone with Cont

We can only guess what prompted Bach to preface this cantata with the first movement of the third Brandenburg Concerto, re-scored to allow for the addition of the above instruments, playing independent parts, to the original triple lines of the strings.

A cantata consisting only of two arias, separated by a recitative, and a chorale obviously needed lengthening to take up the statutory time. Bach could easily have chosen another libretto and if he was able to copy out the movement and add the extra instruments, which meant filling in fifteen lines of score on every page, he cannot have been pressed for time.

2 ARIA
'Ich liebe den Höchsten von ganzem Gemüte, er hat mich auch am höchsten lieb' ('I love the Highest with my whole mind, He holds me also most dear')
A. Ob i, ii, Cont

The incessant activity of the Sinfonia, in common time, gives place to this restful aria, in 6/8 time, which expresses gratitude for God's love for man and is warmly responded to.

3 RECITATIVE
'O Liebe, welcher keine gleich, o unschätzbares Lösegeld!' ('O love, which has no equal, O inestimable ransom')
T. Vln i, ii, iii (unis.), Vla i, ii, iii (unis.), Cont

Bach's emotional response to the text, which contains the words 'God so loved the world . . . my heart take heed . . . be strong . . . before this mighty banner tremble even hell's portals', shows how moved he was by the Father's love for man. The strings reproduce the 'tremble' just before 'Hell's portals' is sung.

4 ARIA
'Greifet zu! fasst das Heil, ihr Glaubenshände' ('Grip fast, grasp Salvation, ye faith's-hands')
B. Vlns and Vlas (unis.), Cont

This beautiful aria is a splendid example of Bach's wonderful

M   161 power to achieve melodic continuity by constantly weaving a few short themes into the musical texture in such a way that their easily recognizable entrances and exits seem inevitable.

5 CHORALE
'Herzlich lieb hab ich dich, O Herr' ('Heartily dear have I Thee, O Lord')
SATB. Ob i, ii, Te, Vln i, ii, iii, Vla i, ii, iii, all with voices, Cont

The first stanza of Martin Schallings's hymn (1571) set to its own melody.

WHIT TUESDAY

Epistle: Acts VIII. 14–17 (The Holy Spirit descends, in Samaria, on those on whom Peter and John have laid hands).
Gospel: John x. 1–10 (Christ, the door of the sheepfold).

Erwünschtes Freudenlicht (Longed for joy-light).
Cantata BWV 184. Leipzig, 1724.

1 RECITATIVE
'Erwünschtes Freudenlicht, das mit dem neuen Bund anbricht durch Jesum, unsern Hirten' ('Longed-for joy-light that dawns with the new covenant through Jesus, our Shepherd')
T. Fl trav i, ii, Cont

The reference to Christ as shepherd, a theme developed in verses 1–16 of the tenth chapter of St John's Gospel for this Sunday, is reflected throughout the libretto, which in this recitative also quotes verse 4 of Psalm XXIII, that in death's dark valley our help and comfort will still be His rod and staff.

The first two movements of the cantata are suffused with a pastoral atmosphere expressed in this lengthy recitative by a constantly repeated triplet figure played mostly in thirds by the two flutes. They are silent for the first half of the arioso into which the recitative runs, the words of which speak of following Jesus joyfully to the grave. These end, as the flutes return, 'Up, up, hasten to Him, transfigured before Him to stand'.

2 DUET
'Gesegnete Christen, glückselige Heerde, kommt, stellt euch bei Jesu mit Dankbarkeit ein' ('Blest Christians, blissful flock, come, unite yourselves with Jesus in gratitude')
S.A. Fl trav i, ii, Vln i, ii, Vla, Cont

A dance-like duet, perhaps of secular origin, with the flutes having joyous pendant phrases of four-note groups of demi-semiquavers. The voices sing in thirds during the greater part of the delightful movement and are given expansive sequential phrases in the middle section the words of which warn the Christian to despise the attractions of the world.

3 RECITATIVE
'So freut euch, ihr auserwählten Seelen! Die Freude gründet sich in Jesu Herz' ('So rejoice, ye chosen souls! Joy establishes itself in Jesus's heart')
T. Cont

The rather lengthy text has references to the hero of Judah, David, who frees us from our enemies and endures the bitterness of the Cross for us, and ends with a florid arioso welcoming the joys of Heaven.

4 ARIA
'Glück und Segen sind bereit, die geweihte Schaar zu krönen' ('Happiness and blessing are ready to crown the consecrated host')
T. Vln solo, Cont

The text of this aria, unlike its charming melody, is rather obscure.

5 CHORALE
'Herr, ich hoff, je, du werdest die in keiner Not verlassen' ('Lord, I hope ever that Thou will not leave those in distress')
SATB. Fl trav i, ii, Vln i, ii, Vla, all with voices, Cont

The eighth verse of Anark von Wildenfels' (?) 'O Herre Gott, dein göttlich Wort', set to its own melody (1527).

6 CHORUS
'Guter Hirte, Trost der Deinen, lass uns nur dein heilsam Wort' ('Good Shepherd, comfort of Thy [people] grant to us only Thy healing word')
SATB. Fl trav i, ii (unis.), Vln i, ii, Vla, Cont

Er rufet seinen Schafen mit Namen und führet sie hinaus (He calls His sheep by name and leads them forth). Solo Cantata BWV 175. Leipzig, 1725. Libretto by Marianne von Ziegler.

1 RECITATIVE
(As above)
T. Fl i, ii, iii, Cont

The brief text of the recitative, verse 3 of the Gospel, which is accompanied by the three flutes over a pedal bass, makes a poetical beginning to the cantata.

2 ARIA
'Komm, leite mich, es sehnet sich mein Geist auf grüne Weide' ('Come lead me, my spirit longs for green pastures')
A. Fl i, ii, iii, Cont

A pastoral aria in 12/8 time with the three flutes (recorders) playing together in sixths. The words of the second section bring a yearning note into the music which is reflected in the chromatic writing.

3 RECITATIVE
'Wo find ich dich? Ach, wo bist du verborgen? O zeige dich mir bald. Ich sehne mich' ('Where find I Thee? Ah, where art Thou hidden? Oh, show Thyself to me soon! I yearn')
T. Cont

4 ARIA
'Es dünket mich, ich seh' dich kommen, du gehst zur rechten Türe ein' ('It seems to me I see Thee come, Thou goest in by the right door')
T. Vln, V'cello picc solo, Cont

This aria is adapted from the seventh movement of the secular cantata 'Durchlauchtster Leopold' which, as has been said before, was a serenade composed in 1717 in honour of the birth-day of Prince Leopold of Anhalt-Cöthen. Whittaker justly says that the light-hearted tripping obbligato for the violoncello piccolo is quite out of keeping with the approach of the Saviour. It does not accord either with such lines as, 'I know Thy gracious voice . . . so that I in spirit thereat am wrathful at him who doubts that Thou the Saviour art'. This is not one of Bach's happy adaptations.

5 RECITATIVE
'Sie vernahmen aber nicht, was es war, das er zu ihnen gesagt hatte' ('But they did not understand what it was that he had said to them')
A.B. Vln i, ii, Vla, Cont

As the alto comes to the end of the above line the bass continues the text, 'Ah yea! We men are often to the deaf to be compared. O fool, mark then when Jesus with thee speaks that it is for thy salvation.'

6 ARIA
'Öffnet euch, ihr beiden Ohren, Jesus hat euch zugeschworen, dass er Teufel, Tod erlegt' ('Open ye both your ears, Jesus has sworn to you that He lays the devil [and] death low')
B. Tr i, ii, Cont

The brilliant parts for the trumpets reinforce the need for the ears of the deaf and foolish to be unstopped. The trumpets are directed to play softly at 'the laying low of death' and again when these words recur, but this time their simple quaver figures are replaced by fanfares of triumph which lead effectively to the recapitulation of the ritornello.

7 CHORALE

'Nun, werter Geist, ich folg' dir, hilf dass ich suche für und für nach deinem Wort ein ander Lebcn' ('Now, honoured spirit, I follow Thee, help so that I seek ever and ever through Thy word another life')

SATB. Fl i, ii, iii, Vln i with S. Vln ii with A. Vla with T. Cont

Verse 9 of Johann Rist's hymn, 'O Gottes Geist, mein Trost und Rat' (1651) set to the Whitsun melody 'Komm, heilger Geist'— an adaptation of the plainsong hymn, 'Come, Holy Ghost, our souls inspire'. The three flutes have independent parts high above the voices to suggest, perhaps, the shining of the morning star mentioned in the chorale verse.

TRINITY SUNDAY

Epistle: Rom. xi. 33–36 (Who can know the riches of the wisdom and
judgements of God).
Gospel: John iii. 1–15 (Nicodemus coming to Christ in the night).

**O heilges Geist- und Wasserbad, das Gottes Reich uns
einverleibet** (O holy Spirit- and waterbath, that God's
kingdom in us incarnates).
Cantata BWV 165. Weimar, 1715. Libretto by Salomo Franck.

1 ARIA
(As above)
S. Vln i, ii, Vla, Fag, V'cello with Cont

Sanford Terry tries to conceal the therapeutic nature of the
title of this cantata by translating it, 'O holy font that washeth
white', but he has been overtaken by detergent advertising!

The words of the aria were presumably inspired by the Gospel
narrative of Christ's words to Nicodemus, 'Except a man be born
of water and the Spirit he cannot enter into the kingdom of God'.
Bach begins the aria with a four-part fugal exposition as if illustrating the complexity of Christ's words. The writing of our names
in the Book of Life is illustrated, typically, by an extended phrase
on 'life'.

2 RECITATIVE
'Die sündige Geburt verdammter Adams-Erben gebieret
Gottes Zorn' ('The sinful birth of Adam's condemned heirs
arouses God's anger')
B. Cont

After some vivid declamation about original sin there comes a
tender little one-bar arioso at the words, 'How blessed is a
Christian'.

3 ARIA
'Jesu, der aus grosser Liebe in der Taufe mir verschriebe
Leben, Heil und Seligkeit' ('Jesus, who from great love in the
baptism to me prescribed life, salvation and blessedness')
A. Cont

This flowing aria in 12/8 time is an illustration of the famous
words of St Paul, 'O felix culpa'. Bach underlines the great gift to
sinful man by repeating, in slightly decorated form, the opening
clause.

4 RECITATIVE

'Ich habe ja, mein Seelenbräutigam da du mich neu geboren, dir ewig treu zu sein geschworen, hoch heil, Gottes Lamm' ('I have indeed, my soul's bridegroom, when Thou me newly created, sworn to Thee to be everlastingly faithful, hail, God's holy Lamb') B. Vln i, ii, Vla, Fag, Cont

A long and impressive accompanied recitative. There is a fine *adagio* outburst at 'Hail, God's holy Lamb' and a sinister phrase for the old serpent, which—as Christ reminded Nicodemus— Moses lifted up in the wilderness, with a poignant reference to the lifting up of Christ on the Cross.

5 ARIA

'Jesu, meines Todes Tod, lass in meinem Leben und in meiner letzten Not' ('Jesu, my death's death, let in my life and in my last need')
T. Vln i, ii, (unis.), Cont

The violins' part consists of groups of semiquavers, and it may be as one commentator has suggested, that Bach took a hint from the ensuing phrase 'salvation snakelet' in writing an accompaniment which could be said to writhe snake-wise.

6 CHORALE

'Sein Wort, sein Tauf, sein Nachtmahl dient wider allen Unfall, der heilge Geist in Glauben lehrt uns darauf vertrauen' ('His Word, His baptism, His communion, serves against all misfortune, the Holy Ghost in faith teaches us thereon to trust')
SATB. Vln i, ii, Vla, Fag, all with voices, Cont

The fifth verse of Ludwig Helmbold's 'Nun lasst uns Gott dem Herren' (1575) set to N. Selnecker's melody (1587).

Höchsterwünschtes Freudenfest (Highest-wished-for joyous feast).
Cantata BWV 194. Leipzig, 1724.

These are the opening words of the second of Bach's four cantatas for Trinity Sunday. The text goes on to tell of the honour of celebrating it in 'the erected sanctuary'. There are twelve numbers in this two-part cantata, but the Holy Trinity is not mentioned at all except in the chorale at the end of Part I and the recitative with which Part II begins. There are references in seven of the remaining numbers to this holy house of prayer, etc., which obviously refer to some other occasion. Bach, in fact, adapted the cantata for this Sunday from the one he composed on 2 November 1723 for the dedication of the new Church and organ at Störmthal, near Leipzig, by substituting the chorale and recitative mentioned above.

The form of the work is broadly speaking that of an orchestral suite—perhaps one composed at Cöthen—which is not extant. No. 1, in French overture form with the chorus entering in the quick section, No. 5, a soprano aria, and No. 10, a duet for soprano and bass, have the characteristic rhythm and mood respectively of a gavotte and a minuet. Two verses are provided for each of the chorales so that all those present would be able more fully to participate.

The organ at Störmthal was considerably lower in pitch than the Leipzig organs, which explains the extraordinarily high-pitched writing for the chorus sopranos—who at one point have to come in rightaway on a top C!—and the bass, who has continually to sing high G's and F's in his recitative and aria.

There is some charming music in the work but the recitatives are not interesting, nor is the tenor aria.

(For a more detailed discussion see Whittaker Vol. I, pp. 264–71.)

Es ist ein trotzig und verzagt Ding um aller Menschen Herze (It is an obstinate and hopeless thing about all men's hearts).

Cantata BWV 176. Leipzig, 1725. Libretto by Marianne von Ziegler.

1 CHORUS
(As above)
SATB. Ob i, ii, Ob da cacc, Vln i, ii, Vla, Cont

The chorus enter simultaneously with the strings in the first bar with these pessimistic words, which Bach sets to a vigorous and condemnatory fugue. The text has no direct relation to the Gospel or Epistle for the day—this comes in the recitative following—but is based on Jeremiah xvii. 9; but later in the Gospel (v. 19) Christ declares that 'men loved the darkness rather than the light; for their works were evil'. The musical texture is highly dramatic and dense.

169

2 RECITATIVE

'Ich meine, recht verzagt, dass Nikodemus sich bei Tage nicht, bei Nacht in Jesu wägt' ('I think, right timidly, that Nicodemus ventures not by day but by night to Jesus')

A. Cont

The text then makes reference to Joshua seeing the sun stand still (Jos. x. 13) until victory came and Nicodemus wishing he could see it set.

3 ARIA

'Dein sonst hell beliebter Schein soll vor mich umnebelt sein, wenn ich nach dem Meister frage, denn ich scheue mich bei Tage' ('Thy otherwise bright beloved gleam shall be before me clouded over, when I ask for the Master, for I am afraid by day')

S. Vln i, ii, Vla, Cont

Bach hails the light that has come into the world (v. 19 of the Gospel) with a delightful and joyous gavotte.

4 RECITATIVE

'So wundre dich, o Meister, nicht, wenn ich dich bei Nacht (ausfrage!') ('So do not wonder, O Master, when I seek Thee out by night!')

B. Cont

Nicodemus confesses his fear of coming to the Master by day. At the end of the arioso that follows Bach added the words, 'Because all who on Thee believe are not lost', which paraphrases v. 15 of the Gospel, 'That whosoever believeth may in Him have eternal life'.

5 ARIA

'Ermuntert euch, furchtsam und schüchterne Sinne, erholet euch, höret, was Jesus verspricht' ('Rouse yourselves, fearful and timid minds, recover yourselves, hear what Jesus promises')

A. Ob i, ii and Ob da cacc (unis.). Cont

The moral is here drawn and Nicodemus is gently rebuked in an aria without da capo, which has no special features.

6 CHORALE

'Auf dass wir also allzugleich zur Himmelspforte dringen, und dermaleinst in deinem Reich ohn' alles Ende singen' ('So that we thus altogether to heaven's gate throng and thereafter in Thy kingdom sing without end')

SATB. As No. 1. Insts. with voices. Cont

Verse 8 of Paul Gerhardt's Trinity hymn, 'Was alle Weisheit

in der Welt' (1653), set to Johann Walther's melody, 'Christ, unser Herr, zum Jordan kam' (1524).

Gelobet sei der Herr (Praised be the Lord).
Chorale Cantata BWV 129. Leipzig 1726 or 1727.

This concise and beautiful work is based on the text of the Trinity hymn by Johannes Olearius with the above title (1665) with the anonymous melody of Johann Heermann's 'O Gott, du frommer Gott' (1679) used in Nos. 1 and 5. All the movements except the last begin with the title line. The three inner movements are arias of continual praise, which never become monotonous.

1 CHORUS
(As above)
SATB. Tr i, ii, iii, Timp, Fl trav, Ob i, ii, Vln i, ii, Vla, Cont

After the joyous opening measures the trumpets and timpani give place to the woodwind and strings, which are given a series of arpeggios swinging up and down as if they are glowing censers of praise. Trumpets then join in and the sopranos begin the chorale melody. At each entry Bach devises new counter-melodies for the lower parts. It is a glorious movement.

2 ARIA
'Gelobet sei der Herr, mein Gott, mein Heil, mein Leben'
('Praised be the Lord, my God, my salvation, my life')
B. Cont

The continuo part is very elaborate, continually repeating a wide-flung figure which the soloist could not be expected to emulate.

3 ARIA
'Gelobet sei der Herr, mein Gott, mein Trost, mein Leben, des Vaters werther Geist, den mir, der Sohn gegeben' ('Praised be the Lord, my God, my comfort, my life, the Father's worthy Spirit, whom the Son has given to me')
S. Fl trav, Vln solo, Cont

The chief feature of this delightful aria in praise of the Holy Spirit, is a little figure heard at once in the continuo part, then on the two solo instruments and running throughout the movement. It is a phrase out of Bach's stockpot and one ought to weary of its incessant repetition, but it is his secret that we do not.

4 ARIA

'Gelobet sei der Herr, mein Gott, der ewig lebet, den Alles lobet, was in allen Lüften schwebet' ('Praised be the Lord, my God, who ever lives, whom everything praises that in all heaven hovers')
A. Ob d'am, Cont

The text ends 'whose name holy is called, God the Father, God the Son, and God the Holy Ghost'. The main melody, pastoral in feeling, has flowing phrases in 6/8 time, and just before the voice comes in the oboe has a little phrase of four descending notes which occurs many times and never fails to charm.

5 CHORALE

'Dem wir das Heilig itzt mit Freuden lassen klingen' ('To whom we the "Holy" now with joy cause to resound')
SATB. As No. 1

The text continues, 'and with the angel host Holy, holy, sing. The whole Christendom heartily praises Him. Praised be my God in all eternity'.

The orchestra has a brilliant independent part except for the flute, which doubles the soprano line an octave higher. Eight times woodwind and strings are given rapid arpeggios as if wafting mankind's praises to Heaven to unite with those of the angelic Host, as in the Chorale with which Part II of the *Christmas Oratorio* ends.

FIRST SUNDAY AFTER TRINITY

Epistle: 1 John IV. 16–21 (God is love).
Gospel: Luke XVI. 19–31 (Dives and Lazarus).

Die Elenden sollen essen, dass sie satt werden, und die nach dem Herrn fragen, werden ihn preisen (The wretched shall eat that they become satisfied and [those] who ask after the Lord shall praise Him).
Cantata BWV 75. Leipzig, 1723.

The three cantatas for this Sunday are all in two parts, the second part being sung after the sermon.

PART I

1 CHORUS
(As above)
SATB. Ob i, ii, Vln i, ii, Vla, Fag, Cont
   The text is Luther's version of Psalm XXII. 26 and the significance of the poignant and brief orchestral introduction with the first oboe's wailing phrases arises from the emphasis, indirect but explicit, in No. 5, which is laid on the sufferings and poverty of Lazarus, who is so touchingly mentioned in the beautiful antiphon 'In Paradisum' in the Latin burial service. At 'those who ask after and praise the Lord', though the voices express these sentiments, the orchestral part remains as pitiful in its appeal. Then comes a consoling and enlivening fugue to the words, 'Your heart shall everlastingly live'.

2 RECITATIVE
'Was hilft des Purpurs Majestät, da sie vergeht? Was hilft der grösste Uberfluss, weil Alles, so wir sehen, verschwinden muss?' ('What avails purple majesty since it passes? What helps the greatest abundance, because all that we see must disappear?')
B. Vln i, ii, Vla, Cont
   Words written with Dives in mind. The text ends with, 'how speedily it comes to pass that riches, lust, splendour, the spirit turns to hell'.

3 ARIA
'Mein Jesus soll mein Alles sein' ('My Jesus shall my all be')
T. Ob i, Vln i, ii, Vla, Cont

173

The voice moves independently of the warmly scored orchestral part at first and then incorporates the latter into its part. The words of the middle section, often accompanied only by the oboe, speak of Christ's precious blood as the 'Christians' purple and all-sweetest joy-wine,' the last words giving Bach a chance for an expansive phrase.

4 RECITATIVE

'Gott stürzet und erhöhet in Zeit und Ewigkeit' ('God casts down and exalts in time and eternity')
T. Cont

Those who seek Heaven in the world are accursed, those who endure hell here will rejoice in Heaven.

5 ARIA

'Ich nehme mein Leiden mit Freuden auf mich' ('I take my sorrow with joy upon me')
S. Ob d'am, Cont

Bach, before somewhat constrained by his libretto, is here relaxed and gives his soprano an exhilarating four-bar florid phrase at 'joy'. The text of the middle section assures that those who bear Lazarus's sufferings patiently take the angels to themselves.

6 RECITATIVE

'Indes schenkt Gott ein gut Gewissen, dabei ein Christe kann ein kleines Gut mit grosser Lust geniessen' ('Meanwhile God gives a good conscience, by which a Christian can enjoy a little possession with great delight')
S. Cont

7 CHORALE

'Was Gott tut, das ist wohlgetan, muss ich den Kelch gleich schmecken der bitter ist nach meinem Wahn' ('What God does that is well done. I must immediately taste the cup which is bitter after my delusion')
SATB. Ob i, Vln i; Ob ii, Vln ii; Vla, Cont

There is to be no fear; at the end all pains will vanish and sweet comfort of heart come. This is the fifth verse of Samuel Rodigast's chorale (1676) with the above title set to its original (1690) melody, straightforwardly sung to a delightfully devised setting for the strings and wind.

PART II

8 SINFONIA
Tr, Vln i, ii, Vla, Cont

This is Bach's first, and last, solely orchestral treatment of a chorale, and it is so fine that one wishes he had composed more of the kind. The trumpet sings out the chorale melody, which the congregation would remember closed Part I.

9 RECITATIVE
'Nur Eines kränkt ein christliches Gemüte: wenn es seines Geistes Armut denkt' ('Only one thing ails a Christian mind: when it thinks of its spirit's poverty')
A. Vln i, ii, Vla, Cont

10 ARIA
'Jesus mach' mich geistlich reich' ('Jesus makes me spiritually rich')
A. Vln i, ii (unis.), Cont

A simply laid out and charming aria. The music beautifully reflects the sentiments of the text.

11 RECITATIVE
'Wer nur in Jesu bleibt, die Selbstverleugnung treibt' ('Who only in Jesus remains, practises self-denial')
B. Cont

12 ARIA
'Mein Herze glaubt und liebt' ('My heart believes and loves')
B. Tr, Vln i, ii, Vla, Cont

The above words suffice Bach for the first section of this aria whose great attraction is the brilliant trumpet obbligato.

13 RECITATIVE
'O Armuth, der kein Reichtum gleicht! Wenn aus dem Herzen die ganze Welt entweicht, und Jesus allein regiert' ('O poverty that no riches equal! When out of the heart, the whole world disappears, and Jesus alone reigns')
T. Cont

The elegantly set text concludes, 'So is a Christian led to God. Grant, God, that we do not lose it by folly.'

14 The score indicates a repeat of No. 7.

O Ewigkeit, du Donnerwort (O Eternity, thou thunderword).
Chorale Cantata BWV 20. Leipzig, 1724.

The factor common to the two cantatas with the above title—the other being BWV 60—is that they both begin with the first verse of Johann Rist's hymn set to Johann Schop's melody 'Wach auf, mein Geist' (1642). This libretto draws on verses i, xi and xvi in their original form in Nos. 1, 7 and 11 and paraphrases the rest.

PART I

1 CHORUS
'O Ewigkeit, du Donnerwort, o Schwert das durch die Seele bohrt' ('O Eternity, thou thunder-word, O sword that through the soul pierces')
SATB. Tr with S. Ob i, ii, iii, Vln i, ii, Vla, Cont

The words of the hymn, which strongly emphasize the everlastingness of eternity for the damned, are used by the librettist to depict the torments of Dives and those like him who have not recognized Christ in the poor and needy. The chorus is cast in the form of a French overture. The trumpet reinforces the splendid melody of the chorale sung in long notes throughout. The only dramatic gesture in the stern orchestral introduction comes with trembling demisemiquavers, which are twice repeated in the course of this section. The time changes from 4/4 to 3/4 at the *vivace*, the agitation grows as the words speak of immeasurable mourning. The music is abruptly halted on a discord, indicating a move into the minor key, and Bach now introduces a high note of drama he has been preparing. It illustrates the words that follow, 'mein ganz erschrocknes Herz' ('My completely affrighted heart'), in broken phrases for the oboes and strings which, as the chorale melody continues on its untroubled course in the top line, appear in the lower voices, and are heard to be a distortion of the melody line.

2 RECITATIVE
'Kein Unglück ist in aller Welt zu finden, das ewig dauernd ist, es muss doch endlich mit der Zeit einmal verschwinden' ('No misfortune is to be found in all the world that is eternally enduring; it must finally with time disappear')
T. Cont

But, the text continues, the pain of eternity has no such limitations, 'as Jesus Himself says, from it there is no redemption' (St Matthew XXIII. 33).

3 ARIA
'Ewigkeit, du machst mir bange, ewig ist zu lange' ('Eternity, thou mak'st me anxious, "ever" is too long')
T. Vln i, ii, Vla, Cont

Long-held notes at the start on the strings and the continuo, then in the voice part, underline the concept of eternity. The music, though moving calmly, conveys a continual sense of unease which breaks out at the mention of flames burning in hell—florid phrases for the soloist which strike terror to the heart and evoke a note of pleading in the instrumental part.

4 RECITATIVE
'Gesetzt, es dau'rte der Verdammten Qual so viele Jahr' ('Granted the damned's torment lasted so many a year')
B. Cont

All pains and troubles suffered by mankind on earth eventually cease, but for the damned there is never an end.

5 ARIA
'Gott ist gerecht in seinen Werken' ('God is just in His works')
B. Ob i, ii, iii, Cont

This needed to be said, with the conviction of an almost sprightly aria in the major key. Those few words suffice Bach for the whole of the first section. But in the middle section there comes a warning that even short sins incur long pain, and this is reiterated impressively just before the *da capo*.

6 ARIA
'O Mensch, errette deine Seele, entfliehe Satans Sklaverei' ('O Man, save thy soul and escape Satan's slavery')
A. Vln i, ii, Vla, Cont

A brief aria, which goes on to speak of the sulphur-hole which torments the damned, but does not gnaw the soul eternally.

7 CHORALE
'So lang ein Gott im Himmel lebt und über allen Wolken schwebt, wird solche Marter währen' ('So long as a God in Heaven lives and over all the clouds soars, will such torment endure')
SATB. As No. 1. Insts. with voices. Cont

There is an enigmatic last line, 'This pain will end when God is no more eternal'. This I find baffling. Terry translates it, 'When God's good time shall give release'.

PART II

8 ARIA
'Wacht auf, verlorne Schaafe, ermuntert euch von Sündenschlafe' ('Wake up, lost sheep, arouse ye from sin-sleep')
B. Tr. Ob i, Vln i; Ob ii, Vln ii; Ob iii, Vla; Cont
  One of Bach's splendid arias with trumpet obbligato. After an hour-long sermon—a hell-fire one, no doubt—this stirring aria must have roused the somnolent. Vividly pictorial phrases for the bass illustrate, 'Wake up, before the trumpet sounds which summons you with fear out of the grave to the judge of all the world'.

9 RECITATIVE
'Verlass, o Mensch, die Wollust dieser Welt, Pracht, Hoffahrt, Reichtum, Ehr'und Geld' ('Forsake, O Man, the delights of this world, splendour, pomp, riches, honour and wealth')
A. Cont
  The first half of this recitative is remarkably imaginative—the continuo leaps up and down, as if stripping the unwary sinner of all he values most.

10 DUET
'O Menschenkind, hör' auf geschwind, die Sünd' und Welt zu lieben' ('O mortal child, cease quickly sin and the world to love')
A.T. Cont
  The librettist must have been glad to recall at this late stage of the cantata that the message of the Epistle for the day (St John IV. 16–21) was that 'God is love'. The long duet, based on the penultimate verse of the hymn, does begin compassionately even though the pains of hell, the howling and gnashing of teeth come into the text.

11 CHORALE
(As at No. 1 except for the last line, 'Take Thou me when it Thee please, Lord Jesu, into Thy joy-tabernacle'.)
SATB. As No. 7

Brich dem Hungrigen dein Brot (Bring the hungry man thy bread).
Cantata BWV 39. Leipzig, 1726.

PART I

1 CHORUS
(As above)
SATB. Fl i, ii, Ob i, ii, Vln i, ii, Vla, Cont

The imaginatively devised orchestral introduction has been taken to represent the breaking of the bread or, which is a much more likely interpretation, the feeble footsteps of the hungry coming up to receive it.

The orchestral prelude ends with a new theme which will be used at the words 'Take into the house', at which point the tottering main theme and the detached notes of the continuo give place to different figuration as if depicting the warm welcome the hungry receive.

The words, to the end of this section, are based on Isaiah LVIII. 7 and 8, 'Is not [the fast I choose] to share the bread with the hungry, and bring the homeless poor into your house, when you see the naked, to cover him and not to hide yourself from your own flesh'. It brings Jesus's words to mind, 'Inasmuch as you do it unto them, you do it unto me' and his denunciation of the careless rich. Isaiah continues, 'Then shall thy light break forth as the morning and thy healing shall spring forth speedily; and thy righteousness shall go before thee.'

Bach sets the paraphrase of these last words to a glorious fugue, with two expositions, and so brings to an end one of his finest choruses and one that is worthy indeed of the inspired words of Isaiah.

2 RECITATIVE
'Der reiche Gott wirft seinen Überfluss auf uns, die wir ohn' ihn nicht den Odem haben' ('The great God throws His abundance on us, who without Him have not breath')
B. Cont

A heartfelt outburst of gratitude and a determination to repay God's goodness by helping our neighbours in distress.

3 ARIA

'Seinem Schöpfer noch auf Erden, nur im Schatten ähnlich werden, ist im Vorschmack selig sein' ('To his Creator yet on earth only in shadow similar to become, is in the foretaste to be blessed')

A. Vln solo, Ob i, Cont

A melodious but unremarkable aria to end the first part of the cantata.

PART II

4 ARIA

'Wohlzutun und mitzuteilen vergesset nicht, denn solche Opfer gefallen Gott wohl' ('Forget not to do well and to share, for such offerings please God well')

B. Cont

The main melody of this aria is characterized by a syncopated little figure. At the close Bach gives an expansive phrase to the 'offering' pleasing to God.

5 ARIA

'Höchster, was ich habe, ist nur deine Gabe' ('Highest, what I have is only Thy gift')

S. Fl i, ii, (unis.), Cont

If Bach meant to lead up from a quite ordinary aria (No. 3) through one of greater attraction and so now to the best of the lot he has certainly achieved his goal. There is a welcome warmth, grace and radiance in the lovely melody for the voice, enchantingly accompanied by the flutes in unison, perhaps illustrating the words of the second section 'When before Thy countenance I already would thankfully appear with my gift, desirest Thou then no offering?'

6 RECITATIVE

'Wie soll ich dir, o Herr, denn sattsamlich vergelten, was du an Leib und Seel' mir hast zu Gut getan' ('How shall I to Thee, Oh Lord, then sufficiently requite, what Thou in body and soul to me has done for good')

A. Vln i, ii, Vla, Cont

A final expression of humble gratitude.

7 CHORALE
'Selig sind, die aus Erbarmen, sich annehmen fremder Not'
('Blessed are they who from pity take an interest in others' needs')
SATB. As No. 1. Insts. with voices. Cont

Verse 6 of David Denicke's 'Kommt, lasst euch den Herren
lehren' (1648) set to Louis Bourgeois' 'Ainsi qu'on oit le cerf'
(1542) and its associated melody. A paraphrase of the beatitude,
very simply set.

SECOND SUNDAY AFTER TRINITY

Epistle: 1 John III. 13–18 (Of Christian brotherly love).
Gospel: Luke XIV. 16–24 (Parable of the great supper).

Die Himmel erzählen die Ehre Gottes und die Veste verkündiget seiner Hände Werk (The heavens declare the glory of God and the firmament proclaims his handiwork).
Cantata BWV 76. Leipzig, 1723.

PART I

1 CHORUS
(As above)
SATB. Tr, Ob i, ii, Vln i, ii, Vla, Cont

The text is verse 1 of Psalm XIX in the first section of the movement, verse 3 in the second section.

The short and triumphant introductory prelude, with the trumpet prominent, leads one to expect the chorus will enter in full cry, but it is the solo bass who declaims—to a fine phrase not again heard—the opening line, accompanied only by the continuo until the last word when the oboes come in, with violins responding, the trumpet silent. Only then does the chorus, with the full orchestra, burst in. When this section has exultantly run its course the solo tenor starts the fugal section. 'There is no language or speech where one hears not their voice'. The three other soloists complete the exposition accompanied only by the continuo, and bring in the chorus, from which point Bach builds up a great structure of glorious sound, withholding the trumpet until the rise to the peak climax.

2 RECITATIVE
'So lässt sich Gott nicht unbezeuget! Natur und Gnade red't alle Menschen an' ('So God lets Himself not be untestified! Nature and mercy address all mankind')
T. Vln i, ii, Vla, Cont

An arioso (*andante*) follows the words which speak of the miracle of the creation of the world, the violins seeming to depict in flowing phrases the spirit of God moving over the face of the waters.

3 ARIA
'Hört, ihr Völker, Gottes Stimme, eilt zu seinem Gnadenthron'
('Hear, ye people, God's voice, hasten to His mercy throne')
S. Vln solo, Cont

This cantata was performed on the second Sunday after Bach
was inducted into the office of Cantor on Monday 31 May 1723
and, after giving the congregation some movements from No. 75
(p. 173) startling to ears accustomed to his predecessor Kuhnau's
very different and conservative style, Bach produced this aria in a
popular melodic style with a foot-tapping rhythm.

4 RECITATIVE
'Wer aber hört, da sich der grösste Haufen zu andern Göttern
kehrt?' ('But who hears, when the greatest crowds to other gods
turn?')
B. Cont

The figure of Belial sitting firm in God's house darkens the
happy scene: it is to this evil spirit the crowds turn, Christians
also running away from Christ.

5 ARIA
'Fahr hin, fahr hin, abgöttische Zunft, sollt' sich die Welt gleich
verkehren, will ich doch Christum verehren.' ('Away, away,
idolatrous tribe. Should the world ever pervert itself, I yet will
Christ honour')
B. Tr, Vln i, ii, Vla, Cont

The trumpet rebukes idolatry with no uncertain sound. The
little figure at the start, in all parts, is always set to 'away' and
also dominates much of the orchestral part.

6 RECITATIVE
'Du hast uns, Herr, von allen Strassen zu dir gerufen'
('Thou hast us, O Lord, from all ways to Thee called')
A. Cont

The arioso that follows the recitative—which thanks God for
His mercies to 'those that sat in darkness'—is planned to run
straight into the chorale after the line, 'Therefore be this prayer
to Thee most submissively made'.

7 CHORALE
'Es woll uns Gott gnädig sein und seinen Segen geben' ('May
God be gracious to us and give His blessing')
SATB. Tr, Vln i, ii, Vla, Cont

The first verse of Luther's 'Es woll' uns Gott genädig sein' (1524) set to its mclody (1525).

PART II

8 SINFONIA
Adagio marked 'After the sermon'
Ob d'am, Vla da gamba, Cont

This is an adaptation of the first movement of the Sonata in E minor for two Claviers and Pedal (BWV 528). A brief *adagio* followed by a lively *vivace*.

9 RECITATIVE
'Gott, segne noch die treue Schar, damit sie seine Ehre durch Glauben, Liebe, Heiligkeit erweise und vermehre' ('God bless still the faithful host, so that through belief, love, holiness, it increases His honour')
B. Vln i, ii, Vla, Vla da gamba, Cont

10 ARIA
'Hasse nur, hasse mich recht, feindlich's Geschlecht' ('Hate only, hate me well, hostile race')
T. Vla da gamba, Cont

The invitation, in which 'hate' is repeated seventeen times in twenty-three bars, is delivered with a masochistic relish. The second section is calmer as regards the vocal part.

11 RECITATIVE
'Ich fühle schon im Geist, wie Christus mir der Liebe Süssigkeit erweist' ('I feel already in my spirit Christ grants me the love-sweetness')
A. Vla da gamba, Cont

Expressive phrases depict the manna falling from Heaven and strengthening brotherly faithfulness.

12 ARIA
'Liebt, ihr Christen, in der Tat, Jesus stirbet für die Brüder' ('Love, ye Christians, Jesus really dies for the brethren')
A. Ob d'am, Vla da gamba, Cont

The scoring is that of the Sinfonia: the text refers to the Epistle for the day about brotherly love.

13 RECITATIVE
'So soll die Christenheit die Liebe Gottes preisen und sie in sich erweisen' ('So shall Christendom praise the love of God and show it within itself')
T. Cont

14 CHORALE
'Es danke, Gott, und lobe dich das Volk in guten Taten' ('Let thank, God, and praise Thee Thy people with good deeds')
SATB. As No. 7
The third verse of Luther's hymn.

Ach Gott, vom Himmel sieh darein (Ah God, from Heaven look thereto).
Chorale Cantata BWV 2. Leipzig, 1724.

The libretto is based on Luther's paraphrase of Psalm XII (1524). The first and last verses are set in their original form in the corresponding numbers of the cantata, the other verses in Nos. 2–5.

1 CHORUS
(As above)
SATB. Vln i, Trb i with S. Vln ii, Ob i, ii, Trb ii with A. Vla, Trb iii with T. Trb iv with B. Cont

This movement is in the motet style of Pachelbel, that is, the chorus accompanied only by an independent continuo part, beginning straightaway with successive entries based on the chorale for T.B.S. The anonymous melody is heard in the alto voice in long notes. The same process occurs before each successive line of the chorale.

These pessimistic words are set with a severity brought out in Bach's use of the archaic form.

2 RECITATIVE
'Sie lehren eitel falsche List, was wider Gott und seine Wahrheit ist' ('They teach empty false deceit which is against God and His truth')
T. Cont

3 ARIA
'Tilg', o Gott, die Lehren, so dein Wort verkehren' ('Exterminate, O God, the teaching which perverts Thy word')
A. Vln solo, Cont

A tirade against heretics and plotters who wish to seize power. The violin solo part contains frenzied phrases of demisemiquaver triplets that dash up and down, while the continuo part, marked *staccato*, breathes out defiance. All this, perhaps, illustrates combat with the enemies of the Church.

4 RECITATIVE
'Die Armen sind verstört, ihr seufzend Ach, ihr ängstlich Klagen bei so viel Kreuz und Not' ('The poor are bewildered, thcir sighing Ah, their anguished laments in so much suffering and want')
B. Vln i, ii, Vla, Cont

These poignant sounds reach the merciful ear of God, who says, 'I must be their helper. I have heard their supplications, the succour's dawn'. God's words are marked *arioso*, and as He speaks the strings rise high above the voice in long notes to illustrate the rise of 'the star of life'.

5 ARIA
'Durchs Feuer wird das Silber rein, durchs Kreuz das Wort bewährt erfunden' ('Through the fire silver becomes pure; through the Cross the word is shown to be proven')
T. Ob i, ii with Vln i; Vln ii, Vla, Cont

The middle section counsels patience in suffering for the Christian.

6 CHORALE
'Das wollst du, Gott, bewahren rein für diesen arg'n Geschlechte' ('That wilt Thou, God, preserve pure for this evil race')
SATB. As No. 1

The sixth and last verse of Luther's hymn.

ST JOHN THE BAPTIST

Epistle: Isa. 1–5 (Prepare ye the way).
Gospel: Luke 1. 57–80 (The birth of John the Baptist and the prophecy of Zacharias).

Ihr Menschen, rühmet Gottes Liebe (Ye men, extol God's love).
Solo Cantata BWV 167. Leipzig, 1723.

1 ARIA
(As above)
T. Vln i, ii, Vla, Cont

The main melody of the aria is in one of Bach's flowing 12/8 measures but it does not seem to me that he had the Jordan in mind, as has been suggested, in choosing this rhythm, but rather wanted to express heartfelt gratitude for God's love—as the text goes on to say—that Zacharias' prophecy was to be fulfilled.

2 RECITATIVE
'Gelobet sei der Herr Gott Israel, der sich in Gnaden zu uns wendet, und seinen Sohn vom hohen Himmelsthron zum Welterlöser sendet' ('Praised be the Lord God of Israel, Who Himself in mercy to us turns and sends His Son from high heaven's throne as world redeemer')
A. Cont

The text goes on to speak of John first coming to prepare the way for the Saviour and, then, Jesus Christ Himself, to redeem mankind with love and mercy and lead them to the heavenly kingdom. These last words are set to a lovely arioso.

3 DUET
'Gottes Wort, das trüget nicht, es geschieht, was er verspricht' ('God's word, that does not deceive: it happens as He promises')
S.A. Ob da cacc obb. Cont

At the start and the five repetitions of 'God's word', the voices are always together and elsewhere echo one another in imitational phrases. The tempo changes from 3/4 to 4/4 at the middle section, 'What He in Paradise and before so many hundred years already promised to the fathers, have we, God be praised! proved'. The 'many hundred years' are illustrated in six-bar

187

florid vocal phrases and in the middle section, the fulfilment of the promise in similar style.

4 RECITATIVE
'Des Weibes Samen kam, nachdem die Zeit erfüllet der Segen, den Gott Abraham, den Glaubensheld, versprochen' ('Of woman's seed came, after the time was fulfilled the blessing, the faith-hero, which God promised to Abraham')
B. Cont

Elizabeth and Zacharias now come into the picture, and mention of the sudden release of his dumbness into the great song of thanksgiving to God. Christians are then exhorted to sing to Him a song of praise. At this point Bach most effectively quotes the first melody line of the chorale that follows.

5 CHORALE
'Sei Lob und Preis mit Ehren, Gott, Vater, Sohn und heiliger Geist' ('Be glory and praise with honour [to] God, Father, Son and Holy Spirit')
SATB. Ob, Vln i, ii, Vla, Cont. Clar with S.

A joyous setting of verse v of Johann Graumann's 'Nun lob, mein Seel, den Herren' (1540)—a version of Psalm CIII—to its associated melody.

Christ, unser Herr, zum Jordan kam (Christ, our Lord, to Jordan came).
Chorale Cantata BWV 7. Leipzig, 1724.

The text is a remodelled version of Luther's hymn with the above title (c. 1524). Verses i and vii are set in their original form in Nos. 1 and 7. The other verses are paraphrased in the rest of the movements. The original melody, possibly by Johann Walther, is used in Nos. 1 and 7.

1 CHORUS
'Christ unser Herr zum Jordan kam nach seines Vaters Willen, von Sanct Johann's die Taufe nahm, sein Werk und Amt zu erfüllen' ('Christ, our Lord to Jordan came according to His Father's will, from St John baptism took, His work and ministry to fulfil')
SATB. Ob d'am i, ii, Vln concertante, Vln i, ii, Vla, Cont

This is one of Bach's finest chorale fantasias. It is cast in concerto form for it is obvious that the composer wishes the solo violin part to stand out prominently. With the continuo, it accompanies the first two entries of the chorus. The chorale melody, in long notes, given to the tenors, is one of the very few instances of their being so singled out in all the chorale fantasias. It is difficult to resist the suggestion that the complex texture is meant to illustrate Bach's picture of the river Jordan. The text continues 'So would He establish for us a bath to wash us from sins, to drown also the bitter death through His own blood and wounds, there prevailed a new life'. These words are the real clue to the heart of the matter which is summed up in the final triumphant phrase at 'life'.

2 ARIA

'Merkt und hört, ihr Menschenkinder, was Gott selbst die Taufe heisst' ('Mark and hear, ye men's children, when God Himself designates the baptism')
B. Cont

These two lines have to suffice for the whole of the first section of this didactic aria, and so involve a lot of repetition. The remarkable feature of the movement is the demisemiquaver figure in the continuo below which, counting the da capo, is heard no less than 129 times. If it is indeed meant to be symbolic of the baptismal water its continual occurrence in the middle section does not consort with the text, which stresses that the water visible to the eye is not water inwardly but God's Spirit and His word, that enable us to reach Heaven.

3 RECITATIVE

'Dies hat Gott klar mit Worten und Bildern dargetan' ('This has God clearly with word and examples demonstrated')
T. Cont

The text speaks of how He openly proclaimed at the baptism His Son as His heir and said, 'This is my dear Son in whom I am well pleased'. Bach puts the quotation, based on St Matthew XXVIII. 19, in inverted commas, i.e. rests before and after. 'He took our lowly state [here the music sinks in pitch] and weak nature. Accept Him, then, as Saviour and Lord and hearken to His holy teaching'.

4 ARIA

'Des Vaters Stimme liess sich hören, der Sohn, der uns mit Blut

erkauft, ward als ein wahrer Mensch getauft' ('The Father's voice lets itself be heard, the Son who with blood redeems us was as a very man baptized')
T. Vln concertante i, ii, Cont

This is a very imaginative aria. The ethereal parts for the two solo violins seem to portray the Holy Spirit, spoken of in the continuation of the text as appearing in the form of a dove. Bach, without stopping the fluttering instrumental phrases, gives moving expression to our redemption through the Son's blood in a long-drawn vocal line at 'redeems'.

5 RECITATIVE
'Als Jesus dort nach seinen Leiden und nach dem Auferstehn aus dieser Welt zum Vater wollte gehn, sprach er in seinen Jüngern' ('When Jesus after His Passion and the resurrection was about to go from this world to the Father, He spoke to His disciples')
B. Vln i, ii, Vla, Cont

The strings come in at the arioso on the words that follow, 'Go ye therefore, and teach all nations' (St Matthew xxviii. 19) using the rising phrase at 'resurrection' a tone higher, proof of the intense care Bach generally took to make recitatives meaningful. The words finish the well-known quotation.

6 ARIA
'Menschen, glaubt doch dieser Gnade, dass ihr nicht in Sünden sterbt' ('Mankind, believe then in this mercy that ye die not in sin')
A. Ob d'am i, ii, Vln i (all in unis.), Vln ii, Vla, Cont

The continuo alone accompanies the first half of the opening and the other lines, after ritornellos, as if Bach wanted to emphasize the importance of the baptismal rite for the Christian.

7 CHORALE
'Das Aug allein das Wasser sieht, wie Menschen Wasser giessen' ('The eyes alone the water sees as mankind's water to flow')
SATB. Ob d'am i, ii, Vln i, ii, Vla, all with voices, Cont

This is verse vii of Luther's hymn.

Freue dich, erlöste Schaar, freue dich, in Zion's Hütten
(Rejoice thee, redeemed host, rejoice thee in Zion's dwellings).
Cantata BWV 30. Leipzig, 1735.

The music of this cantata is adapted, with the exception of the recitatives and the chorale at the end of Part I, from the secular cantata *Angenehmes Wiederau* composed by Bach for a lackey raised to high estate by his patron, Count Brühl, to become 'feudal lord and judge in his own right of Wiederau', a small town on the river Elster. J. C. von Hennicke, this vain person, was flattered by Picander to the extent of suggesting, in a recitative, that Wiederau should now be known as 'Hennicke's Rest'!

Bach, evidently unwilling that his music for this temporary event should be wasted, commissioned Picander to remodel the text of the opening and closing choruses and four of the five arias and to supply new recitatives. Bach may have added the chorale himself.

PART I

1 CHORUS
(As above)
SATB. Tr i, ii, iii, Timp, Fl trav i, ii, Ob i, ii, Vln i, ii, Vla, Org, Cont

There is no orchestral introduction and the delightful syncopated phrase to 'Rejoice' is the only thing that betrays a secular origin. Otherwise 'Zion's dwellings' suits the adapted text better than the original Wiederau's 'pleasant meadows'. 'Pleasant meadows' do not call for trumpets and timpani to praise them.

2 RECITATIVE
'Wir haben Rast, und des Gesetzes Last ist abgetan' ('We have rest, and the law's burden is removed')
B. Org, Cont

3 ARIA
'Gelobet sei Gott, gelobet sein Name, der treulich gehalten Versprechen und Eid' ('Praised be God, praised [be] His name, who faithfully [has] kept promise and oath')
B. Vln i, ii, Vla, Org, Cont

The text ends, 'Sing a song of praise . . . yea sing to each other'. The music goes fairly well with the adapted text but the delightfully florid phrases of triplets illustrating 'praised' are not the kind of thing one would associate with John the Baptist.

4 RECITATIVE
'Der Herold kommt und meld't den König an' ('The herald comes and announces the King')
A. Org, Cont

'His voice shows the way, the light whereby we those blessed meadows can certainly one day behold'. But not those of Wiederau. I hope Bach smiled at this allusion.

5 ARIA
'Kommt, ihr angefocht'nen Sünder, eilt und lauft, ihr Adamskinder' ('Come, ye tempted sinners, hasten and run, you Adam's children')
A. Fl trav, Vln i, ii, Vla, Org, Cont

The charming melody begins, like the opening chorus, with syncopated measures in gavotte-like style. 'There is', Whittaker rightly says, 'absolutely no relation between text and music. . . . It is the worst crime Bach committed against himself.'

6 CHORALE
'Eine Stimme lässt sich hören in der Wüsten, weit und breit' ('A voice makes itself heard in the wilderness wide and far') SATB. S. with Fl trav i, ii, Ob i, ii, Vln i, A. with Vln ii, T. with Vla, Org, Cont

After the frivolous nature of No. 5 the chorale comes as a clear reminder that this is the Feast of St John the Baptist. The chorale is the third verse of Johann Olearius's 'Tröstet, tröstet meine Liebe' for the feast and quotes the Baptist's words about making ready the way for the Lord.

PART II

7 RECITATIVE
'So bist du denn, mein Heil, bedacht, den Bund den du gemacht mit unsern Vätern treu zu halten' ('So art Thou then, my Saviour, minded, the bond which Thou made with our fathers, faithfully to hold')
B. Ob i, ii, Org, Cont

Bach is here wholly attentive to the text, which ends with a vow to live in holiness and fear of God.

8 ARIA
'Ich will nun hassen, und Alles lassen, was dir, mein Gott, zuwider ist' ('I will now hate, and everything abandon, that to Thee, my God, is offensive')
B. Ob d'am, Vln solo, Vln i, ii, Vla, Org, Cont

In the secular cantata this aria, sung by Fate, obsequiously flatters Hennicke. The adaptation is as tasteless as that in No. 5.

9 RECITATIVE
'Und obwohl sonst der Unbestand dem schwachen Menschen ist verwandt so sei hiermit doch zugesagt' ('And although usually the inconstancy is related to the weak man, yet herewith be promised')
S. Org, Cont
The promise is to hold fast and firm our faith.

10 ARIA
'Eilt, ihr Stunden, kommt herbei, bringt mich bald in jene Auen' ('Hasten, ye hours, come hither, bring me soon into those meadows')
S. Vln i, ii (unis.), Org, Cont
The meadows in this aria are those of Heaven—in other words, this is a successful adaptation of what was and remains a charming melody.

11 RECITATIVE
'Geduld, der angenehme Tag kann nicht mehr weit und lange sein' ('Patience, the acceptable day can no longer be far distant')
T. Org, Cont
Bach evidently took trouble over this recitative, which ends with an expressive arioso (*adagio*), 'there will thee no distress more torment'.

12 CHORUS
'Freue dich, geheil'gte Schaar, freue dich in Sions Auen') ('Rejoice ye, holy host, rejoice ye in Zion's meadows')
SATB. As No. 1

THIRD SUNDAY AFTER TRINITY

Epistle: 1 Peter v. 6–11 (Cast your cares upon God).
Gospel: Luke xv. 1–10 (Parable of the lost sheep).

Ich hatte viel Bekümmerniss in meinem Herzen (I had a great affliction in my heart).
Cantata BWV 21. Leipzig, 1723.

PART I

1 SINFONIA
Ob, Vln i, ii, Vla, Fag, Org, Cont

The unknown librettist of this cantata, which Bach marked 'per ogni Tempo' (for any season), concentrates in the first five numbers of this part on the miseries of the lost sheep of the parable and in Part II on the joy when they are found by the Good Shepherd.

No. 1 paints a most moving picture, in the arabesques for the first violin and the oboe, of the lost sheep wandering now here, now there, on the bare mountainside. Bach twice brings the music to a halt on discords, as if the sheep had to pause exhausted and at last give up the search as hopeless. Here the oboe unaccompanied utters a cry of desolation—pitifully broken off as it reaches its high point.

2 CHORUS
'Ich hatte viel Bekümmerniss in meinem Herzen' ('I had a great affliction in my heart')
SATB. As No. 1

The text is based on Psalm xciv. 19, 'When the cares of heart are many thy consolations cheer my soul'. The theme of the free fugue is identical, except that it is in the minor key, with the Weimar G major fugue (BWV 541) for organ.

The *Vivace* with the text of the latter half of the verse is most effectively led up to by an *adagio* bar, preceded and followed by rests, as the chorus sing 'but', and then follows the lively music expressing the consolations with which the Lord refreshes the troubled souls.

3 ARIA
'Seufzer, Tränen, Kummer, Not, Seufzer, Tränen, ängstlich's Sehnen, Furcht und Tod nagen mein beklemmtes Herz' ('Sigh-

194

ing, weeping, trouble, need, anxious longing, fear and death, gnaw my downcast heart')
S. Ob, Org, Cont

This beautiful aria, which returns to the sorrowful mood of the *Sinfonia*, is a duet between oboe and voice, one sometimes echoing the phrases of the other, sometimes the two joining together.

4 RECITATIVE
'Wie hast du dich, mein Gott, in meiner Not, in meiner Furcht und Zagen denn ganz von mir gewandt?' ('Why has Thou Thyself, my God, in my need, in my fear and trembling, then turned completely from me?')
T. Vln i, ii, Vla, Fag, Org, Cont

The sorrowful mood continues in this most expressive recitative, the text of which ends, 'I call, I cry to Thee, but my woe and agony appear to Thee completely unknown'.

5 ARIA
'Bäche von gesalznen Zähren, Fluten rauschen stets einher' ('Streams of salt tears, floods rush continually along')
T. Vln i, ii, Vla, Fag, Org, Cont

The flood of tears is vividly illustrated in the motif for strings and voice, and the 'storms and waves' overwhelming the soul in the middle *allegro* section, which returns to the figuration of the opening *largo* but in a more impassioned variant.

6 CHORUS
'Was betrübst du dich, meine Seele, und bist so unruhig in mir?' ('Why troublest thou thyself, my soul, and art so unquiet in me?')
SATB. As No. 1

The text is taken from Psalm XLII. 5, the form of the music a prelude and fugue, and the opening words are sung by the four soloists. The isolation of the words, 'in me?', two *adagio* chords, is very moving. The words of the rather conventional fugue begin, 'that my countenance's help and my God is'.

PART II

7 RECITATIVE
'Ach, Jesu, meine Ruh, mein Licht, wo bleibest du?' ('Ah Jesu, my rest, my light, where remainest Thou?')
S.B. As No. 4

This recitative, as fine as that in No. 4, is a dialogue between the Soul and Jesus. As the soprano sings the first words the first violin moves slowly up an octave, B flat to B flat, above the stave. To the lost sheep it is still night, but when Jesus answers, 'I am your true friend who even in darkness watches', light breaks in upon her and the violins come in with a sequence expressive of quiet delight.

8 DUET

S: 'Komm, mein Jesu, und erquicke, und erfreu' mit deinem Blicke' B: 'Ja, ich komme und erquicke dich mit meinem Gnadenblicke' (S: 'Come, my Jesus, and revive and rejoice with Thy countenance' B: 'Yes, I come and revive thee with my mercy look')

S.B. Org, Cont

This kind of dialogue was not specifically Lutheran. It can be found in the voluminous writings of such Catholic saints as St Angela of Foligno, but is confined to books not sung in church. The music is charming. Its form, a fairly slow and a quick section (here in 3/8), foreshadows, for example, the Don Giovanni-Zerlina duet in Act 2 of Mozart's opera, but becomes dreadfully coy in such exchanges as, 'Yea, ah yea, I am lost', 'Nay, ah nay, thou art chosen', 'Nay, ah nay, thou hatest me', 'Nay, ah nay, I love thee'.

9 CHORUS

'Sei nun wieder zufrieden, meine Seele, denn der Herr tut dir Gut's' ('Be now again contented, my soul, for the Lord does to thee good things')

SATB. Trb i, ii, iii, iv with Vln i, ii, Vla and Fag; Ob, Org and Cont

The text, verse 7 of Psalm CXVI, is reiterated throughout the course of this long movement but into the texture Bach weaves verses ii and v of Georg Neumark's hymn 'Wer nur den lieben Gott lässt walten', with its melody (1657), giving the former to the tenors, the latter to the sopranos in long notes. It is a fine contrapuntal movement in the Pachelbel style and curiously fascinating as it slowly unwinds.

10 ARIA

'Erfreue dich Seele, erfreue dich Herze, entweiche nun Kummer, verschwinde du Schmerz' ('Rejoice thee, soul, rejoice thee, heart, yield now, sorrows, disappear thou, pain')

T. Org, Cont

The lost sheep is safely returned to the fold, and comforted by Jesus with heavenly delight in this lively aria.

11 CHORUS
'Das Lamm, das erwürget ist, ist würdig zu nehmen Kraft' ('The Lamb, which is slaughtered, is worthy to receive power')
SATB. Tr i, ii, iii, Timp, Ob, Vln i, ii, Vla, Fag, Org, Cont
The text is from Revelations v. 12 which is so familiar in Handel's *Messiah* as 'Worthy is the Lamb'.

The massive start is the prelude to the brilliant fugue beginning, 'Laud and honour and praise, and might, be to our God from everlasting to everlasting'.

Ach Herr, mich armen Sünder straf nicht in deinem Zorn (Ah, Lord, me poor sinner punish not in thine anger).
Chorale Cantata BWV 135. Leipzig, 1724.

The libretto is based on the hymn with the above title by Cyriakus Schneegass (1597); verses i and vi are used in their original form, the intermediate numbers are paraphrased.

1 CHORUS
(As above)
SATB. Ob i, ii, Vln i, ii, Vla, Trb with Cont
The melody used in Nos. 1 and 6 is Hassler's 'Herzlich tut mich verlangen' (1601), best known to us as the 'Passion' chorale. It is given, unusually, to the basses, doubled by trombone and continuo. The final note of the chorale lines is always sustained by the basses and continuo, and acts as an impressive pedal point in the last six bars. The text of this wonderful movement is a sinner's despairing prayer for mercy and forgiveness.

2 RECITATIVE
'Ach heile mich, du Arzt der Seelen, ich bin sehr krank und schwach' ('Ah, heal me, Thou physician of souls, I am very ill and weak')
T. Cont
A flood of tears pours down the sinner's face (illustrated by two phrases of demisemiquavers) and at 'The soul is for terror anxious and afraid' the figure Bach gives to 'terror', with two rests separating the word, vividly depicts a shudder.

197

3 ARIA

'Tröste mir, Jesu, mein Gemüte, sonst versink ich in Tod, hilf mir durch deine Güte aus der grossen Seelennot' ('Comfort me, Jesus, my being, else sink I into death, help me through Thy goodness out of the soul's great distress')
T. Ob i, ii, Cont

After that harrowing recitative the prelude to this aria (C major) falls gratefully on the ear of the listener.

The melody of the first four bars—later sung by the soloist—continually develops expressive phrases, easily discernible to the attentive listener. One of these is a chain of sequences, another the rising and falling figures in the continuo. The words of the second section, 'For in death, all is still, there one remembers Thee not', are a paraphrase of the first line of verse 5 of Psalm VI, 'For in death there is no remembrance of Thee'. It is poignantly illustrated by broken phrases. The third section begins with a touching new melody to the words, 'Beloved Jesus [if] it is Thy will, rejoice my countenance', and at last joy invades the music.

4 RECITATIVE

'Ich bin von Seufzen müde' ('I am with sighing weary')
A. Cont

Gloom returns. The words above are sung to a version of the first line of the chorale melody. The text, full again of despair, ends, 'I grieve me almost to death, and am through mourning old, for my anxiety is manifold'.

5 ARIA

'Weicht, all ihr Übeltäter, mein Jesus tröstet mich' ('Begone, all ye evil-doers, my Jesus comforts me')
B. Vln i, ii, Vla, Cont

The sinner—here a bass—now shakes himself free of his miserable condition, for which he blames the evil-doers, and tardily remembers he has a Saviour. The music is tremendously vigorous, and the ritornello, with an athletically dismissive continuo part, is marked *forte* in all parts at the start. The soloist continually cries, 'Begone! My Jesu comforts me'. In the middle section for a moment the soloist has another vigorous blow at his enemies! Suddenly—a wonderful moment—Bach sets the second melody line of the chorale to 'my Jesus comforts me'.

6 Chorale
'Ehr sei in Himmels Throne mit hohem Ruhm und Preis dem
Vater und dem Sohne' ('Honour be in Heaven's throne with
high renown and praise to the Father and the Son')
SATB. Cornetto, Ob i, ii, Vln i, Vln ii, Vla, all with voices; Cont

The Holy Spirit is then praised in the fifth line of the last
verse of the chorale.

FOURTH SUNDAY AFTER TRINITY

Epistle: Rom. vIII. 18–23 (God's children await the glory of the body's redemption).
Gospel: Luke vI. 36–42 (Be merciful and judge not).

Barmherziges Herze der ewigen Liebe (Merciful heart of eternal love).
Solo Cantata BWV 185. Weimar, 1715. Libretto by Salomo Franck.

1 DUET
(As above)
S.T. Ob (or Tr), Cont

Franck drew on part of the Sermon on the Mount for his libretto, beginning with 'Be merciful, even as your Father is merciful'. Bach gives the paraphrase on this line a lilting melody in 6/4 time with trills in continuo and voice parts (not all marked but clearly meant). Near the conclusion of the first line of the text 'inspire, move my heart through Thee', the oboe begins the anonymous melody of Johann Agricola's hymn, 'Ich ruf zu dir, Herr Jesu Christ' which Bach uses complete in Cantata BWV 177 for this Sunday (p. 202).

2 RECITATIVE
'Ihr Herzen, die ihr euch in Stein und Fels verkehret, zerfliesst und werdet weich' ('Ye hearts which have turned into stone and rock, melt and become soft')
A. Vln i, ii, Vla, Fag, Cont

A rather elaborate setting, with all parts marked *pianissimo* at the start. Franck's commonplace addition to 'Judge not, lest ye be judged' detracts from Christ's words and worse is to come later at 'Forgive and you will be forgiven', when the Christian is exhorted to pile up capital to draw a high rate of interest from God. Bach can do nothing with all this.

3 ARIA
'Sei bemüht in dieser Zeit, Seele, reichlich auszustreuen, soll die Ernte dich erfreuen in der reichen Ewigkeit' ('Be at pains in this time, soul, plentifully to scatter [seed] abroad, [then] will the harvest thee rejoice in abundant eternity')
A. Ob, Vln i, ii, Vla, Fag, Cont

Bach deals with this uninspiring text by painting a picture, *adagio*, of the seed being scattered. The profusion of trills are well in place here, and 'scatter', 'rejoice' and 'eternity' are given florid phrases.

4 RECITATIVE
'Die Eigenliebe schmeichelt sich' ('Self-love deceives')
B. Fag, Cont

The text quotes Christ's words about the mote and the beam, and the blind leading the blind, and both falling in the ditch. In the last bar the continuo obliges with a muddy trill.

5 ARIA
'Das ist der Christen Kunst' ('That is the Christian's art')
B. Fag with Cont

The tempo is *vivace*, the moral to love God and not misjudge your neighbour. This is, musically, mini-Bach.

6 CHORALE
'Ich ruf' zu dir, Herr Jesu Christ' ('I call to Thee, Lord Jesus Christ')
SATB. Tr, Ob, Vln ii, Vla, Fag, all with voices; Vln i, Cont

The first verse of Agricola's hymn, with the first violin moving high above the soprano part.

Ein ungefärbt Gemüte von deutscher Treu und Güte
(An unstained mind of German truth and goodness).
Cantata BWV 24. Leipzig, 1723. Libretto by Erdmann Neumeister.

The unpromising first line of this cantata, and what follows, introduces us to an aria which Whittaker justly called, 'One of the most sterile things Bach ever wrote. The craftsman is present, the composer is not, and for that Neumeister's deadly dull libretto must be blamed.' There are two movements worth mentioning. No. 3 is a chorus which takes its text from St Matthew VII. 12, 'So whatever you wish that men would do to you do to them'. Bach, delivered here from the poetaster, gives the words a lively setting brightened up by the clarino. The other number is the concluding chorale, verse i of Johann Heermann's, 'O Gott, du frommer Gott' (1630), scored as in No. 3, which is given a striking setting. The clarino doubles the soprano part but while the orchestra fills in the spaces between the lines, with lulling phrases all composed of slurred two-quaver groups, the clarino reiterates eight low repeated notes in every bar.

Ich ruf zu dir, Herr Jesu Christ (I call on Thee, Lord Jesus Christ).
Chorale Cantata BWV 177. Leipzig, 1732.

1 CHORUS
'Ich ruf zu dir, Herr Jesu Christ, ich bitt, erhör mein Klagen'
('I call on Thee, Lord Jesus Christ, I ask, hear my lament')
SATB. Ob i, ii, Violino concertante, Vln i, ii, Vla, Cont

The cantata is a setting of Johann Agricola's hymn (1529) appointed to be sung this Sunday, the melody of which is used in No. 1 and the concluding chorale. The texts of the five verses reflect St Luke VI. 36–42, 'Be merciful, even as your Father is merciful' and, 'Judge not, and ye shall not be judged'.

A look at the score focuses attention on a remarkable feature of the elaborate part for the solo violin, a motif entering in the first full bar is repeated no less than 118 times in the course of the movement, stressing the urgency of the prayer to Christ. The sopranos sing the chorale melody, doubled by the first oboe, each line of it being anticipated by independent parts for the other voices. This is one of Bach's most deeply felt chorale fantasias.

2 ARIA
'Ich bitt noch mehr, o Herre Gott, du kannst es mir wohl geben'
('I ask yet more, O Lord God, Thou canst well give it to me')
A. Cont

The continuo derives its first phrases from the first line of the chorale, following this with semiquavers rising in semitones, both of which prayerful motifs are constantly repeated.

3 ARIA
'Verleih, dass ich aus Herzensgrund mein'n Feinden mög' vergeben' ('Grant, that I from heart's depth my enemies may forgive')
S. Ob da cacc, Cont

This aria is more expansive. The oboe da caccia and a continuo part, more varied than in No. 2, add to one's pleasure in the aria.

4 ARIA
'Lass mich kein' Lust noch Furcht von dir in dieser Welt ab-
wenden' ('Let me no desire nor fear in this world turn away
from Thee')
T. Violino concertante, Fag obb, Cont

This is delightful and uplifts the heart at once in the orchestral
introduction with its firm three B flats in the continuo, above
which rises the confident melody expressive of the steadfastness
spoken of in the third and fourth lines of the hymn. The last line,
'Thy mercy which us delivers from death', is twice expressively
repeated, with an especially beautifully shaped phrase at 'dying',
ending with a pause on the last syllable just before the da capo.

5 CHORALE
'Ich lieg im Streit und widerstreb, hilf, o, Herr Jesu Christ, dem
Schwachen' ('I am in conflict and doubt, help, O Lord Jesus
Christ, the weak one')
SATB. Ob i, ii, Vln i, ii, Vla, all with voices, Fag with Cont

A line in No. 4 stresses that works without faith are useless and
this last verse of the hymn, set straightforwardly, emphasizes the
Lutheran dogma.

FIFTH SUNDAY AFTER TRINITY

Epistle: 1 Pet. III. 8–15 (Be patient in affliction).
Gospel: Luke v. 1–11 (The miraculous draught of fishes).

Wer nur den lieben Gott lässt walten (If thou but sufferest
God to guide thee).
Chorale Cantata BWV 93. Leipzig, 1724.

The libretto is based on Georg Neumark's hymn (1657) with
the above title and its melody, with verses i, iv, v and vii set in their
original form in the corresponding numbers in the cantata, the rest
being paraphrased, the melody coming into every number.

1 CHORUS
(As above)
SATB. Ob i, ii, Vln i, ii, Vla, Cont

The libretto which takes its inspiration from the Epistle—
drawing attention to the Gospel only in No. 5—concentrates on
trusting God whatever ills befall, sure of having his help and
counsel.

This chorale fantasia is beautifully designed. The oboes, in the
introductory ritornello, hint at the chorale melody, in canon then
in unison, the strings duetting in thirds with a florid version of the
same motif. Each line of the chorale is prefaced by a short fugato
which is always scored—except in the last line—for two parts (S.
and A. or T. and B.). All parts join, in chords, for the first
bars of the chorale, which is heard in full in the top line, the others
briefly developing their phrases.

2 RECITATIVE AND CHORALE
'Was helfen uns die schweren Sorgen? Sie drücken nur das Herz
mit Centner Pein, mit tausend Angst und Schmerz' ('What avail
us the heavy cares? They only oppress the heart with a hundred-
weight of pain, with a thousand anguishes and pains')
B. Cont

This dialogue is most effective when divided between the solo
and chorus basses, the latter having the lines of the decorated
melody always marked *adagio*. The last two lines are concerned
with 'cross and sorrow', which must be borne with Christ-like
tranquillity.

3 ARIA

'Man halte nur ein wenig stille, wenn sich die Kreuzesstunde naht' ('Endure for a little quietly when the cross's hour approaches')

T. Vln i, ii, Vla, Cont

An unexpectedly simple and delightful aria, with a crisp accompaniment, based on the opening notes of the chorale.

4 DUET AND CHORALE

'Er kennt die rechten Freudenstunden' ('He knows the right joy-hours')

S.A. Vln i, ii, Vla, Cont

The chorale melody is heard in full only on the strings in even notes but the charming duet begins with a decorated version of the melody.

5 RECITATIVE AND CHORALE

'Denk nicht in deiner Drangsalshitze, wenn Blitz und Donner kracht' ('Think not in thy oppression-heat when lightning and thunder crack')

T. Cont

The same pattern as in No. 2, but with a much longer passage of recitative before the final chorale line. It speaks of Peter toiling all night and catching no fish. Then at Jesus's word his net is overwhelmed with them. So with us, Jesus sends sunlight after rain. Bach makes no attempt to depict the miracle.

6 ARIA

'Ich will auf den Herren schau'n, und stets meinem Gott ver-trau'n' ('I shall on the Lord look and ever in my Lord trust')

S. Ob i, Cont

The soprano blends her happy melody with that of the chorale and the oboe's sparkling part is an added enchantment.

7 CHORALE

'Sing, bet und geh auf Gottes Wegen' ('Sing, pray and go in God's ways')

SATB. As No. 4. Instruments with voices; Cont

The seventh verse of the chorale.

Siehe, ich will viel Fischer aussenden (Behold, I will many fishers send out).
Solo Cantata BWV 88. Leipzig, 1726.

Anyone reading the above words would take them to apply to the Gospel of the day, the story of the miraculous draught of fishes and Peter's mission, but in fact the librettist takes his text from Jeremiah XVI. 16, in which God rebukes the Israelites for worshipping false gods and declares they shall be caught by His fishers. The choice of this text was obviously dictated by moral considerations such as the preacher might draw in his sermon after the cantata—a warning to Christians not to desert God. Bach, however, turns the words to his own purpose, associating them with the Gospel text with which Part II begins.

PART I

1 ARIA
'Siehe, ich will viel Fischer aussenden, spricht der Herr' ('Behold, I will many fishers send out, saith the Lord')
B. Cor i, ii, Vln i with Ob d'am i, Vln ii with Ob d'am ii, Vla with Te, Cont

The motif, heard in the first four bars over a pedal bass, is always associated with the first line of the text and is marked *pianissimo* in every part each time it is repeated by the soloist. It leads to gentle phrases of semiquavers, which are introduced into the vocal part. Jesus forgives Peter's lack of trust and bids Peter not to be afraid, this lovely movement seems to say, but it is followed by an *allegro quasi presto*, in which the 6/8 rhythm changes to *alla breve*, with the words, 'And thereafter will I many hunters send out'. The two horns in the score are now brought in to reinforce the hunting call in the soloist's florid phrases on 'hunters'. It comes into all the instrumental parts in the last section of the aria.

2 RECITATIVE
'Wie leichtlich könnte doch der Höchste uns entbehren' ('How easily could then the Highest with us dispense')
T. Cont

The moral is posed here in the last sentence of the text, 'And yields He to us the enemy's cunning and malice?'

3 ARIA
'Nein! Nein! Gott ist allezeit geflissen, uns auf gutem Weg zu
wissen unter seiner Gnaden Schein' ('No! No! God is always
anxious to know us on the good road under His mercy-light')
T. Ob d'am i, ii, Vln i, ii, Vla, Cont

This aria is a masterly illustration of the wavering of mankind
between doubt and faith, with the latter confirmed by the
final ritornello.

PART II

4 INTRODUCTION AND ARIOSO
'Jesus sprach zu Simon' ('Jesus said to Simon'): 'Fürchte dich
nicht, denn von nun an wirst du Menschen fahen' ('Fear thou not,
for from henceforth wilt thou catch men')
T.B. Vln i, ii, Vla, Cont

The tenor sings the first words before the bass's arioso accompanied only by the continuo, which repeats one figure throughout,
as if confirming Peter's mission.

5 DUET
'Beruft Gott selbst, so muss der Segen auf allem unsern Tun im
Übermasse ruh'n' ('If God himself calls, must the blessing on
all our doings in plenteousness rest')
S.A. Ob d'am i, ii, Vln i, ii (unis.) Cont

At the repetition of 'Ever fear and sorrow' the accompaniment
sinks, but confidence returns at last with the use of the prevailing
motif to the odd words beginning 'The talent which He to us has
given, He will with interest again have', a prosaic notion that
baffles Bach!

6 RECITATIVE
'Was kann dich denn in deinem Wandel schrecken, wenn dir,
mein Herz, Gott selbst die Hände reicht?' ('What can thee, then,
in thy conduct affright, if to thee, my heart, God Himself reaches
his hands?')
S. Cont

A very expressive recitative with emphasis on putting troubles
—'weariness, envy, torment and falsehood'—into proper per-
spective. It ends with an exhortation to go joyfully on, these
things will be seen to have been for the good of the soul.

7 CHORALE
'Sing, bet und geh auf Gottes Wegen' ('Sing, pray and go in God's ways')
SATB. Ob d'am i, ii, Vln i, ii, Vla, Te, all with voices, Cont

Verse vii of Georg Neumark's 'Wer nur den lieben Gott lässt walten' (1657) set to his melody.

SIXTH SUNDAY AFTER TRINITY

Epistle: Rom. vi. 3–11 (We may not live in sin).
Gospel: Matt. v. 20–26 (Agree with thine adversary).

Es ist das Heil uns kommen her (It is the salvation to us come hither).
Chorale Cantata BWV 9. Leipzig, 1732.

1 CHORUS
(As above)
SATB. Fl trav, Ob d'am, Vln i, ii, Vla, Cont

The librettist ignores the Epistle and Gospel and bases his text upon the twelve verses of the hymn with the above title by Paul Speratus with its original melody (1524) in Nos. 1 and 7. The other verses are paraphrased in the remaining movements. The hymn emphasizes the Lutheran doctrine of justification by faith, not works, which is not one that cries out for music!

The chief interest of the chorus, in which the chorale in long notes is given to sopranos, is the way in which little fugatos, all varied in figuration but all with entries in the same order (A.T.B.), follow on each choral entry.

2 RECITATIVE
'Gott gab uns ein Gesetz, doch waren wir zu schwach, dass wir es hätten halten können' ('God gave us a commandment, yet were we too weak to be able to keep it')
B. Cont

And a good deal more in this vein.

3 ARIA
'Wir waren schon zu tief gesunken, der Abgrund schluckt' uns völlig ein' ('We were already too deeply sunk, the abyss swallowed us completely')
T. Vln, Cont

A cry of distress and fear of death that no one answers draws really committed music from Bach. The jagged vocal line requires a very able singer.

4 RECITATIVE
'Doch musste das Gesetz erfüllet werden, deswegen kam das Heil der Erden, des Höchsten Sohn, der hat es selbst erfüllt und seines Vaters Zorn gestillt' ('Yet must the law be fulfilled: there-

P   209

THE CHURCH CANTATAS OF J. S. BACH

fore came the salvation of the world, the Highest's Son, who has
fulfilled it Himself and calmed IIis Father's anger')
B. Cont

5 DUET
'Herr, du siehst statt guter Werke auf des Herzens Glaubens-
stärke' ('Lord, thou lookest instead of good works, on the heart's
faithfulness')
S.A. Fl trav, Ob d'am, Cont
    Bach, for his part, is faithful to the canonic treatment he im-
parts to the instrumental prelude and the parts of the soloists,
but the 'good works of the heart' are not allowed to come in and
give true life to faith.

6 RECITATIVE
'Wenn wir die Sünd aus dem Gesetz erkennen, so schlägt es
uns das Gewissen nieder' ('When we the sin through the law
recognize, then conscience strikes it down')
B. Cont
    The routine nature of the declaration shows that Bach could
find nothing better for this last dose of dogma.

7 CHORALE
'Ob sich's anliess, als wollt er nicht, lass dich es nicht erschrecken'
('Though it appeared as if He would not, let it not alarm thee')
SATB. As No. i. Insts. with voices. Cont

Vergnügte Ruh', beliebte Seelenlust (Pleasant rest, beloved
soul's desire).
Solo Cantata BWV 170. Leipzig, 1726.

1 ARIA
(As above)
A. Ob d'am, Vln i, ii, Vla, Cont
    The text of the aria is based on the Epistle, in which the main
idea is a death and a resurrection to a new life. Bach sees the
text in the light of the first words and writes one of his most
beautiful melodies, in the manner of a slumber song, to illustrate
it. The exquisite final ritornello ascends with gentle ecstasy.

2 RECITATIVE
'Die Welt, das Sündenhaus, bricht nur in Höllenlieder aus und
sucht durch Hass und Neid des Satans Bild an sich zu tragen'
('The world, the house of sin, breaks only into songs of Hell, and
seeks through hatred and envy to impress Satan's image upon
itself')
A. Cont

The text continues with a passage based on the Gospel (St
Matthew v. 22), the 'evil of calling your neighbour "Raca"
[fool]'. This is a finely declamatory number.

3 ARIA
'Wie jammern mich doch die verkehrten Herzen die dir, mein
Gott, so sehr zuwider sein' ('How grieve me then the perverted
hearts which to Thee, my God, are so much opposed')
A. Vln i, ii and Vla (unis.) Org obb. Cont

In the accompaniment to this aria Bach dispenses, as in some
other cantatas (see BWV 105, p. 231), with string basses and
continuo but, exceptionally, gives the two treble lines to the
organ without use of the pedals. At the words 'when they themselves only in revenge and hatred rejoice' voice and organ are
given continual furious rushes of demisemiquavers which break
out again when the 'perverted heart' is accused of adopting
Satan's wiles. Near the close of this violent music the tenor has
to sustain a trill of a bar and a half. In between the two outbursts,
and after the second one, voice and organ repeat the despairing
chromatic measures at the start of the aria.

4 RECITATIVE
'Wer sollte sich demnach wohl hier zu leben wünschen, wenn
man nur Hass und Ungemach für seine Liebe sieht?' ('Who
should accordingly desire to live here when one only sees
hatred and evil for His love?')
A. Vln i, ii, Vla, Cont

The strings are needed to express the expected answer that we
must love our enemy as God, who is love Himself, commanded us.

5 ARIA
'Mir ekelt mehr zu leben, drum nimm mich, Jesu, hin' ('I am
averse to living longer, so take me, Jesu, away')
A. Ob d'am with Vln i, Vln ii, Vla, Org obb. Cont

This is a strange aria. The voice part begins with an augmented
fourth (D–G sharp), following, of course, the introductory

ritornello but nevertheless suggesting an instrumental original. The organ part this time employs the pedals but only to play octaves swinging down in a helpless sort of way. Whittaker thinks one of Bach's sons may have filled in this part to help his father! The words above suffice Bach for the whole of the first part of the aria.

THE VISITATION OF THE
BLESSED VIRGIN MARY

Epistle: Isa. xi. 1–5 (A rod shall come out of Jesse).
Gospel: Luke i. 39–56 (Mary's Magnificat).

Herz und Mund und Tat und Leben (Heart and mouth and deed and life).
Cantata BWV 147. Leipzig, 1723.

It was from this cantata that the chorale known as 'Jesu joy of man's desiring' was extracted and subjected to a number of instrumental arrangements which took no note of Bach's scoring (in which a trumpet doubles the voice part), thereby giving a sentimental rather than a joyous impression. The text of Nos. 1, 3, 5 and 7, by Salomo Franck, was intended for the fourth Sunday in Advent of 1716, and so has no connection with the Feast of the Visitation, but it is thought that Bach, in 1723, added the remaining five numbers, including the above chorale, played at the end of Part I, and repeated at the end of the work.

PART I

1 CHORUS
'Herz und Mund und Tat und Leben muss von Christo Zeugnis geben, dass er Gott und Heiland sei' ('Heart and mouth and deed and life must of Christ testimony give that he God and Saviour is')
SATB. Tr, Ob i, ii with Vln i, ii; Vla, Fag, Cont

Trumpet and bassoon lead off in the introduction to this brilliant and exhilarating chorus but are silent during the fugal exposition to the words above until they re-enter at its completion. A delightful feature of the movement is the little motif below shared by the imitative phrases of all the vocal parts. There is a second fugal exposition to the same text as before with the voices entering in the reverse order to the first one and so now BTAS.

2 RECITATIVE
'Gebenedeiter Mund, Maria macht ihr Innerstes der Seelen

durch Dank und Rühmen kund' ('Blessed mouth, Mary makes
her innermost soul through thanks and praises known')
T. Vln i, ii, Vla, Cont

The text, expressively accompanied, alludes to the 'Magnificat'
and its message, and rebukes the obdurate spirits who ignore it.

3 ARIA
'Schäme dich, o Seele, nicht, deinen Heiland zu bekennen'
('Be not ashamed, O soul, thy Saviour to confess')
A. Ob d'am, Cont

Pleasantly flowing but of no particular interest.

4 RECITATIVE
'Verstockung kann Gewaltige verblenden bis sie des Höchsten
Arm vom Stuhle stösst' ('Obstinacy can the mighty delude, till
the Highest's arm hurls them from their seat')
B. Cont

The text is, of course, a paraphrase of 'He hath put down the
mighty from their seat', but does not go on to exalt the humble
and meek.

5 ARIA
'Bereite dir, Jesu, noch itzo die Bahn, mein Heiland, erwähle die
glaubende Seele und siehe mit Augen der Gnade mich an'
('Prepare Thee, Jesu, then now the way, my Saviour, choose
the believing soul, and look with eyes of grace on me')
S. Vln solo, Cont

The violin solo part, as Whittaker truly says, might be a study
for the D minor Prelude in Book I of The 48, though taken at a
somewhat slower pace. The triplets are confined to the solo
violin part and make a delightful accompaniment to the happy
voice part going along the prepared way.

6 CHORALE
'Wohl mir, dass ich Jesum habe, o wie feste halt' ich ihn' ('Well
for me that I have Jesus, O how fast I hold Him')
SATB. As No. 1 (without Fag)

This is verse vi of Martin Jahn's hymn, 'Jesu, meiner Seelen
Wonne' (1661), set to Johann Schop's melody to Johann Rist's,
'Werde munter, mein Gemüte'. There is no need to comment on
this well-known and beautiful setting.

PART II

7 ARIA

'Hilf, Jesu, hilf, dass ich auch dich bekenne in Wohl und Weh, in Freud' und Leid' ('Help, Jesu, help, that I even Thee acknowledge in weal and woe, in joy and sorrow')

T. Cont, V'cello, Violone

The text harks back to the alto solo, No. 3, also by Franck. The continuo part begins with the motif of the cry the tenor utters and then is given phrases of descending semiquaver triplets in almost every succeeding bar. It is a remarkably vivid movement.

8 RECITATIVE

'Der höchsten Allmacht Wunderhand wirkt im Verborgenen der Erden' ('The highest Almighty's wonder-hand works in the secret parts of the earth')

A. Ob da cacc i, ii, Cont

The text tells the story of John leaping in his mother's womb when Elizabeth told Mary that she too was with child. Bach realistically depicts the incident.

9 ARIA

'Ich will von Jesu Wunden singen und ihm der Lippen Opfer bringen' ('I will of Jesu's wounds sing and to Him the lips' offering bring')

B. Tr. Ob i, ii with Vln i, ii; Vla, Cont

A fine aria in which Bach takes advantage of the reference to 'the holy fire', spoken of later, to give the bass some fiery illustrative phrases.

10 CHORALE

'Jesus bleibet meine Freude, meines Herzens Trost und Saft' ('Jesus remains my joy, of my heart comfort and sap')

SATB. As No. 6

This opening line of verse xvii of Martin Jahn's hymn suggested the title by which the chorale arrangements are known.

Meine Seel erhebt den Herren (My soul doth magnify the Lord).
Chorale Cantata BWV 10. Leipzig, 1724.

In this cantata the German translations of the original Latin are set in Nos. 1, 5 and 7 to the canticle's associated melody (*Tonus Peregrinus*), the other four numbers being paraphrased.

1 CHORUS
'Meine Seel erhebt den Herren und mein Geist freuet sich Gottes, meines Heilandes, denn er hat seine elende Magd angesehen. Siehe, von nun an werden mich selig preisen alle Kindes Kind' ('My soul doth magnify the Lord and my spirit rejoices itself in God, my Saviour, for He has regarded his poor handmaiden. Behold, from now henceforth shall me blessed praise all children's children')
SATB. Tr, Ob i, ii, Vln i, ii, Vla, Cont
The presence of the trumpet and the exuberant joy of the music, instrumental and vocal, indicate that Bach wished to concentrate on the last line of the text above and not to draw attention to Mary's humility as he does so beautifully in the third movement of the Latin 'Magnificat'. The chant sung by the sopranos and in the second section—beginning at 'Behold'—by the altos, and already heard on the trumpet in the introductory ritornello, is the German version of the plainsong psalm tone, the *Tonus Peregrinus*. At the repetition of 'shall me blessed praise', as the plainsong ends, all voices join in a tumult of rejoicing.

2 ARIA
'Herr, der du stark und mächtig bist, dessen Name heilig ist' ('Lord, Thou who strong and mighty art, whose name is holy')
S. Ob i, ii (unis.), Vln i, ii, Vla, Cont
The aria begins with the first violins, unaccompanied, swiftly ascending two octaves to the powerful main theme of the movement, but after the soprano's three cries of 'Lord' and the remainder of the line, the music quietens at 'God, whose name is holy'.

3 RECITATIVE
'Des Höchsten Güt und Treu wird alle Morgen neu, und währet

immer für und für' ('The Highest's goodness and faithfulness is every morning new and endures always for ever and ever')
T. Cont

Paraphrases of verses v–vi, with a pictorial representation of the proud and arrogant being scattered like chaff.

4 ARIA
'Gewaltige stösst Gott vom Stuhl hinunter in den Schwefelpfuhl' ('God thrusts the mighty from the seat down into the brimstone pool')
B. Cont

A highly dramatic aria which makes, 'Deposuit potentes de sede' in Bach's Latin *Magnificat* pale by comparison. The thudding low C's in the continuo bass part show that the mighty are being thrust down well and truly into the brimstone pool, but the meek are exalted and the hungry filled.

5 DUET
'Er denket der Barmherzigkeit und hilft seinem Diener Israel auf' ('He remembers mercy and succours His servant Israel')
A.T. Ob i, ii, Tr, Cont

This movement is the gem of the cantata. The appealing figure on the continuo at the start is taken over by the soloists. As in the corresponding movement of Bach's Latin *Magnificat* the oboes (here with the trumpet, at a much lower pitch) play the *Tonus Peregrinus*.

6 RECITATIVE
'Was Gott den Vätern alter Zeiten geredet und verheissen hat' ('What God to the fathers of old has spoken and promised')
T. Vln i, ii, Vla, Cont

At the line, 'His seed must extend itself so greatly, as sand on the ocean and sand in the firmament', Bach introduces on the strings, to the end of the recitative, the sound of waves gently lapping on the shore.

7 CHORALE
'Lob und Preis sei Gott dem Vater und dem Sohn und dem heiligen Geiste' ('Glory be to the Father and to the Son and to the Holy Spirit')
SATB. Tr, Ob i, ii, Vln i, ii, Vla, all with voices; Cont

The doxology. The sopranos have the first phrase of the *Tonus Peregrinus*, sung twice, and completed in the last line.

Epistle: Rom. vi. 19–23 (The wages of sin is death).
Gospel: Mark viii. 1–9 (Christ feeds the four thousand).

Ärgre dich, o Seele, nicht (Trouble thyself not, O Soul).
Cantata BWV 186. 1723. Libretto by Salomo Franck.

PART I

1 CHORUS
(As above)
SATB. Ob i, ii with Vln i, ii, Te with Vla, Fag, Cont

The text of the opening chorus is a paraphrase of St Matthew xi. 3–10, which has no connection with this Sunday's Gospel, and it substantiates the opinion that Bach set Franck's libretto, written for the Third Sunday in Advent, in 1716 and got him to revise it for this Sunday, or did so himself. The brief text, twice repeated, is concerned with Christ's reply to the imprisoned John the Baptist's doubts, 'Are you he who is to come or shall we look for another?' Christ told the messenger to relate the miracles He had accomplished but the words of the chorus continue, 'that the all-highest light, God's splendour and image itself in servant-form veils'. The text is, of course, aimed at strengthening those weak in faith, hence the force of the music.

2 RECITATIVE
'Die Knechtsgestalt, die Not, der Mangel, trifft Christi Glieder nicht allein' ('Servitude, distress, want, affect Christ's members not alone')
B. Cont

The arioso at the close, 'Lord, how long wilt Thou me forget', is the chief point of interest in this recitative.

3 ARIA
'Bist du, der mir helfen soll, eilst du nicht mir beizustehen?' ('Art Thou He who shall help me, hurriest Thou not to stand by me?')
B. Cont

The doubts return. 'My mind is full of doubt, Thou rejectest perhaps my supplication, yet O soul, doubt not, let reason not thee ensnare.' The soul is directed to behold its helper, Jacob's light, in the scriptures.

4 RECITATIVE
'Ach, dass ein Christ so sehr für seinen Körper sorgt' ('Ah, that a Christian so much for his body cares')
T. Cont

The body must return to earth, the salvation of the soul lies in Jesus. Here again the long arioso is the centre of interest and there is a most expressive phrase at the close to the words, 'Taste and see then how friendly Jesus is' (Psalm xxxiv. 8)

5 ARIA
'Mein Heiland lässt sich merken in seinen Gnadenwerken' ('My Saviour lets Himself be seen in His mercy-works')
T. Ob da cacc, Cont

Bach's first use of an oboe da caccia obbligato part is the most interesting feature of the aria, which shows we are still with St John's doubts.

6 CHORALE
'Ob sich's anliess, als wollt er nicht, lass dich es nicht erschrecken' ('Though it appeared as if He would not, let it not alarm Thee')
SATB. Ob i, ii, Vln i ii, Vla, Cont

Verse xii of Paul Speratus's hymn, 'Es ist das Heil uns kommen her' (see p. 209) is a fine extended chorale setting.

PART II

7 RECITATIVE
'Es ist die Welt die grosse Wüstenei: der Himmel wird zu Erz, die Erde wird zu Eisen, wenn Christen durch den Glauben weisen dass Christi Wort ihr grösster Reichthum sei' ('The world is the great wilderness; heaven becomes as brass, the earth becomes as iron, when Christians through faith show that Christ's word is their greatest riches')
B. Vln i, ii, Vla, Cont

By this time any perceptive member of the Leipzig congregation should have become irritated. There is no mention of Christ having compassion on the hungry multitude. Bach is defeated by the text.

8 ARIA
'Die Armen will der Herr umarmen mit Gnaden' ('The poor will the Lord embrace with mercy')
S. Vln i, ii (unis.), Cont

219

At last in this moving aria there is a reference to the compassion of Christ for the hungry multitude and a forgetfulness of self. The violin's part is particularly expressive.

9 RECITATIVE
'Nun mag die Welt mit ihrer Lust vergehen, bricht gleich der Mangel ein, doch kann die Seele freudig sein' ('Now may the world with its pleasures pass away, even if want breaks in, still can the soul be joyful')
A. Cont
This recitative ends with an arioso marked *adagio* where the people who walk in darkness are mentioned.

10 DUET
'Lass, Seele, kein Leiden von Jesu dich scheiden, sei, Seele, getreu' ('Let, soul, no sorrow from Jesus thee separate, be, soul, faithful')
S.A. Ob i, ii, Te, Vln i, ii, Vla, Cont
Joy breaks in with the prospect of a 'crown through mercy as reward'. The music, in 3/8 time, trips delightfully along with its varied rhythm enlivening all parts of the score. (It is probable that the cantata ended with a repeat of No. 1.)

Was willst du dich betrüben, o meine liebe Seel' (Why wilt thou thyself trouble, oh my dear soul).
Chorale Cantata BWV 107. Leipzig, 1724.

Verses i–vi, set in the corresponding numbers of the cantata, are those of Johann Heerman's hymn, 'Was willst du dich betrüben' (1690).

1 CHORUS
(As above)
SATB. Fl trav i, ii, Ob d'am i, ii, Vln i, ii, Vla, Cor da cacc, Org, Cont
The chorale melody is given to the sopranos, strengthened by an oboe da caccia in a decorated form, with chordal writing, independent of the melody, in the lower voices. The movement, which has an intimate and consoling effect, closes with the promise of happiness and well being. This is not a chorale fantasia but rather a chorale with an independent orchestral setting.

2 RECITATIVE
'Denn Gott verlässet keinen, der sich auf ihn verlässt' ('For God
forsakes no one who himself on Him relies')
B. Ob d'am i, ii, Org, Cont
The soul is told how joyful he will be when he finds how God
delivers him from troubles.

3 ARIA
'Auf ihn magst du es wagen, mit unerschrock'nem Mut' ('On
Him mayst thou it venture with unaffrighted courage')
B. Vln i, ii, Vla, Org, Cont
The aria begins with a confident melody, marked *vivace*, which
the singer takes over, but when he reaches the word, 'unaffrighted', the fragmented vocal line implies the exact opposite. At
'pursue' in 'Thou wilt with Him pursue what for thee is useful and
good' Bach gives the soloist an elaborate slow trill to suggest, as it
were, the divine huntsman and the hound. The first violin and the
continuo part are very lively throughout.

4 ARIA
'Wenn auch gleich aus der Höllen der Satan wollte sich dir
selbst entgegenstellen und toben wider dich' ('Although from
Hell Satan would place himself in thy way and rage against
thee')
T. Cont

5 ARIA
'Er richt's zu seinen Ehren, und deiner Seligkeit soll 's sein' ('He
ordains it to His honour, and your blessedness must it be')
S. Ob d'am i, ii, Org, Cont
At the close of the aria Bach introduces a line of the chorale
melody, with touching effect, as the soprano ends with the words,
'What God ordains, that happens', repeating the last two words.

6 ARIA
'Drum ich mich ihm ergebe, ihm sei es heimgestellt' ('Therefore I
myself to him surrender, to Him be it left')
T. Fl trav i, ii (unis.), Org, Cont
This is the fourth aria in succession and fortunately, in expressing the end to doubts, it is an attractive one. The continuo part is
pizzicato throughout, which helps to liven up the music that much
more. The flutes carol away delightfully.

7 CHORALE
'Herr, gieb, dass ich dein' Ehre, ja all' mein Leben langs von
Herzengrund vermehre' ('Lord, grant that I Thine honour, yea,
all my life long from heart's depth increase')
SATB. As No. 1

This is the fourteenth verse of David Denicke's 'Ich will zu
aller Stunde' (1646) set to the melody of 'Von Gott will ich nicht
lassen'. An extended setting, the chief feature being the delightful
6/8 dotted quaver parts for the instruments.

**Es wartet alles auf dich, dass du ihnen Speise gebest zu
seiner Zeit** (There wait all things on Thee that Thou to
them give food in its time).
Cantata BWV 187. Leipzig, 1726.

PART I

1 CHORUS
(As above)
SATB. Ob i, ii, Vln i, ii, Vla, Cont

The words of this fine chorus are based on verses 27–28 of
Psalm CIV, beginning. 'These wait all upon Thee, that thou
mayest give them their meat in due season'. The rise of a fourth on
the first violins in the first bar of the introduction becomes the
leading motif in the first and third chorale sections but it is
followed here by another motif for the oboes in thirds with the
violins playing a *staccato* counter motif below them. This bar and
the subsequent use of its material suggested to Whittaker 'the
waving of corn in the breeze and the movement of a sickle'. It
could be so but it could equally be the pleasure and gratitude of
the hungry at being fed!

2 RECITATIVE
'Was Kreaturen hält das grosse Rund der Welt!' ('What creatures
contains the great sphere of the world!')
B. Cont

A tribute of praise to the multitudinous miracle of creation for
which all earth's gold could not pay.

3 ARIA
'Du Herr, du krönst allein das Jahr mit deinem Gut' ('Thou,
Lord, Thou crownest alone the year with Thy blessing')
A. Ob i with Vln i, Vln ii, Vla, Cont

An attractive feature of this pleasant aria is the tying of the
third quavers in each of the bars (3/8 time) to the first one of the
next bar in the accompaniment almost throughout, while the
soloist is given a flowing legato melody.

PART II

4 (ARIA)
'Darum sollt ihr nicht sorgen noch sagen: was werden wir essen,
was werden wir trinken? womit werden wir uns kleiden?' ('Therefore shall ye not sorrow nor say: what shall we eat, what shall we
drink? wherewith shall we ourselves clothe?')
B. Vln i, ii (unis.), Cont

The words, which come from St Matthew vi. 31–32, are set in
the simple straightforward style Bach usually adopts for Christ's
sayings.

5 ARIA
'Gott versorget alles Leben, was hienieden Odem hegt' ('God
provides for all life, which here below breath preserves')
S. Ob solo, Cont

The style of this aria is in complete contrast to No. 4. Oboe and
voice share the expansive florid phrases of the first section. The
tempo then quickens from *adagio* to *un poco allegro* for the next
section, in plainer style, 'yield ye sorrows, His faithfulness is also
mindful of me and for me daily becomes new through many love-
gifts of the Father'. The *staccato* phrases for the oboe happily
reflect gratitude for the 'gifts'.

6 RECITATIVE
'Halt ich nur fest an ihm mit kindlichem Vertrauen' ('Hold I only
fast to Him with childlike faith')
S. Vln i, ii, Vla, Cont

Another expression of gratitude and trust, and the acceptance
of any trials that may come, all of which He has suffered for us
before.

223

7 CHORALE
'Gott hat die Erde schön zugericht't, lässt an Nahrung mangeln
nicht' ('God has arranged the earth beautifully, and permits no
want of nourishment')
SATB. As No. 1. Insts. with voices. Cont

Verses iv and vi of the anonymous 'Singen wir aus Herzensgrund' (1569) set to its original melody (1589).

EIGHTH SUNDAY AFTER TRINITY

Epistle: Rom. VIII. 12–17 (We are joint heirs with Christ).
Gospel: Matt. VII. 15–23 (Beware of false prophets).

Erforsche mich, Gott, und erfahre mein Herz, prüfe mich und erfahre, wie ich's meine (Search me, God, and learn my heart, prove me, and learn how I purpose it). Cantata BWV 136. Leipzig, 1723.

1 CHORUS
(As above)
SATB. Cor, Ob i, Ob ii d'am, Vln i, ii, Vla, Cont

Verse 23 of Psalm CXXXIX is the origin of the text of this chorus but the pleasantly ambling melody announced by the horn in its first three measures and repeated three times by the sopranos, with similar quaver figuration in the underparts, has no apparent connection with the text and once set in motion it could continue *ad lib.* There is, however, a slight sense of urgency in the homophonic phrases to 'prove me' near the close. The orchestral part is equally uneventful.

2 RECITATIVE
'Ach, dass der Fluch, so dort die Erde schlägt, auch derer Menschen Herz getroffen' ('Ah, that the curse which there strikes the earth, also smote men's hearts')
T. Cont

An allusion to the fall (Genesis III. 17). The moral is drawn that good fruit cannot be hoped for when the soul is afflicted by a curse. Bach, afflicted by such a text, cannot bring forth good music.

3 ARIA
'Es kommt ein Tag, so das Verborg'ne richtet vor dem die Heuchelei erzittern mag' ('There comes a day which the hidden [things] judges, before which hypocrisy may tremble')
A. Ob d'am i, Cont

The musical temperature rises considerably higher in this quite dramatic aria whose text follows the Gospel for the day.

The music of the monitory first section is followed by a brief *presto* (6/8) for voice and continuo only and that by an expressive ·

Q   225 *adagio* (4/4) in which the repetition of the 'There comes a day', differently set, acquires a deeper meaning.

4 RECITATIVE
'Die Himmel selber sind nicht rein, wie soll es nur ein Mensch vor diesem Richter sein!' ('The heavens themselves are not pure, how shall a mere man be before this Judge?')
B. Cont

This obscure text draws better music from Bach than No. 2. There is a brief and carefully devised arioso at the closing words, '[he has] in Christ, however, righteousness and strength'.

5 DUET
'Uns treffen zwar der Sünden Flecken, so Adams Fall auf uns gebracht' ('On us indeed fall the sin's stains which Adam's fall brought on us')
T.B. Vln i, ii (unis.), Cont

A strange text for a duet, calling forth music mostly of a routine character. It is at its best in the middle section where the words speak of the cleansing power of Jesu's wounds.

6 CHORALE
'Dein Blut, der edle Saft, hat solche Stärk' und Kraft, dass auch ein Tröpflein kleine die ganze Welt kann reine' ('Thy blood, the honoured essence has such strength and might that even a small droplet can cleanse the whole world')
SATB. Cor, Ob i, ii, Vln ii, Vla, all with voices; Vln i, Cont

Verse ix of Johann Heermann's, 'Wo soll ich fliehen hin' (1630) set to its associated melody, 'Auf meinen lieben Gott'. The first violin is given an expressive melody high above the voices.

Wo Gott, der Herr, nicht bei uns hält, wenn unsre Feinde toben (If God, the Lord, hold not with us when our enemies rage).
Chorale Cantata BWV 178. Leipzig, 1724.

The libretto is based on Justus Jonas' hymn (1524) with the above title which is itself a conflation of Psalm cxxiv and the Gospel of the day.
Verses i, ii, iv, v, vii and viii are set in their original form to its anonymous melody (1535), iii and vi are paraphrased in those numbers in the cantata.

1 CHORUS
(As above)
SATB. Ob i, ii, Vln i, ii, Vla, Cor with S. Cont

The enemy the libretto attacks is Christians who have become false prophets against whom the faithful are exhorted to fight with sure hope that the foe will be defeated.

Bach sounds the call to battle—without recourse to trumpets—in the tremendously vigorous orchestral introduction. It combines most effectively at various points, in all parts, a dotted quaver rhythm and rushing semiquavers and through the tumult the first line of the chorale rings out confidently, with a sustained chord at 'holds'. The second line depicts the rage of the foe.

2 RECITATIVE AND CHORALE
'Was Menschen Kraft und Witz anfäht, soll uns billig nicht schrecken' ('What men's strength and wit can do shall us justly not affright')
SATB. A. Cont

The chorus sings the chorale in long notes accompanied by marching quavers and each line of the text is followed by recitatives in which the soloist declaims against the evil forces. This is one of Bach's finest treatments of such exchanges.

3 ARIA
'Gleichwie die wilden Meereswellen mit Ungestüm ein Schiff zerschellen so raset auch der Feinde Wuth und raubt das beste Seelen-Gut' ('Even as the wild sea-waves with impetuosity a ship dash to pieces so rages also the enemy's wrath and robs the soul's best possession')
B. Vln i, ii (unis.) Cont

Bach seizes on the imagery to depict a spiritual fight at sea as vividly as the battle on land in No. 1. The foe plan to sink 'Christ's little ship'. Bach paints the surge and thunder of the waves, also giving long pictorial phrases to the soloist on 'sea-waves'.

4 CHORALE
'Sie stellen uns wie Ketzern nach, nach unserm Blut sie trachten' ('They lie in wait for us as heretics, after our blood they aspire')
T. Ob d'am i, ii, Cont

The tenor sings a rhythmic variant of the chorale melody to an *ostinato* type of accompaniment, maintained throughout.

227

5 CHORALE
'Aufsperren sie den Rachen weit, nach Löwen-Art mit brüllendem
Getöne' ('They open their jaws wide in lion fashion, with roaring
sounds')
SATB. Cont

A highly dramatic setting, with another *ostinato*-type accompaniment for the continuo, a series of rising arpeggios. Solo tenor
and alto are given recitatives between most of the lines. The bass
has the first and last of these, in the latter fiercely foretelling that
God will destroy the foolish prophets with the fire of his anger.

6 ARIA
'Schweig, schweig nur, taumelnde Vernunft' ('Be silent, be silent
now, tottering reason')
T. Vln i, ii, Vla, Cont

The godly are not lost, for the Cross upholds faith against
reason and the door of mercy is always open to those who hope
on Jesus.

7 CHORALE
'Die Feind' sind all' in deiner Hand, dazu all' ihr' Gedanken'
('The enemies are all in Thine hand, their thoughts also')
SATB. As No. 1. Insts. with voices. Cont

The two last verses of the chorale.

Es ist dir gesagt, Mensch, was gut ist (It is to thee declared,
man, what good is).
Cantata BWV 45. Leipzig, 1726.

PART I

1 CHORUS
(As above)
SATB. Fl. trav i, ii with Ob, i, ii, Vln i, ii, Vla, Cont

The text is from Micah VI. 8. The declaration is driven home
by constant repetition of the above words, in varied groupings of
the voices, culminating in a long fugue. This done, the terms of
the declaration are revealed, 'namely, God's word to hold, and
love to exercise, and humble to be before thy God'. Then comes a
modified recapitulation of the opening words.

2 RECITATIVE
'Der Höchste lässt mich seinen Willen wissen und was ihm
wohlgefällt' ('The Highest lets me know His will and what to
Him is well-pleasing')
T. Cont

3 ARIA
'Weiss ich Gottes Rechte was ist das mir helfen kann' ('I know
God's justice what [it] is that can help me')
T. Vln i, ii, Vla, Cont

The text mentions punishment for transgression against
obedience, the sharp reckoning demanded of God's servants; but
the agreeable music only reflects this in its second section where
'drohet' ('threaten') has extended runs.

PART II

4 ARIOSO
'Es werden viele zu mir sagen an jenem Tage, Herr' ('Many will
say to me on that day, Lord')
B. Vln i, ii, Vla, Cont

This movement, in spite of its length, is marked *arioso*, a term
Bach usually uses when Christ is speaking in person. The text is
St Matthew VII. 22–23, condemning evil-doers who claim to have
prophesied and worked miracles in His name, 'Depart from me—
I know you not.' Christ's indignation is expressed with vigour, and
even has two extended runs, exceptional in other of His utterances
Bach set. The frequent swinging octaves in the continuo add to
the strength of the denunciation.

5 ARIA
'Wer Gott bekennt aus wahrem Herzensgrund' ('Who God
acknowledges from the true heart's-core')
A. Fl trav i, Cont

The text goes on to declare that, 'he must everlastingly burn
who calls Him Lord only with his mouth'. Unlike No. 3, the
music does really reflect this dire pronouncement, especially at
'ever burn'.

6 RECITATIVE
'So wird denn Herz und Mund selbst von mir Richter sein, und
Gott will mir den Lohn nach meinem Sinn erteilen' ('So will then

229

heart and mouth themselves of me judge be, and God will bestow on me the reward according to my character')
A. Cont

7 CHORALE
'Gib, dass ich tu mit Fleiss, was mir zu tun gebühret, wozu mich dein Befehl in meinem Stande führet' ('Grant, that I do with diligence, what for me to do is seemly, to which me Thy command in my station guides')
SATB. As No. 1. Insts. with voices. Cont

Verse ii of Johann Heermann's, 'O Gott, du frommer Gott' (1630), set to its associated melody, 'Die Wollust dieser Welt' (1679).

NINTH SUNDAY AFTER TRINITY

Epistle: 1 Cor. x. 6–13 (Take heed lest ye fall).
Gospel: Luke xvi. 1–9 (Parable of the unjust steward).

Herr, gehe nicht ins Gericht mit deinem Knecht (Lord, enter not into judgement with Thy servant).
Cantata BWV 105. Leipzig, 1723.

1 CHORUS
(As above)
SATB. Cor and Ob i with Vln i, Ob ii with Vln ii, Vla, Cont

We come here to one of the best librettos Bach ever had to set and to which he responded with one of his greatest cantatas. The text is from Psalm CXLIII. 2. The lamenting theme, on horn and oboe, the throbbing continuo part (quavers, in groups of two) bring before us the anguished penitent who pours out his guilty soul in the first section of the chorus. The succeeding words, 'For before Thee becomes no living person righteous', are set to a fugue in quick time.

2 RECITATIVE
'Mein Gott, verwirf mich nicht, indem ich mich in Demuth vor dir beuge' ('My God, cast me not away, whilst I bend myself in humility before Thee')
A. Cont

A moving confession of guilt, denying and concealing nothing.

3 ARIA
'Wie zittern und wanken der Sünder Gedanken indem sie sich unter einander verklagen, wiederum sich zu entschuldigen wagen' ('How tremble and totter the sinner's thoughts while they accuse one another and again dare to excuse themselves')
S. Ob, Vln i, ii, Vla

There is no continuo part. Bach gives the lowest line to the violas in quavers and the middle part to the violins in semiquavers, the latter depicting the trembling of a guilty soul who tries to excuse herself: oboe and voice underline her distress. In the middle section the voice, at 'So is an anguished conscience torn through its own torture', leaps up a seventh on 'anguished' and ends with a jagged phrase on the last words of the text before the da capo of the instrumental introduction.

231

4 RECITATIVE
'Wohl aber dem, der seinen Bürgen weiss, der alle Schuld
ersetzet' ('But how happy he who his surety knows, who all guilt
indemnifies')
B. Vln i, ii, Vla, Cont

In this beautiful arioso the continuo part is given repeated
octave leaps, *pizzicato* throughout, as the soloist sings of 'the death-
hour striking'. The strings move gently above as the soloist sings
of the body being carried to the grave, to be received at last into
the eternal mansions by the Saviour.

5 ARIA
'Kann ich nur Jesum mir zum Freunde machen so gilt der
Mammon nichts bei mir' ('If I can only make a friend of Jesus,
Mammon is worth nothing to me')
T. Cor, Vln i, ii, Vla, Cont

A happy aria with exuberant rushes of demisemiquavers on the
first violin, expressive of a purged conscience, mixed with contempt—wild phrases on the first violin—for all that Mammon
represents.

6 CHORALE
'Nun, ich weiss, du wirst mir stillen, mein Gewissen das mich
plagt' ('Now I know Thou wilt calm my conscience which tortures
me')
SATB. Vln i, ii, Vla, Cont

Verse xi of Johann Rist's 'Jesu, der du meine Seele' (1641), set
to its associated melody (1663).

This is one of Bach's most imaginative settings of a chorale. The
trembling figures that accompanied the soprano aria (No. 3) now
accompany the chorus, who pause at the end of each line; and
make us see the unhappy soul, lonely and outcast. At the next
two lines of the chorale, the semiquavers become quaver triplet
groups, then normal quaver groups, followed by crotchet–quaver
triplets in 12/8 time, and ending with two chromatic phrases in
4/4 time.

Was frag' ich nach der Welt und allen ihren Schatten
wenn ich mich nur an dir, mein Jesu, kann ergötzen
(What ask I from the world and all its shadows, if I myself
can delight only in Thee, my Jesus).
Chorale Cantata BWV 94. Leipzig, 1724.

1 CHORUS
(As above)
SATB. Fl trav, Ob i, ii, Vln i, ii, Vla, Org, Cont

The libretto is based on Georg Michael Pfefferkorn's hymn
(1667), set in Nos. 1, 3, 5 and 8 to its associated melody, 'O Gott,
du frommer Gott' (1679). The other verses are paraphrased.

As in all the cantatas for this Sunday the librettists do not come
to terms with Christ's commendation of the unjust steward, who is
advised to make friends with Mammon. This movement is in the
familiar style of an extended chorale, with the bright orchestral
part filling in between the chorale entries.

2 ARIA
'Die Welt ist wie ein Rauch und Schatten, der bald verschwindet
und vergeht' ('The world is like smoke and shadow which soon
disappears and dissolves')
B. Cont

Both voice and continuo depict a disintegrating universe, with
long runs on 'world'. The first line of the chorale is repeated
at the close.

3 RECITATIVE AND CHORALE
'Die Welt sucht Ehr und Ruhm bei hocherhabnen Leuten' ('The
world seeks honour and glory among exalted folk')
T. Ob i, ii, Org, Cont

A continual exchange between the chorale text with moral
reflections on it in the recitatives between. The chorale sections,
marked *arioso*, are all accompanied differently. The general
sense of the recitatives reproaches the proud man, a sort of tycoon
whose pretensions are 'blown away' by death, and exhorts the
Christian to seek spiritual treasures.

4 ARIA
'Betörte Welt, auch dein Reichthum, Gut und Geld ist Betrug

233

und falscher Schein' ('Befooled world, even thy wealth, goods and money are deception and illusion')
A. Fl trav, Cont

This aria puts the unjust steward in his place. The amazing part for the flute may well depict his ill-gained but attractive profits: but when the tempo changes to *allegro*, he is left to count his gains whereas the Christian holds to Jesus as *his* wealth.

5 RECITATIVE AND CHORALE
'Die Welt bekümmert sich' ('The world grieves')
B. Org, Cont

The lines of the hymn, always marked *adagio*, are linked to the recitatives in this not very successful movement. The text is world despising, ending once more with the line, 'What ask I from the world?'

6 ARIA
'Die Welt kann ihre Lust und Freud, das Blendwerk schnöder Eitelkeit, nicht hoch genug erhöhen' ('The world can its desire and joy, the sham of mean emptiness, not extol high enough')
T. Vln i, ii, Vla, Org, Cont

Gold is alluded to in this aria as 'yellow filth' and Bach's delightful fugue-like setting pictures these profiteers, in low-pitched phrases for the strings, mixing the gold.

7 ARIA
'Es halt' es mit der blinden Welt, wer nichts auf seine Seele hält' ('Let him hold with the blind world, who thinks nothing of his soul')
S. Ob d'am solo, Cont

The charming melodies for the oboe solo and voice contradict the world-despising text but are perfectly compatible with the words of the middle section, 'I will only Jesus love since God, after all, made the world and all in it is not Mammon'.

8 CHORALE
'Was frag ich nach der Welt' ('What ask I from the world')
SATB. As No. 1. Insts. with voices. Cont

Verses vii–viii of the hymn, which declare 'My Jesus is my life, my treasure, my possession'.

Tue Rechnung! Donnerwort! (Make a reckoning! Thunder-word).
Solo Cantata BWV 168. Leipzig, 1725. Libretto by Salomo Franck.

1 ARIA
(As above)
B. Vln i, ii, Vla, Cont

Here, as in the previous cantata, the parable of the unjust steward is applied to the Christian soul. God is to be paid what is owing, and quickly! The solo bass appears here in the role—in present-day terms—of the income-tax inspector presenting his final demand. In this splendid bass aria the declamatory phrases for the voice are accompanied in the first section by imperious dotted quaver figures on the strings, with a triplet figure on the continuo.

2 RECITATIVE
'Es ist nur fremdes Gut, was ich in diesem Leben habe' ('It is only borrowed property that I have in this life')
T. Ob d'am i, ii, Cont

The unjust steward makes his excuses, praying that the mountains may fall on him and conceal him from God's anger.

3 ARIA
'Kapital und Interessen meiner Schulden gross und klein müssen einst verechnet sein' ('Capital and interest of my debts great and small must some day be reckoned')
T. Ob d'am i, ii (unis.), Cont

The debts are all put down in God's account book, 'as with steel and diamond stone'.

4 RECITATIVE
'Jedoch, erschrocknes Herz, leb' und verzage nicht' ('Yet, terrified heart, live and despair not')
B. Cont

God is referred to as the Security, who has all debts remitted, and the text goes on to counsel the Soul, free of debt, to use worldly wealth prudently, give to the poor, and so rest with untroubled conscience in heaven.

5 ARIA
'Herz, zerreiss' des Mammons Kette, Hände, streuet Gutes aus'
('Heart, rend Mammon's chains, hands, give away possessions')
S.A. Cont

No one has ever satisfactorily explained Christ's words about making friends with Mammon as a matter of expediency—surely He spoke ironically—so the librettist played for safety in this cantata and gave Bach a chance to break 'the chains' with a delightful duet which prays for a 'soft death bed' and a 'firm house' that will last for ever when earthly possessions turn to dust.

6 CHORALE
'Stärk mich mit deinem Freudengeist, heil mich mit deinen Wunden' ('Strengthen me with Thy joy-spirit, heal me with Thy wounds')
SATB. Ob d'am i, ii, Vln i, ii, Vla, all with voices; Cont

The eighth verse of Bartholomäus Ringwaldt's 'Herr Jesu Christ, du höchstes Gut' (1588) set to its melody (1593).

Epistle: 1 Cor. XII. 1–11 (Spiritual gifts are diverse).
Gospel: Luke XIX. 41–48 (Jesus weeps over Jerusalem).

Schauet doch und sehet, ob irgend ein Schmerz sei, wie mein Schmerz (Behold then and see if there is any sorrow like my sorrow).
Cantata BWV 46. Leipzig, 1723.

1 CHORUS
(As above)
SATB. Fl i, ii, Tr or Cor da tirarsi, Ob da cacc i, ii, Vln i, ii, Vla, Cont

One could not give greater praise to Bach's setting of the above words, from the Lamentations of Jeremiah 1. 12, than to say it can be placed without qualification beside Victoria's 'O vos omnes qui transitis per viam' in his Office of Holy Week.

Bach's chorus is even more heart-rending in its original form here than in the better-known adaptation he made of the movement in the 'Qui tollis' of the *B Minor Mass*—in which the vocal parts are practically identical with the original—by reason of the deeply expressive orchestral introduction of sixteen bars, whereas in the B Minor Mass the movement begins on the last beat of the bar with which 'Domine Deus' ends. A fugue follows—*un poco allegro*—to the words 'for the Lord has made me full of lamentations on the day of his grim anger', the exposition of which is—as so often with Bach—accompanied only by the continuo up to the soprano entry. It is a fine fugue but, in my view, rather destructive of the profound impression made by the first section. Christ wept over Jerusalem—but not in anger.

2 RECITATIVE
'So klage du, zerstörte Gottesstadt, du armer Stein- und Aschenhaufen' ('So mourn thou, destroyed God's city, thou poor stone and ash heap!')
T. Fl i, ii, Vln i, ii, Vla, Cont

A little motif of mourning on the flutes is repeated in every bar of this movement, with sustained chords on the strings below. The librettist compares the destruction of the city to that of Gomorrah.

3 ARIA
'Dein Wetter zog sich auf von Weitem, doch dessen Strahl bricht

endlich ein' ('Thy tempest gathered in the distance, now the storm at last breaks')
B. Tr or Cor da tirarsi, Vln i, ii, Vla, Cont

A magnificent aria with thudding notes for strings and continuo and a brilliant trumpet part. At 'and must be to Thee insufferable', all parts are marked *pianissimo*.

4 RECITATIVE
'Doch bildet euch, o Sünder, ja nicht ein, es sei Jerusalem allein vor andern Sünden voll gewesen' ('Then do not imagine to yourselves, Oh sinners, yea, Jerusalem has not above all others been full of sins')
A. Cont

The text is based on St Luke XIII. 5 'Unless you repent you will all perish'.

5 ARIA
'Doch Jesus will auch bei der Strafe der Frommen Schild und Beistand sein' ('Yet Jesus will even by the chastisement of the godly, shield and helper be')
A. Fl i, ii, Ob da cacc i, ii (unis.)

Compassion breaks in during the first part of this aria in which Jesus is spoken of as 'gathering the faithful lovingly in as His sheep, as His chickens' (St Matthew XXIII. 37). The tender music, however, is followed in the second section by a dramatic outburst of vengeance against sinners with a promise that Christ will secure the survival of the godly.

A remarkable feature of the aria is the use of the two oboi da caccia as the continuo part.

6 CHORALE
'O grosse Gott der Treu', weil vor dir Niemand gilt als dein Sohn Jesus Christ' ('O great God of truth, since before Thee no man is worthy but Thy Son, Jesus Christ')
SATB. Fl i, ii, Vln i, ii, Vla, Tr or Cor da tirarsi with S., Cont

The ninth verse of Balthasar Schnurr's 'O Grosser Gott von Macht' set to its original melody (1632). This is an extended setting with the lines separated by the passages for the flutes, two to each part, exceptional in Bach's practice.

Nimm von uns, Herr, du treuer Gott (Take from us, Lord,
Thou faithful God).
Chorale Cantata BWV 101. Leipzig, 1724.

1 CHORUS
(As above)
SATB. Fl trav, Ob i, ii, Te, Vln i, ii, Vla, Cont, Cornetto, Trb i, ii, iii
double the SATB. lines

This is one of Bach's most austere and splendid choruses, made
more sombre by the nature of the scoring with the brass doubling
the voice parts. The orchestral prelude ends with a short mourning
motif constantly present throughout and movingly developed in
the third and fifth ritornellos. The only ray of light is provided
by the flute doubling the chorale melody, sung in long notes by
the sopranos, an octave above. The text prays that our sins may be
taken from us and that we may be spared from 'pestilence, fire,
and great suffering'. Verses i, iii, v, vii of Martin Moller's hymn
(1584) as above with its associated melody 'Vater unser im
Himmelreich' (1539) are set in Nos. 1, 3, 5, 7. The remainder
are paraphrased, with all but No. 2 quoting the melody.

2 ARIA
'Handle nicht nach deinen Rechten mit uns bösen Sünden-
Knechten lass' das Schwert des Feinde ruh'n' ('Deal not according
to Thy law with us evil sins'-servants, cause the sword of the enemy
to rest')
T. Vln solo, Cont

If Bach meant the lively violin solo which continually contradicts the sense of the text to represent the light-mindedness of a
sinner he has certainly succeeded; or was it an ingenious way of
beguiling the ears of the congregation with the obbligato part so
that the medicine of the vocal part, which does reflect the sense of
the text, would be much more palatable?

3 RECITATIVE AND CHORALE
'Ach! Herr Gott, durch die Treue dein wird unser Land in Fried
und Ruhe sein' ('Ah! Lord God, through Thy faithfulness,
Thine will our land in peace and rest be')
S. Cont

Four alternations of verse iii of the chorale and its melody, considerably altered, with the texts of the recitative between.

4 ARIA
'Warum willst du so zornig sein?' ('Why wilt Thou so angry be?')
B. Ob i, ii, Te, Cont

The bass sings the opening line only of the chorale melody twice in this remarkable movement, following it each time with a free part, greatly developed after the repetition but always in the voice and oboe parts with phrases imitative of the four last descending notes of the chorale. The same phrase is given to oboes and taille in the middle section of the aria. The prayer here is for the flames of God's jealousy to cease, for Him to have patience with our weak flesh.

5 RECITATIVE AND CHORALE
'Die Sünd hat uns verderbet sehr, so müssen auch die Frömmsten sagen, und mit betränten Augen klagen' ('The sin has sorely destroyed us, so must even the godly say, and with tearful eyes lament')
T. Cont

The same pattern as in No. 4, and another cry for the Helper to come to the aid of the weaklings.

6 DUET
'Gedenk an Jesu bittern Tod, nimm, Vater, deines Sohnes Schmerzen und seiner Wunden Pein zu Herzen' ('Remember Jesu's bitter death, take, Father, Thy Son's sufferings and His wounds' pain to Thy heart')
S.A. Fl trav, Ob da cacc, Cont

The chorale melody, but not all of it, is woven into this beautiful duet, a heartfelt plea for mercy at all times and a realization of the payment and the ransom money the love of the Saviour gladly gave for us.

7 CHORALE
'Leit uns mit deiner rechten Hand und segne unsre Stadt und Land' ('Lead us with Thy right hand and bless our town and land')
SATB. Insts. with voices. Cont

Herr, deine Augen sehen nach dem Glauben! (Lord,
Thine eyes look towards the faith!).
Cantata BWV 102. Leipzig, 1726.

PART I

1 CHORUS
(As above)
SATB. Ob i, ii, Vln i, ii, Vla, Cont

No direct reference is made to the Gospel in the libretto of this
cantata but the emphasis is again laid on the wrath of God and
not on Jesu's weeping over the destruction of Jerusalem to come
'because you did not know the time of your visitation'. The text of
this chorus comes from Jeremiah v. 3, 'O Lord, do not thy eyes
look for truth? Thou hast smitten them, but they felt no anguish
. . . they refused to take correction, they have made their faces
harder than a rock: they have refused to repent'. Bach repeats the
opening line four times before coming to 'thou smitest them',
graphically illustrated in the broken phrases of the fugato that
follows, accompanied only by detached staccato phrases for the
oboes. A return to the first line leads to a full-scale fugue where the
text refers to 'the sinners with faces harder than rocks who refuse
to reform'. The texture becomes dense in this astonishing fugue,
which seems to burn with wrathful fire. The last words are those
of the first line. The diversity of themes in the orchestral introduction is used to good effect in the course of this powerful movement.

2 RECITATIVE
'Wo ist das Ebenbild, das Gott uns eingepräget, wenn der
verkehrte Wille sich ihm zuwider leget?' ('Where is the image,
that God stamps on us, when the perverted will itself contrary to
Him sets?')
B. Cont

3 ARIA
'Weh der Seele, die den Schaden nicht mehr kennt!' ('Woe to the
soul which harm no more knows!')
A. Ob, Cont

The slurred two-quaver phrases in the continuo part, expressive
of woe, are present almost throughout the aria and the voice part
is declamatory of the text.

4 ARIOSO
'Verachtest du den Reichtum seiner Gnade, Geduld und Lang-
mütigkeit?' ('Despisest thou the riches of His grace, patience and
long-suffering?')
B. Vln i, ii, Vla, Cont

The librettist turns here to Romans II. 4–5, which speaks of
those who presume on God's kindness, forbearance and patience
but who, by reason of their impenitence, will incur His wrath on
the day of judgement. Bach powerfully emphasizes this dire
warning.

PART II

5 ARIA
'Erschrecke doch, du allzu sich're Seele!' ('Fear then thou too
certain soul!')
T. Fl trav solo or Vln picc, Cont

Bach repeats 'Fear then' three times to detached and angular
phrases in this aria, which again berates the presumptuous soul.
God's wrath at the sinner's enjoyment of sin may be delayed but
will prove all the more terrible when it strikes. The first phrases
prophesying this are menacing and burst out angrily as the music
continues. The flute—or more effectively, as Bach realized, the
violino piccolo—is given an extraordinarily descriptive part.

6 RECITATIVE
'Beim Warten ist Gefahr; willst du die Zeit verlieren?' ('In the
waiting is danger; wilt thou the time lose?')
A. Ob i, ii, Cont

At last there is a note of compassion and of penitence expressed
by the little motif on the oboes which, as so often with Bach, is
maintained throughout.

7 CHORALE
'Heut' lebst du, heut' bekehre dich, eh' morgen kommt, kann's
ändern sich' ('Today livest thou, today mend thy ways, before
tomorrow comes it can alter')
SATB. Fl trav, Ob i, ii, Vln i, ii, Vla, all with voices; Cont

This is verses vi and vii of Johann Heermann's hymn 'So wahr
ich lebe, spricht dein Gott' (1630) set to its customary melody,
'Vater unser im Himmelreich'.

ELEVENTH SUNDAY AFTER TRINITY

Epistle: 1 Cor. xv. 1–10 (Of Christ's resurrection).
Gospel: Luke xviii. 9–14 (Parable of the Pharisee and the Publican).

**Mein Herze schwimmt im Blut, weil mich der Sünden
Brut in Gottes heilgen Augen zum Ungeheuer macht**
(My heart swims in blood because in God's holy eyes sin's
brood makes me a monster).
Solo Cantata BWV 199. Weimar, 1714.

1 RECITATIVE
(As above)
S. Vln i, ii, Vla, Fag, Violone, Cont
The lamentation of a guilty conscience, all too aware of the
fruits of original sin, and deeply ashamed.

2 ARIA
'Stumme Seufzer, stille Klagen, ihr mögt meine Schmerzen
sagen, weil der Mund geschlossen ist' ('Dumb sighs, secret
laments, ye are able to tell my afflictions, because my mouth is
closed')
S. Ob solo, Violone, Cont
The beautiful melody for the oboe in the introduction, rising up
in its last four phrases before the voice enters, depicts an interior
grief that no words can express. The groups of two slurred notes,
representative of tears, so often used by Bach, are constant in the
vocal part; their shedding is hoped to show the sign of atonement,
and a short passage of recitative which leads to the *da capo* speaks
of a heart stricken beyond healing.

3 RECITATIVE
'Doch Gott muss mir genädig sein, weil ich das Haupt mit Asche,
das Angesicht mit Tränen wasche' ('But God must be gracious
to me because I lave my head with ashes, my face with tears')
S. Vln i, ii, Vla, Fag, Violone, Cont
At the close there is a hopeful cry 'Ah, yea, His heart breaks [i.e.
softens] and my soul sings'.

4 ARIA
'Tief gebückt und voller Reue, lieg' ich, liebster Gott, vor Dir'

243

('Lowly bent and full of repentance lie I, dearest God, before Thee')
S. Vln i, ii, Vla, Fag, Violone, Cont

One of Bach's most lovely and moving arias with poignantly drawn-out phrases for the voice at 'repentance' and, just before the *da capo*, three repetitions of 'Geduld' ('patience').

5 RECITATIVE
'Auf diese Schmerzensreu fällt mir alsdann dies Trostwort bei' ('On this painful repentance falls to me then this comfort-word')
S. Violone, Cont

6 CHORALE
'Ich, dein betrübtes Kind, werf alle meine Sünd' ('I, thy troubled child, cast [away] all my sins')
S. Vla obb, Violone, Cont

The third verse of Johann Heermann's 'Wo soll ich fliehen hin' (1630). The soul finds saving grace in the wounds of Christ.

7 RECITATIVE
'Ich lege mich in diese Wunden, als in den rechten Felsenstein' ('I lay myself in these wounds, as in the true rock')
S. Vln i, ii, Vla, Fag, Violone, Cont

The repentant sinner's heart now expands in faith and joy, which Bach reflects in a run down and up the scale at 'gladly'.

8 ARIA
'Wie freudig ist mein Herz, da Gott versöhnet ist' ('How joyful is my heart, since God is reconciled')
S. Ob, Vln i, ii, Vla, Fag, Violone, Cont

The first quick movement in the cantata, an outburst of new-found joy, with farewell to grief and salvation assured.

Siehe zu, dass deine Gottesfurcht nicht Heuchelei sei
(See to it that thy God-fearing be not hypocrisy).
Cantata BWV 179. Leipzig, 1723.

1 CHORUS
(As above)
SATB. Vln i with S. Vln ii with A. Vla with T. Cont

The text is taken from Ecclesiasticus 1. 28–29, which includes the line, 'Be not a hypocrite in men's sight and keep a watch over your lips'.

The basses have the rather lengthy subject of this fugal chorus and the tenors invert it, and the same pattern is followed by soprano and altos. 'False' (heart) is given a chromatically descending phrase in all parts which tells powerfully in the final *stretto*. The effect of the movement is of a stern but controlled denunciation.

2 RECITATIVE
'Das heut'ge Christentum ist leider schlecht bestellt' ('The present Christendom is unfortunately badly ordered')
T. Cont

The text takes its cue from Revelations III. 16. 'So because you are lukewarm and neither cold nor hot I will spew you out of my mouth.' These are hypocritical Christians who go to church and perform outward observances like the Pharisees.

3 ARIA
'Falscher Heuchler Ebenbild können Sodoms Äpfel heissen' ('False hypocrites' likeness can Sodom's apples be called')
T. Ob i, ii with Vln i, Vln ii, Vla, Cont

The 'apples' may look attractive but are filled with filth. This aria puts into high relief the pitiable state of him who dares to stand up to God.

4 RECITATIVE
'Wer so von innen wie von aussen ist, der heisst ein wahrer Christ, so war der Zöllner in dem Tempel' ('Who then is from within as from without, he is called a true Christian, as was the publican in the temple')
B. Cont

Here the abrupt declamation of the first recitative about the Pharisees gives place to a lyrical vocal line, especially sensitive when the words speak of the publican smiting his breast.

5 ARIA
'Liebster Gott, erbarme dich, lass mir Trost und Gnad erscheinen' ('Beloved God, have Thou pity, let comfort and mercy to me appear')
S. Ob da cacc i, ii, Cont

The warning at the end of the recitative is heeded in this beautiful aria by a penitent sinner whose abasement is touchingly conveyed by the continually down-curving phrases for the oboe. Later in the aria at 'help me Jesus, Lamb of God, I sink in deep mire', the soprano descends from A flat above the stave to B natural below it.

6 CHORALE
'Ich armer Mensch, ich armer Sünder, steh hier vor Gottes Angesicht' ('I poor man, I poor sinner, stand here before God's countenance')
SATB. As No. 1, but with Ob i, ii, all with voices. Cont

The first verse of Christoph Tietze's hymn (1663) set to Georg Neumark's 'Wer nur den lieben Gott lässt walten'. The harmonization is most lovely. Bach is evidently touched to the heart by the words.

Herr Jesu Christ, du höchstes Gut (Lord Jesus Christ, thou highest good).
Chorale Cantata BWV 113. Leipzig, 1724.

1 CHORUS
(As above)
SATB. Ob i, ii, Vln i, ii, Vla, Cont

The libretto is based on Bartholomäus Ringwaldt's hymn with the above title (1588) with the melody (1593) associated with it. Verses i, ii, iv and viii are set in their original form in the corresponding numbers; the rest are paraphrased. The chorale is sung in a simple harmonization to a melodious accompaniment which may be intended to illustrate the reference in the second line to Christ as the well-spring of goodness, but unable to free the troubled conscience of this soul.

2 CHORALE
'Erbarm dich mein in solcher Last, nimm sie aus meinem Herzen' ('Have pity on me in such trouble, take it from my heart')
A. Vln i, ii (unis.), Cont

The soloist sings the melody in long notes placed in a neutral kind of setting.

The soul brings to mind the atonement for sinners suffered by Jesus on the Cross, without which they would have perished eternally.

3 ARIA
'Fürwahr, wenn mir das kommet ein, dass ich nicht recht vor

Gott gewandelt' ('Truly, when to me that appears, that I not rightly before God walked')
B. Ob d'am i, ii, Cont

Self-knowledge will bring 'trembling fear and pain'. The music, in 12/8 time, takes account of the text only in an ascending chromatic phrase sung to 'trembling' and twice more at 'break' in the line '. . . my heart would break if to me Thy word not comfort promised', otherwise the movement goes melodiously on its way regardless.

4 RECITATIVE
'Jedoch dein heilsam Wort, das macht mit seinem süssen Singen' ('Nevertheless Thy healing word, that causes with its sweet songs')
B. Cont

The bass sings the whole of the fourth verse with a running accompaniment, but with recitative sections following on each line. The 'sweet songs' bring refreshment and comfort to the soul whose conscience no longer torments him.

5 ARIA
'Jesus nimmt die Sünder an, süsses Wort voll Trost und Leben' ('Jesus accepts the sinners, sweet word full of comfort and life')
T. Fl trav, Cont

There is no question of a neutral kind of accompaniment in this delightful aria. It is indeed full of comfort and life. The solo flute carols joyously away—he has a brilliant part—and the tenor begins with the two charming phrases the flute has already played. There is a lovely phrase to the words, 'He gives the soul tranquillity', with a long note on 'rest' (Ruh).

6 RECITATIVE
'Der Heiland nimmt die Sünder an, wie lieblich klingt das Wort in meinen Ohren' ('The Saviour accepts the sinners, how pleasantly rings the word in my ears')
T. Vln i, ii, Vla, Cont

The text continues with a very familiar quotation from St Matthew XI. 28, and there are also quotations from 2 Samuel XII. 13, 2 Chronicles XXXIII. 12; these I must leave interested listeners to look up. There is also an allusion to the contrite tax-gatherer and the publican.

7 DUET

'Ach Herr, mein Gott, vergib mir's doch, womit ich deinen Zorn
erreget' ('Ah Lord, my God, forgive me it then wherewith I
Thine anger have provoked')
S.A. Cont

This return to the angry God is disappointing after the fine
recitative in No. 6, and fails to convince. Bach gives runs of extravagant length, eight bars of semiquavers, to 'provoke' and to
'laid': the yoke of sin laid on the soul by Satan.

8 CHORALE

'Stärk mich mit deinem Freudengeist, heil mich mit deinen
Wunden' ('Strengthen me with Thy joy-spirit, heal me with Thy
wounds')
SATB. (No instruments indicated)

TWELFTH SUNDAY AFTER TRINITY

Epistle: 2 Cor. III. 4–11 (Ministers of a new Covenant).
Gospel: Mark VII. 31–37 (The deaf man cured).

Lobe den Herrn, den mächtigen König der Ehren
(Praise the Lord, the mighty King of honours).
Chorale Cantata. BWV 137. Leipzig, 1725.

1 CHORUS
(As above)
SATB. Tr i, ii, iii, Timp, Ob i, ii, iii, Vln i, ii, Vla, Cont

In 1725 the twelfth Sunday after Trinity was followed a few days later by the annual Service for the Inauguration of the Leipzig Town Council and so Bach, perhaps pressed for time, chose a libretto that would do duty on both occasions though this meant that there could be no direct reference to the Gospel of the Sunday. For libretto Bach set all five verses of a hymn by Joachim Neander (1680) with its associated and anonymous melody (1665) in the same archaic style as in the well-known Easter Chorale Cantata *Christ lag in Todesbanden* (BWV 4), but gave verses 2–4 to soloists. Each verse begins with the first words of the title 'Lobe den Herrn', but Bach manages to avoid the monotony the continual praise in each verse might engender. The exuberantly joyful orchestral introduction to verse 1 leads to a *fugato* begun by the altos followed by tenors and basses, with a subject derived from a theme in the introduction. As this ends the sopranos make a most effective entry with the fine triple-time chorale, not put into long notes but left in its original rhythm. This pattern, with orchestral ritornellos between the lines, is repeated except for a massive chordal entry at 'Come in multitudes, psaltery and harps awake'.

2 ARIA
'Lobe den Herrn, der alles so herrlich regieret' ('Praise the Lord, who all things so gloriously governs')
A. Vln solo, Cont

This aria, with violin obbligato, is perhaps best known in the transcription Bach made for the last of the six Schübler Chorale Preludes for Organ. He marked the phrasing of the violin part—much more effective here than on the organ—very carefully so as to lend it as much variety as possible. The alto has a decorated form of the chorale melody.

3 DUET
'Lobe den Herrn, der künstlich und fein dich bereitet' ('Praise the Lord, who skilfully and beautifully prepares thee')
S.B. Ob i, ii, Cont

A richer elaboration of the melody with in the second half of the duet some striking chromatic passages. This is the finest movement in the cantata.

4 ARIA
'Lobe den Herrn, der deinen Stand sichtbar gesegnet' ('Praise the Lord, who thy state visibly blessed')
T. Tr, Cont

In this aria the solo tenor part acts as a counter melody to the solo trumpet's playing of the chorale. A striking feature of the lively string bass continuo is the thirty-four repetitions of its first four bars.

5 CHORALE
'Lobe den Herrn, was in mir ist, lobe den Namen' ('Praise the Lord, what is in me, praise His name')
SATB. As No. 1

Oboes, strings and continuo double the voice parts in this resplendent concluding verse. The three trumpets have independent parts, with the first trumpet rising to a ringing high C in the last bar.

Geist und Seele wird verwirret, wenn sie dich, mein Gott, betracht' (Spirit and soul becomes disordered when it contemplates Thee, my God).
Solo Cantata BWV 35. Leipzig, 1726.

PART I

1 SINFONIA
Ob i, ii, Te, Vln i, ii, Vla, Org obb. Cont

This oddly designed cantata consists of two *sinfonias* and three arias all derived from instrumental sources, only the two recitatives being newly composed material. It is, however, the only one of the three cantatas for this Sunday that concerns itself with the Gospel—the healing of the deaf man.

The first *sinfonia* opens with the nine bars that survive of a harpsichord concerto in D minor (BWV 1059), the remainder of the movement presumably adapting the rest. It is a lively enough piece with no special qualities.

2 ARIA
'Geist und Seele wird verwirret, wenn sie dich, mein Gott, betracht' ('Spirit and soul becomes disordered when it contemplates Thee, my God')
A. As No. 1

This aria must have taken its music from the slow movement, in the rhythm of a siciliano, from the above concerto. The text speaks of the wonder and exultation that filled the people at the deaf and dumb being healed. The voice part is rather awkwardly fitted in, the organ obbligato having the most interesting part in the movement.

3 RECITATIVE
'Ich wundre mich, denn alles, was man sieht' ('I marvel, for all that one sees')
A. Org, Cont

The text marvels at the deaf, dumb and blind healed by Christ.

4 ARIA
'Gott hat Alles wohl gemacht, seine Liebe, seine Treu, wird uns alle Tage neu' ('God has all things done well, His love, His faithfulness becomes to us every day new')
A. Org obb. Cont.

Another elaborate manual organ part with the continuo doubling the pedal. It is thought the music may have been derived from a gamba or a cello sonata movement.

PART II

5 SINFONIA
As No. 1

The finale, presumably, of the harpsichord concerto.

6 RECITATIVE

'Ach starker Gott, lass mich doch dieses stets bedenken' ('Ah powerful God, let me then this ever remember' (St Mark VII. 34))
A. Org. Cont

7 ARIA

'Ich wünsche mir, bei Gott zu leben, ach! wäre doch die Zeit schon da' ('I desire with God to live, ah, would then that the time were already here')
A. As No. 1

The figuration of the organ obbligato part in this movement certainly suggests the finale of one of the lost violin concertos. Bach utilizes its brilliant triplet figures in the second half of the movement for the last word of 'my torment-full life end'.

Lobe den Herrn, meine Seele; und vergiss nicht, was er dir Gutes getan (Praise the Lord, my soul, and forget not what He to thee of good has done).
Cantata BWV 69. Leipzig, c. 1743.

1 CHORUS

(As above)
SATB. Tr i, ii, iii, Timp, Ob i, ii, iii, Fag, Vln i, ii, Vla, Cont

Bach composed the first version of this cantata in 1723 at Leipzig (BWV 69a) for the Inauguration of the Town Council: he also used it as the cantata on the Sunday (the Twelfth after Trinity) of the week in which the Council was held. Some time between 1743 and 1750 Bach revised the cantata for the same two occasions, retaining Nos. 1, 3 and 5, but using new texts for the recitatives—which consorted better with the Gospel for the Sunday—and a different chorale at the close.

The text, based on Psalm CIII. 2, serves Bach for the whole length of the magnificent opening chorus.

Altos and tenors, then sopranos and basses, sing the first half of the Psalm verse and then all join in a climax of general acclamation. There follow two fugues, the first begun by the sopranos, the second with a much less florid subject, by the tenors. This second fugue is combined with the first one. Just before the da capo there is an even more triumphant climax than the one mentioned above.

2 RECITATIVE
'Wie gross ist Gottes Güte doch! Er bracht uns an das Licht und
er erhält uns noch' ('How great then is God's goodness. He
brought us to the light and He upholds us still')
S. Fag, Cont

Newly composed except for the first phrase to the above words.

3 ARIA
'Meine Seele, auf! erzähle, was dir Gott erwiesen hat' ('My soul,
arise! Tell what God has shown thee')
A. Ob, Vln i, Fag, Cont

This aria was scored, in the earlier version of the cantata, for
tenor, flute and oboe da caccia. All the movements except, of
course, the secco recitatives, which are always in 4/4 time in the
cantatas, are in triple rhythm (as before in BWV 137), befitting
the basic theme of the cantata. This melodiously flowing aria
is in 9/8.

4 RECITATIVE
'Der Herr hat grosse Ding an uns getan, denn er versorget und
erhält, beschützet und regiert die Welt' ('The Lord to us great
things has done, for he supplies and maintains, protects and
governs the world')
T. Vln i, ii, Vla, Fag, Cont

The secco recitative of BWV 69a is replaced here by an accompanied recitative to the new text in which the strings in the
arioso of the concluding section movingly underline the prayer
that God will protect 'our land' from harm and make its people
ready to bear what chastisements He may send.

5 ARIA
'Mein Erlöser und Erhalter, nimm mich stets in Hut und Wacht'
('My Redeemer and preserver, take me ever in protection and
guard')
B. Ob d'am with Vln i, ii, Vla, Fag, Cont

Solo bass singers should bless Bach for the many fine arias he
has given them: this is one of the best. The prayer becomes deeply
moving at the words 'Stand by me in suffering and sorrow'—
phrases which Bach has carefully marked *pianissimo* for the oboe and
continuo. The aria ends with 'then sings my mouth with joys,
God hath all things done well'.

6 CHORALE

'Es danke, Gott, und lobe dich, das Volk in guten Taten' ('May thank, God, and praise Thee the folk in good deeds')

SATB. Tr i, ii, iii, Timp, Ob i, ii, iii, Vln i, ii, Vla with voices. Fag, Cont

This is verse iii of Luther's 'Es woll uns Gott genädig sein' (see p. 184). A notable feature of the setting is the 'Amen' cadences (e.g., G, F sharp, G) at the end of each pause mark in the chorale, played by trumpets and timpani. At the last of these the first trumpet ascends to a triumphant high D.

THIRTEENTH SUNDAY AFTER TRINITY

Epistle: Gal. III. 15-22 (The promises made to Abraham).
Gospel: Luke x. 23-37 (The parable of the Good Samaritan).

Du sollst Gott, deinen Herren, lieben (Thou shalt God, thy Lord, love).
Cantata BWV 77. Leipzig, 1723.

1 CHORUS
(As above)
SATB. Tr, Vln i, ii, Vla, Cont

Bach, meditating on the words, adds a comment in quoting the melody to Luther's chorale, 'These are the holy ten commandments' (1524). The repeated notes in this melody are already anticipated in the second bar of the introductory ritornello and are woven into the vocal parts also. A unique feature is the giving of the chorale itself only to the trumpet in canon, with the continuo a fifth below in long notes.

2 RECITATIVE
'So muss es sein! Gott will das Herz für sich alleine haben' ('So must it be! God will have the heart for himself alone')
B. Cont

3 ARIA
'Mein Gott, ich liebe dich von Herzen, mein ganzes Leben hangt dir an' ('My God, I love Thee from my heart, my whole life hangs on Thee')
S. Ob i, ii, Cont

A quietly fervid expression of 'love from the heart', happily accompanied by the oboe. Bach gives florid phrases to 'ever' and 'burns' in the line, 'Let me then know Thy law, and in love so burn, that I can ever love Thee'.

4 RECITATIVE
'Gib mir dabei, mein Gott, ein Samariterherz, dass ich zugleich den Nächsten liebe' ('Give me thereby, my God, a Samaritan-heart, that I at the same time my neighbour may love')
T. Vln i, ii, Vla, Cont

The prayer is haloed in string-tone and the repeated notes of the chorale come here and there into the tenor's phrases.

255

5 ARIA
'Ach, es bleibt in meiner Liebe lauter Unvollkommenheit' ('Ah, there remains in my love only imperfection')
A. Tr, Cont

This aria is very expressive of humility in recognizing the imperfections of the will, which make it fail to do what God desires for it, and it too desires. The use of the trumpet may seem strange but from other instances of such use in Bach's time—and earlier—it would not have seemed so to his hearers.

6 CHORALE
No words or instruments are indicated in the manuscript. The melody is the anonymous *Ach, Gott, vom Himmel sieh darein* to which Carl Zelter fitted the eighth verse of David Denicke's *Wenn einer alle Ding verstünd* (1657), 'Du stellst, mein Jesu, selber dich'.

Allein zu dir, Herr Jesu Christ (Alone on Thee, Lord Jesus Christ).
Chorale Cantata BWV 33. Leipzig, 1724.

1 CHORUS
(As above)
SATB. Ob i, ii, Vln i, ii, Vla, Org, Cont

The libretto is based on Johannes Schneesing's hymn with the above title (1540) set in Nos. 1 and 6 to its original melody (*c.* 1541). The remaining verses are paraphrased.

In this chorus each line of the nine in the hymn is separated from the next by ritornellos developed from the orchestral introduction. The chorale melody, sung by the sopranos, and the lower parts are always treated quite simply. It falls to the orchestra, therefore, to express the happiness that confidence in the Saviour brings, whatever troubles befall, and this it does in the uprushing scales for the oboes, followed by the violins, in the introduction. The pendant phrases with repeated notes, two or more bars at a time, are a distinctive and combative feature in the instrumental parts almost throughout. Whittaker points out that the treatment of the fifth line, 'From the beginning is nothing ordained', gives the clue to these assertive repeated notes—which here also enter the lower voice parts—and was Bach's way of hitting out at the Calvinistic doctrine of predestination.

2 RECITATIVE

'Mein Gott und Richter, willst du mich aus dem Gesetze fragen, so kann ich nicht, weil mein Gewissen widerspricht, auf tausend eines sagen' ('My God and Judge, wilt Thou question me upon the law, yet can I not, because my conscience contradicts, in a thousand once answer')
B. Org, Cont

The emotional climate changes, as so often in the librettos, from confidence to uncertainty and awareness of the burden of personal sins, but this gives place, in a short arioso at the close, to the hope that the burden will be lifted.

3 ARIA

'Wie furchtsam wankten meine Schritte, doch Jesus hört auf meine Bitte und zeigt mich seinem Vater an' ('How fearfully faltered my steps, yet Jesus hears my prayer and points me to His Father')
A. Vln i (muted), Vln ii, Vla, Org, Cont

A superb aria, most imaginatively scored. The arpeggios in the continuo are marked organ *staccato*, string bass *pizzicato*, violin ii and viola *pizzicato*, above which the muted first violin plays the poignant melody, with a motif that prevails throughout in one form or another.

The burden of sin, continually reiterated, still lies heavy on the soul, but hope is not dimmed and leads to a moving expression of humble gratitude at the line, 'He has for me done enough with His words of comfort'.

4 RECITATIVE

'Mein Gott, verwirf mich nicht, wiewohl ich dein Gebot noch täglich übertrete, von deinem Angesicht' ('My God, cast me not away from Thy presence, though I Thy commandment daily violate')
T. Org, Cont

This anguished prayer ends, 'Good deeds will be active through love'.

5 DUET

'Gott, der du die Liebe heisst, ach, entzünde meinen Geist' ('God, Thou who art called love, ah, kindle my spirit')
T.B. Ob i, ii, Org, Cont

The essential sentence is, 'Grant that I from pure impulse, may love my neighbour as myself'.

The last section, which prays that if enemies disturb his rest God will send help, has some lovely phrases on 'rest', a word Bach always dwells on tenderly.

6 CHORALE
'Ehr' sei Gott in dem höchsten Thron, dem Vater aller Güte' ('Honour be to God on the highest throne, the Father of all goodness')
SATB. As No. 1. Insts. with voices. Org, Cont

Ihr, die ihr euch von Christo nennet (You, who yourselves call after Christ).
Solo Cantata BWV 164. Leipzig, 1725. Libretto by Salomo Franck.

1 ARIA
(As above)
T. Vln i, ii, Vla, Cont
The libretto is wholly concerned with the parable of the Good Samaritan (St Luke x. 23–37) read in the Gospel for the day, and in this aria professing Christians are upbraided for the lack of pity they show forth in their lives. Their hearts are stony, not loving. It is difficult to relate such a text to the flowing melody, in 9/8 time, which violins i and ii announce in the orchestral introduction and with which the tenor begins. It makes very pleasant listening but the explanation sometimes given that it is a picture of the good man going down from Jerusalem to Jericho without a care is too ingenious.

2 RECITATIVE
'Wir hören zwar, was selbst die Liebe spricht, die mit Barmherzigkeit den Nächsten hier umfangen, die sollen vor Gericht Barmherzigkeit erlangen' ('We hear verily what love says, "They who with mercy the neighbour here embrace shall before the Judgement seat obtain mercy" ')
B. Cont
This paraphrase of the fifth Beatitude is set as an arioso. The text that follows speaks of the ignoring of the sighs of the neighbours and of Christ knocking vainly at the door of our hearts and

wringing His hands. The priest and Levite enter, the pitiless men
who pour neither oil nor wine on the wounds of the afflicted man.

3 ARIA
'Nur durch Lieb' und durch Erbarmen werden wir Gott selber
gleich' ('Only through love and through pity do we become like
to God Himself')
A. Fl trav i, ii, Cont

The text continues: feeling for the pains of others awakens pity
in Samaritan-like hearts, who feel these pains also. The 'tear
motif', denoting compassion, is prominent in this moving little
aria.

4 RECITATIVE
'Ach, schmelze doch durch deinen Liebesstrahl des kalten Herzens
Stahl' ('Ah, melt then through Thy love-beam the cold heart's
steel')
T. Vln i, ii, Vla, Cont

A heartfelt prayer to show love and pity to all, friend or foe,
heathen or Christian.

5 DUET
'Händen, die sich nicht verschliessen, wird der Himmel aufgetan'
('To the hands which themselves do not close up is Heaven
opened')
S.B. Fl trav i, ii, Ob i, ii, Vln i, ii (all unis.), Cont

To give the top part to six instruments accompanied only by
the continuo suggests that Bach wanted the melodies of the first
and middle sections to come out strongly.

Falling and rising sixths characterize the main melody in the
two instrumental parts, expressing the striving in the line, 'To
hearts which strive after love will God Himself give His heart'.

6 CHORALE
'Ertöt' uns durch dein Güte, erweck uns durch dein Gnad'
('Mortify us by Thy grace, awaken us by Thy mercy')
SATB. Ob i, ii, Vln i, ii, Vla, all with voices; Cont

The fifth verse of Elisabeth Kreutziger's Christmas hymn, 'Herr
Christ, der einig Gott's Sohn', so beautifully set in Cantata 22
(p. 92).

FOURTEENTH SUNDAY AFTER TRINITY

Epistle: Gal. v. 16–24 (Walk in the Spirit).
Gospel: Luke XVII. 11–19 (The healing of the lepers).

Es ist nichts Gesundes an meinem Leibe (There is nothing healthy in my body).
Cantata BWV 25. Leipzig, 1723.

1 CHORUS
(As above)
SATB. Cornetto, Trb i, ii, iii, Fl i, ii, iii unis., Ob i, ii, Vln i, ii, Vla, Cont

The text is taken from Psalm XXXVIII. 3. The despairing groups of three quavers, off the beat, are maintained by the orchestra for the first forty bars. Woodwind and brass enter in bar fifteen, with Hassler's melody used for the penitential hymn, 'Ach Herr, mich armen Sünder' ('Ah Lord, me poor sinner'), best known to us as the 'Passion' chorale. The first phrases are reflected in the chorus parts in which 'threatening' ('through Thy anger'), is extended over four bars, first by the soprano and alto, then by the tenors and basses. At 'there is no peace for my sins' the orchestra is silent until the next entry of the chorale melody and again before the closing bars. This is one of three instances known, in the cantatas, in which the trombones are used other than with the voices.

2 RECITATIVE
'Die ganze Welt ist nur ein Hospital, wo Menschen, von unzählbar grosser Zahl und auch die Kinder in der Wiege, an Krankheit hart darniederliegen' ('The whole world is but a hospital, where men in uncountably great number, and also children in cradles, lie low in illness')
T. Cont

A catalogue of all the evils and troubles that result from Adam's fall.

3 ARIA
'Ach, wo hol' ich Armer Rat? Meinen Aussatz, meine Beulen, kann kein Kraut noch Pflaster heilen, als die Salb aus Gilead' ('Ah, where can I, poor man, obtain advice? My leprosy, my boils can no herb nor plaster heal, except the balm of Gilead')
B. Cont

260

This clinical text, set to fragmented phrases, did not inspire Bach. The last line offers some comfort, 'Only thou, my physician, Lord Jesus, knowest the soul's best cure'.

4 RECITATIVE
'O Jesu, lieber Meister, zu dir flieh ich' ('Oh Jesu, beloved Master, to Thee I fly')
S. Cont

A prayer to be made clean from the leprosy of sin.

5 ARIA
'Öffne meinen schlechten Liedern, Jesu, dein Genaden-Ohr' ('Open to my poor songs, Jesu, Thy gracious ear')
S. Fl i, ii, iii, Ob i with Vln i, Ob ii with Vln ii. Vla, Cont

At last a beautiful aria, preceded by a long ritornello, in the confident key of C major. The three flutes, echoed by the other instruments, underline 'when I in the higher choir shall with the angels sing, my thanksgiving will better ring'. The leper is at last healed and, like the Samaritan in the Gospel, returns to give thanks.

6 CHORALE
'Ich will alle meine Tage rühmen deine starke Hand' ('I shall all my days extol Thy strong hand')
SATB. As No. 1. Insts. with voices. Cont

The last verse of Johann Heermann's 'Treuer Gott, ich muss dir klagen' (1630) set to its associated melody, Louis Bourgeois' 'Ainsi qu'on oit le cerf' (1542).

Jesu, der du meine Seele (Jesus, Thou who my soul). Chorale Cantata BWV 78. Leipzig, 1724.

1 CHORUS
(As above)
SATB. Fl trav, Ob i, ii, Vln i, ii, Vla, Cor with S. Cont

This cantata, by far the finest of the three Bach composed for this Sunday, begins with one of his greatest choral movements. The libretto is based on Johann Rist's hymn (1641) with the above title, set unaltered in Nos. 1 and 7 to its associated melody, with the remaining verses paraphrased. The chorale is relevant to the Gospel insofar as it expresses fervent gratitude for being healed of the leprosy of sin, but at a price. 'Jesu, Thou who my soul hast torn through Thy bitter death out of the devil's dark hole . . . Be then, O God, my refuge.' The short introduction contains the dominant motif in the continuo, an *ostinato* bass of ancient origin and familiar in Dido's death-song in Purcell's opera. Above it the orchestra have a confident theme worked here and there into the texture. A third theme begins on the continuo as the altos and tenors enter with the *ostinato* theme. The chorale melody is given to the sopranos; doubled by the horn and the flute an octave above. At 'Be then, O God, my refuge', Bach directs the organ to play with the continuo an octave above. The cadence bars are marked *piano*.

An hour or so spent learning how to follow with a score will be rewarding—as it always is in some degree or another. It will show the listener the full majesty of the architecture and expression of this unforgettably poignant movement.

2 DUET

'Wir eilen mit schwachen, doch emsigen Schritten, o Jesu, o Meister, zu dir' ('We hasten with weak, yet eager, steps, O Jesus, O Master, to Thee')

S.A. Org and V'cello, Violone

There could not be a greater contrast between the tremendous chorus in No. 1 and this enchanting duet. The violone plays *pizzicato* throughout, the organ and cello depict the eager footsteps. The voices begin in canon at the fourth, then join, in sixths or thirds, ending the first section tenderly echoing 'to Thee'. The duet breathes Bach's love of his Saviour.

3 RECITATIVE

'Ach! ich bin ein Kind der Sünden. Ach! ich irre weit und breit' ('Ah, I am a child of sin! Ah, I err far and wide')

T. Cont

An outburst of anguish because the leprosy of sin is still to be found in the soul, and a prayer that it be forgiven.

4 ARIA

'Dein Blut, so meine Schuld durchstreicht, macht mir das Herze wieder leicht und spricht mich frei' ('Thy blood, which erases my guilt, makes the heart again light for me and declares me free')

T. Fl trav, Violone, Cont

The flute expresses the lightness, as also does the violone part, which again is marked *pizzicato* throughout.

5 RECITATIVE
'Die Wunden, Nägel, Kron und Grab, die Schläge, so man dort dem Heiland gab' ('The wounds, nails, crown and grave, the blows which one there gave to the Saviour')
B. Vln i, ii, Vla, Cont

These are victory signs; but then the tempo changes to *vivace* for the Judgement the damned will hear pronounced, emphasized by loud chords on the strings and followed by an *adagio*, 'Thou changest it to blessing'. A most expressive arioso follows, the words of which offer a heart full of sorrow for the precious blood shed on the Cross.

6 ARIA
'Nun du wirst mein Gewissen stillen, so wider mich um Rache schreit' ('Now wilt Thou my conscience quieten which cries against me for vengeance')
B. Ob i, Vln i, ii, Vla, Cont

An aria of no great consequence and possibly an adaptation from some other source.

7 CHORALE
'Herr, ich glaube, hilf mir Schwachen, lass mich ja verzagen nicht' ('Lord, I believe, help me, weak one, let me yea not despair')
SATB. As No. 1. Insts. with voices. Cont

The last verse of the chorale, full of trust in the Saviour.

Wer Dank opfert, der preiset mich (Who offers thanks, he praises me).
Cantata BWV 17. Leipzig, 1726.

PART I

1 CHORUS
(As above)
SATB. Ob i, ii, Vln i, ii, Vla, Cont

The text is that of Psalm L. 23, in the Lutheran version. The allusion here is to the Samaritan leper who alone returned to give thanks to Christ for healing him.

A flowing and melodious chorus in which 'who thanks' is continually repeated. The closing pages are warmly expressive.

2 Recitative

'Es muss die ganze Welt ein stummer Zeuge werden von Gottes hoher Majestät, Luft, Wasser, Firmament und Erden' ('The whole world must be a silent witness of God's high majesty; air, water, firmament and earth')
A. Cont

3 Aria

'Herr, deine Güte reicht so weit der Himmel ist' ('Lord, Thy goodness reaches as far as Heaven')
S. Vln i, ii, Cont

A delightful aria. The text is based on Psalm LVII. 10.

PART II

4 Recitative

'Einer aber unter ihnen, da er sahe, dass er gesund worden war kehrete und preiste Gott mit lauter Stimme' ('But one of them, when he saw that he was healed, turned round and praised God with a loud voice')
T. Cont

And this was the Samaritan.

5 Aria

'Welch Übermass der Güte schenkst du mir' ('What abundance of goodness givest Thou me')
T. Vln i, ii, Vla, Cont

An enchanting aria. The first phrase on the first violins, sung after the opening words, lingers in the memory as we follow the happy man making his way home. There is no *da capo* of the vocal part but fortunately the opening ritornello is repeated.

6 Recitative

'Sieh meinen Willen an, ich kenne, was ich bin' ('Look on my will, I know what I am')
B. Cont

The Samaritan sums up all he has received in his healing, a sound mind, body and spirit and the treasures of love, peace, justice and joy in the Lord's Spirit.

7 CHORALE
'Wie sich ein Vat'r erbarmet üb'r seine jungen Kindlein klein
so tut der Herr uns Armen' ('As a father takes pity on his small
young children, so does the Lord on us poor ones')
SATB. As No. 1. Insts. with voices. Cont

The third verse of Johann Graumann's 'Nun lob, mein Seel,
den Herren' (1540) set to a melody of 1540. The text is based on
Psalm CIII.

Epistle: Gal. v. 25–vi. 10 (The fruits of the Spirit).
Gospel: Matt. vi. 23–34 (Avoid worldly cares. Seek first the Kingdom of
God).

Warum betrübst du dich, mein Herz? (Why troublest thou thyself, my heart?).
Chorale Cantata BWV 138. Leipzig, 1723.

1 CHORUS
(As above)
SATB. Ob d'am i, ii, Vln i, ii, Vla, Cont

The hymn whose first three verses are quoted in Nos. 1, 3 and
7 of this cantata is thought to be by Hans Sachs and to have been
written in 1560, the anonymous melody five years later. The words
express faith and trust but the self-regarding commentaries
(recitatives) that come into Nos. 2–4 betray the opposite.

The first oboe d'amore plays the first line of the chorale melody
in the few introductory bars, the violins anticipating the solo
tenor's entry, 'Why troublest thou thyself, my heart?', which
the chorus repeat. The same pattern follows in the second and
third lines. 'Grievest thou and bearest pain only about the
temporal good?' Then the solo alto laments the heavy cares that
oppress her, punctuated by tearful phrases for the oboes. This is
answered by the two last lines of the chorale for the chorus,
'Trust thou thy Lord God, who has all things created'.

2 RECITATIVE
'Ich bin veracht', der Herr hat mich zum Leiden am Tage seines
Zorns gemacht' ('I am despised, the Lord has created me to suffer
on the day of His anger')
B. Cont

The assurance goes unheeded in this highly emotional outburst, which speaks of having to drink the bitter cup of tears, not
the wine of joy.

3 CHORALE AND RECITATIVE
'Er kann und will dich lassen nicht' ('He can and will not leave
thee')
SATB. As No. 1

In this second verse of the chorale, first violins double the melody, joining it to short phrases between the first three lines. 'He can and will not leave thee, He knows right well what thee lack, Heaven and earth is His.' The soprano, now representing the troubled soul, complains, in the recitative, that 'God cares for the birds and the beasts and gives them their food, but what crust of bread is there for me, poor child?' The chorus, in lines 4–5, assure her of the Father's awareness of her need but she breaks in again, 'I am forsaken. . . . Who regards my grief?' The chorus repeats the last two lines, more elaborately harmonized.

4 RECITATIVE
'Ach süsser Trost! Wenn Gott mich nicht verlassen und nicht versäumen will, so kann ich in der Still' und in Geduld mich fassen' ('Ah sweet comfort! If God will not forsake and not neglect me, then can I in silence and patience compose myself')
T. Cont

5 ARIA
'Auf Gott steht meine Zuversicht, mein Glaube lässt ihn walten' ('On God stands my confidence, my faith lets him rule')
B. Vln i, ii, Vla, Cont
The confidence is expressed in the simple and open-hearted melody of this lengthy aria which has lively parts for first violin and continuo.

6 RECITATIVE
'Ei nun, so will ich auch recht sanfte ruhn' ('Ah now, so will I even right softly rest')
A. Cont

7 CHORALE
'Weil du mein Gott und Vater bist, dein Kind wirst du nicht verlassen' ('Because Thou art my God and Father, Thy child wilt Thou not forsake')
SATB. As No. 1
Verse iii of the chorale, with the melody not this time doubled by the oboe. The score is black with sweeping unison demisemiquavers for the violins which it is difficult to interpret except as exuberant joy in the certainty of the Father's care, as opposed to the melancholy of Nos. 2 and 3.

267

Was Gott tut, das ist wohlgetan (What God doth, that is well done).
Chorale Cantata BWV 99. Leipzig, 1724.

Bach composed three cantatas with this title but the librettos only have in common the first and last verses of the hymn by Samuel Rodigast (1676) in Nos. 99 and 100 and the first verse in No. 98. The first and last verses of the chorale in No. 99 are set in Nos. 1 and 6 to its melody, the other verses are paraphrased.

1 CHORUS
(As above)
SATB. Fl trav, Ob d'am, Vln i, ii, Vla, Cor with S. Cont

The strings introduce the attractive melody, which is obviously derived from that of the chorale, and then give place to the woodwind, with the oboe d'amore playing the melody, the flute carolling above. The sopranos have the chorale melody in long notes, always anticipating the entry of the lower and independent parts.

2 RECITATIVE
'Sein Wort der Wahrheit stehet fest, und wird mich nicht betrügen' ('His word of truth stands fast and will me not deceive')
B. Cont

3 ARIA
'Erschüttre dich nur nicht, verzagte Seele, wenn dir der Kreuzes-Kelch so bitter schmeckt' ('Do not be shocked, despondent soul, when the suffering-cup so bitter tastes to thee')
T. Fl trav, Cont

The flute has demisemiquaver phrases in most of its part in this expressive aria, perhaps depicting the fears of 'the despondent soul', but an extended passage at 'the sweetness hidden lies', the flute rising to a sustained high E, is a measure of reassurance.

4 RECITATIVE
'Nun, der von Ewigkeit geschlossne Bund bleibt meines Glaubes Grund' ('Now, the from-eternity-made covenant remains my faith's ground')
A. Cont

5 DUET
'Wenn des Kreuzes Bitterkeiten, mit des Fleisches Schwachheit

streiten' ('If the Cross's bitterness with the flesh's weakness strives')

S.A. Fl trav, Ob d'am, Cont

The text reflects St Paul's words in the Epistle for this Sunday about the antagonism between spirit and flesh. It is hammered home by the constant use of repeated notes in the instrumental and vocal parts. The struggle is vividly depicted whenever 'struggle' comes into the voice parts.

6 CHORALE

'Was Gott tut, das ist wohlgetan, dabei will ich verbleiben' ('What God does, that is well done, by that will I stand')

SATB. As No. 1. Insts. with voices

Verse vi of the chorale straightforwardly set.

Jauchzet Gott in allen Landen! (Praise God in all lands!). Solo Cantata BWV 51. Leipzig, 1730.

1 ARIA

(As above)

S. Tr, Vln i, ii, Vla, Cont

Although Bach composed this cantata for the Fifteenth Sunday after Trinity he indicated on the score that it was also for general use. The libretto is relevant to the Gospel, 'Seek first the Kingdom of God', and to the Epistle, which extols the fruits of the Spirit.

It is hard to believe that Bach had at any time a boy in his choir capable of performing this virtuoso aria and competing with the brilliant trumpet part so often in duet with the voice. One can only hope, since women's voices were forbidden in the organ loft, that he did find a treble able to tackle it, and to touch C above the stave here and in the 'Alleluia' of the final number. It is one of the few cantatas that sound at home in the concert hall. The text calls on all men to praise God and bring an offering to One who stands by them in time of need—the trumpet is silent in this one solemn section. The aria is immensely exhilarating and enjoyable.

2 RECITATIVE

'Wir beten zu dem Tempel an, da Gottes Ehre wohnet, da dessen Treu, so täglich neu, mit lauter Segen lohnet' ('We

269

adore in the temple where God's honour dwells as His goodness, daily new, with pure blessings rewards')
S. Vln, i, ii, Vla, Cont

The text of this movement is based on Psalms cxxxviii. 2 and xxvi. 8. The recitative, a very expressive arioso, falls into two sections. The first has a gently pulsating string accompaniment, the second merely the continuo to illustrate that the mouth is only able to stammer in feeble praise of God's wonders (hardly the case in No. 1!) but that He well understands this. The stammer is depicted in an extended and angular phrase.

3 ARIA
'Höchster, mache deine Güte ferner alle Morgen neu' ('Highest, make Thy goodness farther every morning new')
S. Cont

A fresh-sounding aria in 12/8 time, with four groups of three quavers in each bar most of the way through, many decorative phrases in the vocal part, and a prolonged run on the last word of 'that we Thy children may be called'.

4 CHORALE
'Sei Lob und Preis mit Ehren, Gott, Vater, Sohn, heiligem Geist' ('Be laud and praise and honour to God, Father, Son and Holy Spirit')
S. Vln i solo, Vln ii, Cont

The fifth verse of Johann Graumann's 'Nun Lob, mein Seel, den Herren', set to its associated melody (1540).

An extended doxology with a joyous accompaniment for the violins and continuo and three fairly long ritornellos, the last of which leads directly, with a change of tempo from 3/4 to 2/4, to a scintillating 'Alleluia' in which the trumpet enters again into the score. All parts contribute to this glorious Coda.

Was Gott tut, das ist wohlgetan (What God does, that is well done).

Chorale Cantata BWV 100. Leipzig, 1732. Libretto by Samuel Rodigast.

The text, verses i and vi, and the music are substantially the same as in Cantata 99 (see p. 268). Two horns and timpani are added to the scoring of the opening chorus. The whole of the hymn is set and the melody of the chorale, only heard complete in Nos. 1 and 6, does, as Terry says, pervade the whole cantata. Every movement begins with the opening line.

1 CHORUS
(As above)
SATB. Cor i, ii, Timp, Fl trav, Ob d'am, Vln i, ii, Vla, Org, Cont

2 DUET
A.T. Org, Cont
One of Bach's 'walking-basses' in the continuo, supporting the soloists in this moderately interesting movement.

3 ARIA
S. Fl trav solo, Org, V'cello
The solo flute part, with its swirls of demisemiquavers, recalls a similar happening also on the flute in the third movement of Cantata 99 where it is difficult to divine its purpose. In this third verse, however, there is mention of 'healing medicine' being poured into the soul by God and perhaps Bach meant to illustrate its miraculous effect!

4 ARIA
B. Vln i, ii, Vla, Org, Cont
This verse, in which the key line is 'He is my light, my life in joy and sorrow', is set to an attractively syncopated melody. It has copious dynamic marks perhaps suggested by the antithesis of 'joy and sorrow' even though used at other points.

5 ARIA
A. Ob d'am, Org with V'cello, Violone
Sorrow enters momentarily into this verse. 'Must I now taste the cup, which is bitter according to my delusion . . . yet at the last I shall be rejoiced with sweet comfort in my heart; then yield all pains'.
A beautifully flowing melody with aspiring phrases in the oboe d'amore part and pathos free from any morbidity in the vocal lines.

6 CHORALE
SATB. As No. 1. Insts. with voices
A brilliant orchestral setting to the simply harmonized chorale.

Epistle: Eph. III. 13–21 (Paul prays that the Ephesians may perceive the love of God).

Gospel: Luke VII. 11–17 (The raising of the son of the widow of Nain).

Komm, du süsse Todesstunde (Come thou sweet death's hour).
Solo Cantata BWV 161. Weimar, 1715. Libretto by Salomo Franck.

1 ARIA
(As above)
A. Fl i, ii, Org, Cont

The two recorders introduce the lovely melody of this aria and thereafter share it with the voice. From time to time the organ plays, in single notes in the treble, the melody by Hans Leo Hassler (1601) to the hymn by Christoph Knoll (1605), 'Herzlich tut mich verlangen', the words of which are a prayer to depart in peace without fear. In Terry's translation the second verse ends, 'Then clothed in radiant glory, before my God I'll sing of His great love the story, O Death where is Thy sting'. The words of the aria allude to the episode of Samson finding a swarm of bees in the lion he had torn apart 'as one tears a kid'. Hence the familiar line, 'Out of the lion came forth sweetness' (Judges, XIV. 8). The soul finds this sweetness in the jaws of death and in the middle section prays, 'Make my departure sweet, delay not, that I my Saviour may kiss'.

Bach was fortunate in knowing that the introduction of the chorale on the organ would at once be understood by the congregation.

2 RECITATIVE
'Welt, deine Lust ist Last, dein Zucker ist mir als ein Gift verhasst'. ('World, thy pleasure is burden, thy sugar is by me as a poison hated')
T. Cont

'Roses are thorns, tormenting my soul, pale death is my dawn before the sun of glory and the bliss of heaven rise and so I yearn for the last hour of death'. This very expressive recitative ends with a moving arioso, 'I desire with Christ to pasture, I long from this world to depart.'

3 ARIA
'Mein Verlangen ist, den Heiland zu umfangen, und bei Christo

bald sein' ('My longing is the Saviour to embrace and with Christ soon to be')
T. Vln i, ii, Vla, Cont

This aria is, as melody, rather dry and the longing of the soul 'to be dissolved and to be with Christ' is reticently expressed.

4 RECITATIVE
'Der Schluss ist schon gemacht, Welt, gute Nacht, und kann ich nur den Trost erwerben, in Jesu Armen bald zu sterben, er ist mein sanfter Schlaf' ('The ending is already made, world, good-night, and can I only comfort win soon to die in Jesu's arms, He is my soft sleep')
A. Fl i, ii, Vln i, ii, Vla, Cont

'Recitative' is a bald word to denote the content of this exquisite movement. At the prayer to die in Jesu's arms the voice, continuo, and flutes—in that order—gently descend the scale. One *sees* the soul sinking to rest, the roses covering the grave till the awakening—a hint here of the melody of No. 1—and one *hears* the bells tolling—swinging octaves in the continuo, strings *pizzicato*, the first flute high above. The four chords at the close seem to pronounce 'Requiem aeternam'.

5 CHORUS
'Wenn es meines Gottes Wille, wünsch ich, dass des Leibes Last heute noch die Erde fülle' ('If it is my God's will I wish that the body's burden today the earth fills')
SATB. As No. 4

In the instrumental introduction the tear-motif of the opening aria is recalled, but now becomes one of joy, as the outburst of demisemiquavers on the flutes betokens.

6 CHORALE
'Der Leib zwar in der Erden von Würmern wird verzehrt' ('The body indeed in the earth by worms is destroyed')
SATB. As No. 4. Fl i, ii, obb.

This is the fourth verse of Christoph Knoll's hymn, the melody of which, by Hassler, was heard in No. 1. The words continue, 'But awakened shall be through Christ beautifully transfigured'. This explains, surely, the melody for the flutes high above the chorale, though one commentator interpreted it as the writhing of the worms in the grave.

Christus, der ist mein Leben (Christ, who is my life).

Chorale Cantata BWV 95. Leipzig, 1723.

The four cantatas Bach composed for this Sunday are all meditations on death. This seems curious at first in view of the widow's son being restored to life, but the miracle is evidently used by the librettists as symbolic of our resurrection to eternal life. No. 95 is unique in using four chorales, two in No. 1, the third in No. 3, and the fourth in No. 7.

1 CHORUS
(As above)
SATB. Cor, Ob d'am, Ob i, ii, Vln i, ii, Vla, Cont

The first verse of the anonymous hymn 'Christus, der ist mein Leben' (1609) is set to Melchior Vulpius's melody of the same date. There is no hint of morbidity in this cantata. The tranquil melody on the oboes, the ascending scales on the first violins, show simply a desire to leave a world of which the soul has grown weary and go to its eternal home. Both chorales in the movement are sung in simple four-part harmony except for the moment in the first at 'dying is my gain'. The voices at 'dying' build a chord downwards on successive sustained notes ending on a discord, with a quaver rest after it and a pause mark. This is one of the most wonderful and visionary passages in the cantatas. Between the two chorales the solo tenor bursts in, carolling like a lark, 'with joy, oh yes with heart's delight will I from here depart'. The orchestra continues on its severe way as before.

The second chorale is the first verse of Luther's version of 'Nunc dimittis', 'Mit Fried und Freud ich fahr dahin' ('In peace and joy I now depart'), with his melody (1524). It follows the tenor's last words, 'My parting words are on my lips, ah might I this day sing them'. The chorale is marked *allegro*, the horn anticipates each line and with the oboes doubles the voice parts.

2 RECITATIVE
'Nun, falsche Welt, nun hab ich weiter nichts mit dir zu tun' ('Now, false world, now I have nothing further with thee to do') S. Ob d'am i, ii (unis.), Cont

At once there follows:

3 CHORALE
'Valet will ich dir geben, du arge, falsche Welt' ('Farewell will I to thee give, thou wicked, false world') S. As No. 2

This is the first verse of Valerius Herberger's hymn (1613) with the above title, set to Melchior Teschner's melody (1613). Three motifs unite in this most beautiful movement: the chorale melody, the arpeggios in the continuo, and a joyous, gradually ascending motif for the oboes d'amore.

4 RECITATIVE
'Ach, könnte mir doch bald so wohl gescheh'n dass ich den Tod, das Ende aller Not in meinen Gliedern könnte seh'n' ('Ah, could it to me then soon so well happen, that I could see death, the end of all distress, in my limbs')
T. Cont

5 ARIA
'Ach, schlage doch bald, sel'ge Stunde' ('Ah, strike then soon, blessed hour')
T. Ob d'am i, ii, Vln i, ii, Vla, Cont

The strings and continuo play *pizzicato* throughout. The parts are laid out to imitate bells small and large. A poignant chord underlines the anxious words, 'Only call soon (thou most beloved of holy bells)'. The lovely melody keeps the soloist at the top of the stave most of the time but a good singer can express the full beauty of his part without strain.

6 RECITATIVE
'Denn ich weiss dies und glaub es ganz gewiss, dass ich aus meinem Grabe ganz sichern Zugang zu dem Vater habe' ('For I know this, and believe it quite certainly, that I from my grave have quite a sure way to the Father')
B. Cont

7 CHORALE
'Weil du vom Tod erstanden bist, werd ich im Grab nicht bleiben' ('Because Thou from death art arisen I shall not in the grave remain')
SATB. Vln i, ii, Vla, Cont (Cor, Ob d'am i, ii with S.)

The fourth verse of Nikolaus Hermann's 'Wenn mein Stündlein vorhanden ist' (1560) set to his melody (1569).

The first violin rises high above the voices with a melody that makes one picture the soul free of the body and about to ascend to its Maker.

275

Liebster Gott, wann werd ich sterben? (Beloved God, when shall I die?).
Cantata BWV 8. Leipzig, 1724.

1 CHORUS
(As above)
SATB. Fl trav, Ob d'am i, ii, Vln i, ii, Vla, Cor with S. Cont

The libretto is based on Caspar Neumann's hymn with the above title (c. 1700). Verses i and iv are set in Nos. 1 and 6 to Daniel Vetter's melody (1713), the other verses being paraphrased. Spitta, so often concerned to deny Bach's tonal pictorialism, was moved by the beauty of the instrumental introduction to write (Vol. 2, p. 432), 'the sound of tolling bells, the fragrance of blossoms pervade it—the sentiment of a churchyard in spring time'.

The poetic scoring supports this interpretation. As in Cantata 95 (see p. 274), the strings play an unvarying figure, *pizzicato*, tranquilly moving throughout, and from time to time the flutes reiterate very high-pitched phrases of six semiquavers while the continuo has deep low tones. These high, medium and low 'tolling bells' accompany the long breathed melody for the oboes d'amore. It expresses shades of gentle regret—for the world pictured here is beautiful—but not of mourning of the un-Christian kind formerly denoted by black clerical vestments and dismal lay clothes.

2 ARIA
'Was willst du dich mein Geist entsetzen, wenn meine letzte Stunde schlägt?' ('Why wilt thou, my soul, be terrified, when my last hour strikes?')
T. Ob d'am, Cont

The continuo is marked *pizzicato* for the bells here toll throughout the aria. The voice part is at first punctuated by rests, as if to suggest momentary fear of death, but the melody it takes over from the oboe d'amore mediates comfort and trust. Bach, just before the end of the first section, gives the voice single detached notes, three to a bar, on the word 'strikes', as if a bell was ringing also in the mind of the singer.

3 RECITATIVE
'Zwar fühlt mein schwaches Herz, Furcht, Sorgen, Schmerz, wo

wird mein Leib die Ruhe finden?' ('Indeed, my weak heart feels
fear, sorrow, pain, where will my body find rest?')
A. Vln i, ii, Vla, Cont

4 ARIA
'Doch weichet, ihr tollen, vergeblichen Sorgen' ('Then vanish,
you mad fruitless cares')
B. Fl trav, Vln i, ii, Vla, Cont

The tempo, 12/8, is that of the opening movement, but here is
used for one of Bach's gigue-like arias of uninhibited joy. The flute,
in the quite lengthy orchestral introduction, announces in joyous
rushes the return of trust in the mercy of God. The delicious
melody gives place in the second section to another melody,
equally captivating, at the words, 'Nothing that pleases me
belongs to the world', and now, as the voice and continuo part
show, the bells ring out joyfully and yet another enchanting melody
comes at, 'Appear to me thou blessed joyous morning, transfigured and glorious before Jesus to stand'. The flute has a
final ecstatic roulade in the closing bars.

5 RECITATIVE
'Behalte nur, o Welt, das Meine' ('Retain only, O world, my
belongings')
S. Cont

The moral is that the real treasures are laid up in Heaven.

6 CHORALE
'Herrscher über Tod und Leben, mach einmal mein Ende gut'
('Lord over death and life, make once for all my ending good')
SATB. Insts. with voices

The flute doubles the melody at the octave in this final verse of
the chorale.

Wer weiss, wie nahe mir mein Ende! (Who knows how
near is my end!).
Chorale Cantata BWV 27. Leipzig, 1726.

1 CHORUS
(As above)
SATB. Cor, Ob i, ii, Vln i, ii, Vla, Cont

The first verse of the Countess of Schwarzburg-Rudolstadt's
hymn (1695) with the above title set to Georg Neumark's, 'Wer

nur den lieben Gott lässt walten' (1657) is sung in a straight-forward style in this chorale fantasia. The introductory bars have a motif for the violins almost throughout, of four quaver phrases with swinging octaves, as it were the march of time, in the continuo, and a lamenting melody on the oboes. The words continue, 'Time departs, death arrives . . . my God, I beg through Christ's blood make my end good'.

The mood is tearful and at its most poignant in the prayer to Christ.

2 RECITATIVE
'Mein Leben hat kein ander Ziel, als dass ich möge selig sterben, und meines Glaubens Anteil erben' ('My life has no other aim, than that I may die blessed, and my faith's portion inherit')
T. Cont

3 ARIA
'Willkommen! will ich sagen, wenn der Tod ans Bette tritt. Fröhlich will ich folgen, wenn er ruft, in die Gruft' ('Welcome, will I say, when death steps to my bed. Joyfully will I follow, when He calls, into the grave')
A. Ob da cacc, Org obb. Cont

This movement is thought by some commentators to have its origin in one for gamba and harpsichord. The continuo doubles the bass of the organ part throughout. The melody given out in the long instrumental introduction by the oboe da caccia is attractive and reflects the joyful sentiment of the text but this is not a distinctive movement.

4 RECITATIVE
'Ach, wer doch schon im Himmel wär! Ich habe Lust zu scheiden, und mit dem Lamm . . . mich in der Seeligkeit zu weiden. Flügel her!' ('Ah, who were then already in Heaven! I desire to depart and with the Lamb . . . myself in blessedness to pasture. Wings hither!')
S. Vln i, ii, Vla, Cont

The singer repeats the order to be airborne, which is accom-panied both times by uprushes of the first violin as the wings, symbolically, sprout!

5 ARIA
'Gute Nacht, du Weltgetümmel' ('Good night, thou world-confusion')
B. As No. 4

These few words suffice Bach for the whole of the first section of the aria. 'Good night' is set to a lovely lyrical phrase, simply accompanied, 'world-confusion' to agitated groups of semi-quavers in the instrumental parts. A short and quicker section, again simply set, has the words, 'Now I make conclusion with Thee. I stand already with the beloved God in heaven.' The opening line of the aria is repeated but to new music, and peace comes in the quiet instrumental postlude.

6 CHORALE
'Welt, ade! ich bin dein müde, ich will nach dem Himmel zu, da wird sein der rechte Friede und die ew'ge stolze Ruh' ('World adieu! I am weary of thee, I will go to heaven, there will be the true peace and eternal stately calm')
SSATB. As No. 1. Insts. with voices

The first verse of Johann Georg Albinus's hymn with the above title (1649), to a melody by Johann Rosenmüller (1682) set to five-part harmony and adopted by Bach. There is no other such instance in the cantatas.

SEVENTEENTH SUNDAY AFTER TRINITY

Epistle: Eph. IV. 1–6 (Exhortation to unity).
Gospel: Luke XIV. 1–11 (Christ heals the dropsical man).

Bringet dem Herrn Ehre seines Namens, betet an den Herrn in heil'gem Schmuck (Bring to the Lord honour of His name, pray to the Lord in holy adornment). Cantata BWV 148. Leipzig,?1723. Libretto by Picander emended by Bach.

1 CHORUS
(As above)
SATB. Tr, Vln i, ii, Vla, Cont

This is thought to be the first libretto by Picander set by Bach and it may well be that the emendations the latter made are the psalm verses in this chorus and No. 3. The text of No. 1 is from Psalm XCVI. 8, 'Give unto the Lord the glory due unto his name: bring an offering, and come into his courts'. There is no special relation between the libretto and the Gospel or Epistle for the day.

This is one of Bach's brilliant D major choruses. The chorus begin in four-part harmony unaccompanied except by the strong and decisive continuo bass. The text is continually repeated and treated fugally in the section leading up to the second of the three ritornellos.

2 ARIA
'Ich eile, die Lehre des Lebens zu hören, und suche mit Freuden das heilige Haus' ('I hasten, the teaching of life to hear, and seek with joy the holy house')
T. Vln solo, Cont

Words like 'hasten' and 'joy' always cause Bach to accelerate and so we get the expected runs on these words. The solo violin, which is kept going with little rest from start to finish, has some delightful phrases with trills in this very lively movement.

3 RECITATIVE
'So wie der Hirsch nach frischem Wasser schreit, so schrei ich, Gott, zu dir' ('Even as the hart crieth after the fresh water, so cry I, God, to Thee')
A. Vln i, ii, Vla, Cont

The text begins with the first verse of the well-loved Psalm XLII and goes on to pay tribute to the holy and precious Sabbath celebration. The expressive setting shows how much the words appealed to Bach.

4 ARIA
'Mund und Herze steht dir offen, Höchster, senke dich hinein' ('Mouth and heart stands to Thee open, Highest, sink Thyself therein')
A. Ob i, ii, iii, Cont

In the first section the last line of the text above is treated differently at each of its two repetitions as Bach meditates upon it. The middle section, 'I in Thee and Thou in me, faith, love, endurance, hope, shall be my repose-bed' is set to more intimate music, with a long-sustained note at 'repose'.

5 RECITATIVE
'Bleib auch, mein Gott, in mir, und gieb mir deinen Geist, der mich nach deinem Wort regiere' ('Remain also, my God, in me, and give me Thy Spirit, which according to Thy word may govern me')
T. Cont

The soul expresses hope that he may so live as to be worthy to hold the great Sabbath with God, the beloved.

6 CHORALE
'Führ auch mein Herz und Sinn' ('Guide also my heart and mind')
SATB. Instrumentation not stated

As Bach provided no verse to the anonymous melody of this chorale, Spitta's suggestion of the eleventh verse of Johann Heermann's hymn 'Wo soll ich fliehen hin' (1630) to an anonymous melody (1609) was adopted by the editors of the Bach Society Edition of the Cantatas.

Wer sich selbst erhöhet, der soll erniedriget werden
(Whoever himself exalteth he shall abased be).
Cantata BWV 47. Weimar, 1726. Libretto by Johann F. Helbig.

1 CHORUS
(As above)
SATB. Ob i, ii, Vln i, ii, Vla, Cont

281

The virtue of humility, the theme of the libretto, is at once pronounced in a paraphrase of Jesus' words in the Gospel for the day. Everyone even slightly familiar with Bach's organ works will recognize the massive opening chords of the long introductory ritornello as those of the Prelude (and Fugue) in C minor (BWV 546) composed at Weimar, and he draws on other material from the Prelude in the course of this powerful movement. There are two expositions of the fugue, the subject of which, begun by the tenor, is designed to describe the self-exaltation of the proud and, in a tremendous passage, the proud are held up to contempt.

2 ARIA
'Wer ein wahrer Christ will heissen, muss der Demut sich befleissen, Demut stammt aus Jesu Reich' ('Who a true Christian would be called must apply himself to humility, humility springs from Jesu's kingdom')
S. Org obb. Cont

In the middle section of this aria, Bach emphasizes, in long sustained notes, that arrogance is akin to the Devil, and pride that is stubbornly maintained will cause God to reject such souls.

3 RECITATIVE
'Der Mensch ist Kot, Stank, Asch und Erde' ('Man is dirt, dust, ashes, and earth')
B. Vln i, ii, Vla, Cont

Bach's contempt for the proud is vividly expressed. The text refers to Christ's humility. The proud soul is exhorted to do penance and follow in Christ's footsteps.

4 ARIA
'Jesu, beuge doch mein Herze unter deine starke Hand dass ich nicht mein Heil verscherze' ('Jesu, bend then my heart under Thy strong hand, that I may not lose my salvation through folly')
B. Ob, Vln, Cont

Arrogance is to be execrated and Bach sees to it that it is in his florid phrases on the word 'haughtiness'.

5 CHORALE
'Der zeitlichen Ehr' will ich gern entbehr'n, du wollst mir nur das Ew'ge gewähr'n' ('Temporal honour will I gladly forgo if Thou wilt only the eternal grant me')
SATB. As No. 1. Insts. with voices

The eleventh verse of Hans Sachs's 'Warum betrübst du dich, mein Herz' (1560) set to an anonymous melody.

Ach, lieben Christen, seid getrost (Ah, dear Christians, be comforted).
Cantata BWV 114. Leipzig, 1724.

1 CHORUS
(As above)
SATB. Ob i, ii, Vln i, ii, Vla, Cor with S. Cont
This libretto is based on Johannes G. Gigas's hymn with the above title (1561) set to its accustomed melody, 'Wo Gott der Herr nicht bei uns hält'. This is used in Nos. 1, 4 and 7 (verses i, iii, vi). The remaining verses are paraphrased in the other movements.

Christians must humbly bear the punishments that fall on them and try to understand and be comforted by the thought that they are beneficial to the soul.

The orchestral prelude is an excellent example of Bach's superb musical architecture. He presents two themes simultaneously: (a) oboes and first violins; (b) second violins, and continuo; the latter, joyful in character, is complementary to the former, which is serious. A third, with its series of repeated notes, could portray contrition. These motifs pervade the whole movement: they are not developed but continually rearranged in the various orchestral parts and hardly ever heard singly. The chorale is sung in long notes by the sopranos, the independent lower parts being simply but effectively laid out.

2 ARIA
'Wo wird in diesem Jammertale für meinen Geist die Zuflucht sein?' ('Where will in this lamentation vale be refuge for my spirit?')
T. Fl trav solo, Cont
It is the beautiful obbligato for the flute that carries the deep emotion of this aria, the tenor's part being declamatory. He asks the question seven times and his persistence is rewarded in the vivacious and lyrical music of the middle section of the aria, with the flute contributing wide-flung phrases of delight. The words that inspire this outburst are 'Alone to Jesu's Father-hands will I myself in weakness turn'.

3 RECITATIVE
'O Sünder, trage mit Geduld, was du durch deine Schuld dir selber zugezogen' ('O Sinner, bear with patience what thou through thy guilt hast caused to thyself')
B. Cont

This brings us back to the beginning—the rejoicing was premature.

4 CHORALE
'Kein Frucht das Weizenkörnlein bringt, es fall' denn in die Erden' ('No fruit the wheat-grain brings unless it fall into the earth')
S. Cont

Jesus's words in the Gospel (St John XII. 24), 'Except a grain of wheat fall into the earth and die, it abideth by itself alone; but if it die, it beareth much fruit'. The detached phrases in the continuo suggest the sowing of the grain.

5 ARIA
'Du machst, o Tod, mir nun nicht ferner bange, wenn ich durch dich die Freiheit nur erlange' ('Thou makest me, O death, now not further anxious, if I through thee only attain freedom')
A. Ob i, Vln i, ii, Vla, Cont

The moral of Jesus's words is drawn in this predominantly joyful aria in the middle section of which the words recall Simeon's 'Nunc dimittis', and look forward to the day when, pure and transfigured, the soul is called to its Redeemer.

6 RECITATIVE
'Indes bedenke deine Seele und stelle sie dem Heiland dar' ('Meanwhile consider thy soul and bring it before the Saviour')
T. Cont

7 CHORALE
'Wir wachen oder schlafen ein, so sind wir doch des Herren' ('We wake or sleep, yet are we indeed the Lord's')
SATB. As No. 1. Insts. with voices. Cont

The sixth verse of the chorale.

EIGHTEENTH SUNDAY AFTER TRINITY

Epistle: 1 Cor. 1. 4–8 (Paul gives thanks for the grace of God given to the Corinthians).

Gospel: Matt. XXII. 34–46 (The first great commandment . . . What do you think of Christ? Whose Son is he?).

Herr Christ, der ein'ge Gottessohn (Lord Christ, the only Son of God).

Chorale Cantata BWV 96. Leipzig, 1724.

1 CHORUS
(As above)
SATB. Fl picc, Vln picc, Ob i, ii, Vln i, ii, Vla, Cor, Trb with A. Cont

The libretto is based on Elisabeth Kreutziger's hymn (1524) with the above title. Verses i and v are set to the original melody in Nos. 1 and 6. The other verses are paraphrased.

This is one of the few cantatas in which the *cantus firmus* is placed, in long notes, in the alto part, in which its entry always precedes the entry of the other parts. The main theme, heard in the melodious prelude, swings along at a lively pace, with the flute in unison with the violino piccolo. The reason for the bright scoring is made clear in the fifth line, 'He is the morning star . . . clear beyond all other stars'. Bach reserves a specially attractive phrase for the sopranos, rising ever upward at 'morning star'.

2 RECITATIVE
'O Wunderkraft der Liebe, Gott an sein Geschöpfe denkt' ('O wonder-power of love, God on His creation thinks')
A. Cont

In eloquent phrases the text speaks of the mystery of the birth of Christ by a woman of 'maiden purity', who came to open Heaven to us and defeat Satan.

3 ARIA
'Ach, ziehe die Seele mit Seilen der Liebe, O Jesu, ach, zeige dich kräftig in ihr' ('Ah, draw the soul with cords of love, O Jesu, ah, show Thyself mightily in it')
T. Fl trav solo, Cont

A most charming aria with a little semiquaver 'lift' in the flute solo, frequent in the voice part also, that seems to express sheer happiness.

285

The text prays that the soul, illuminated by faith, may burn and thirst after its Saviour.

4 RECITATIVE
'Ach führe mich, o Gott, zum rechten Weg' ('Ah, lead me, O God, to the right way')
S. Cont

A note of distrust, as so often in the librettos of the cantatas. The text is a prayer not to follow the promptings of the flesh.

5 ARIA
'Bald zur Rechten, bald zur Linken, lenkt sich mein verirrter Schritt' ('Now to the right, now to the left, turns itself my erring step')
B. Ob i, ii, Vln i, ii, Vla, Cont

Bach cannot resist depicting this indecisive wavering by giving the violins an up-going little motif, the oboes the reverse.

6 CHORALE
'Ertöt uns durch dein Güte, erweck uns durch dein Gnad' ('Mortify us through Thy goodness, awaken us through Thy grace')
SATB. Cor, Ob i, ii, Vln i, ii, Vla, all with voices, Cont

Gott soll allein mein Herze haben (God shall alone my heart have).
Solo Cantata BWV 169. Leipzig, 1726.

1 SINFONIA
Ob i, ii, Te, Vln i, ii, Vla, Org obb. Cont

Bach adapted the first and second movements of his E major Concerto for Clavier (BWV 1053), composed in the 1730s, in the first and fifth numbers of this cantata. The part for the harpsichord is transferred to the organ (one manual and pedals). It is another example of using a movement that has no connection at all with the libretto, which combines the grace Paul found in the Corinthians with Christ's revelation of the greatest commandment.

2 ARIOSO AND RECITATIVE
(As above)
A. Cont

The opening two bars for the continuo have a memorable phrase that recurs in the three sections of the arioso, which are separated by two passages of recitative and in the third beautifully expanded.

The text of the first recitative rejects the claims of the world, the second continues the thought at the end of the arioso following, 'I find in Him the highest good', and the succeeding arioso emphasizes 'alone'. A short concluding recitative reiterates conclusively the opening words.

3 ARIA
A. Org obb. Cont

The text of the first section is the same as that of the second arioso but more expansively set to the new melody. The words of the middle section express the certainty that in bad times the loving God will be with the soul. The attractive alto part deserved a less florid accompaniment than that of the organ obbligato.

4 RECITATIVE
'Was ist die Liebe Gottes? Des Geistes Ruh', der Sinnen Lustgeniess', der Seele Paradies' ('What is the love of God? The spirit's repose, the senses' delight-enjoyment, the soul's paradise')
A. Cont

5 ARIA
'Stirb in mir, Welt, und alle deine Liebe, dass die Brust sich auf Erden für und für in der Liebe Gottes übe' ('Die in me, world, and all thy love, that the breast disciplines itself on earth for ever and ever in the love of God')
A. Vln i, ii, Vla, Org obb. Cont

The music is an adaptation of the second movement, a siciliano, of the harpsichord concerto: the continuo's detached octaves persist throughout. The vocal line is independent of the orchestral part and as in No. 3 Bach gives the singer an expressive melody.

6 RECITATIVE
'Doch meint es auch dabei mit eurem Nächsten treu, denn so steht in der Schrift geschrieben' ('Moreover, do well also by your neighbour, for so stands [it] written in the Scripture')
A. Cont

The next line sums up the theme of the cantata, 'Thou shalt love God and thy neighbour'.

7 Chorale
'Du süsse Liebe, schenk uns deine Gunst, lass uns empfinden der Liebe Brunst' ('Thou sweet love, give us Thy grace, let us experience love's ardour')
SATB. As No. 1. Insts. with voices

The third verse of Luther's 'Nun bitten wir den heiligen Geist' (1524) set to its melody—one of the few vernacular pre-Reformation hymn-tunes.

ST MICHAEL

Epistle: Rev. XII. 7–12 (War in heaven).
Gospel: Matt. XVIII. 1–11 (Whoso humbleth himself is greatest in Heaven).

Herr Gott, dich loben alle wir (Lord God, we all Thee praise).
Chorale Cantata BWV 130. Leipzig, 1724.

1 CHORUS
(As above)
SATB. Tr i, ii, iii, Timp, Ob i, ii, iii, Vln i, ii, Vla, Cont

The libretto is based on Paul Eber's hymn (*c.* 1554) with the above title set in Nos. 1 and 6 to the melody of Louis Bourgeois' 'Or sus, serviteurs du Seigneur' (1551), known to us as that of the 'Old Hundredth'.

The opening chorus is one of praise and thanks to God for the creation of the angels, 'who float round Thee on Thy throne'.

Four motifs appear simultaneously in the introductory ritornello, all arpeggios: trumpets ascend, oboes descend, strings alternate high and low groups of semiquavers and the continuo booms out detached octaves. These motifs become interchangeable and, as there are two others to come, the texture is very rich. The *cantus firmus* is given to the sopranos in long notes.

2 RECITATIVE
'Ihr heller Glanz und hohe Weisheit zeigt, wie Gott sich zu uns Menschen neigt' ('Their bright appearance and high wisdom shows, how God inclines Himself to us men')
A. Cont

The text goes on to pray that the angels may guard the 'poor little group from the fury of Satan'.

3 ARIA
'Der alte Drache brennt vor Neid, und dichtet stets auf neues Leid' ('The old dragon burns with envy and ruminates continually on new affliction')
B. Tr i, ii, iii, Timp, Cont

The text gives Bach an opportunity for vivid tone painting. The trumpet fanfares explain themselves but the thudding repeated notes of the timpani may represent the restless scheming of the Evil one. The congested vocal part shows 'the poor little

U 289

group' struggling to evade him. The fanfares proclaim the presence of the angels but the conflict is still in progress as the aria ends.

4 RECITATIVE
'Wohl aber uns, dass Tag und Nacht die Schar der Engel wacht, des Satans Anschlag zu zerstören' ('Well for us, that day and night the host of angels watches to destroy Satan's onslaught') S.T. Vln i, ii, Vla, Cont

The text speaks of Daniel in the lions' den and the three holy children in the fiery furnace. The angels saved them and will save us, give them praise.

5 ARIA
'Lass, o Fürst der Cherubinen, dieser Helden hohe Schar immerdar deine Glaübigen bedienen' ('Let, O Prince of the Cherubim, the heroes' high host always Thy believers serve') T. Fl trav, Cont

The text, as in the closing chorale of No. 19 below, mentions believers being carried up to Heaven in Elijah's chariot. Bach here provides exactly what is wanted, a most tuneful and indeed an enchantingly melodious movement.

6 CHORALE
'Darum wir billig loben dich, und danken dir, Gott, ewiglich' ('Therefore we justly praise and thank Thee, God, eternally') SATB. As No. 1. Insts. with voices. Tr i, ii, iii, Timp, Cont

The last two verses of Paul Eber's hymn. The brass come in effectively at the end of each line, with the first trumpet twice running up to high C.

Es erhub sich ein Streit (There arose a strife).
Cantata BWV 19. Leipzig, 1726.

Johann Christoph Bach, who seems to have been as stubborn a character as his nephew became, was naturally attracted to the violent war between the good and the bad angels depicted in the Revelation of St John and composed a cantata in twenty-two parts (two five-part choirs, four trumpets and timpani, strings, organ and bass continuo). Johann Sebastian had the work performed at Leipzig and it made a great impression. Johann Christoph's libretto, written before the operatic recitative and *da capo* aria invaded church music, is based wholly on biblical texts.

1 CHORUS
(As above)
SATB. Tr i, ii, iii, Timp; Vln i, Ob i; Vln ii, Ob ii; Vla, Te. Cont

The basses burst straight into the description of the battle with the powerful fugue subject that unleashes writhing groups of semiquavers as the other voices and instruments come in. At the second exposition the voices enter in the reverse order (SATB). There is a sudden pause before the middle section which tells how 'the blustering serpent and hellish dragon storm against the heaven with raging vengeance'—the trumpets mutter on low notes here with sinister effect. Then Michael appears as conqueror and with the host that surrounds him overthrows Satan's ferocity. At this point Johann Christoph ended his chorus but Bach fell victim quite unnecessarily to the convention of the *da capo* aria and so the strife begins again, leaving the final result uncertain.

2 RECITATIVE
'Gottlob, der Drache liegt. Der unerschöpfte Michael und seiner Engel Schaar hat ihn besiegt' ('God be praised, the dragon falls. The inexhaustible Michael and his angels' host has defeated him')
B. Cont

Bach illustrates by the drop of a seventh (F sharp to low G) the fall, but nothing else in the vivid text, which describes Satan chained and roaring in the darkness while angels guard the faithful.

3 ARIA
'Gott schickt uns Mahanaim zu, wir stehen oder gehen, so können wir in sicherer Ruh, vor unsern Feinden stehen' ('God sends us to Mahanaim whether we stand or move, so can we stand in sure calmness before our enemies')
S. Ob d'am i, ii, Cont

Mahanaim is the name of the place where Jacob met the angels of God; the reference comes from Genesis XXXII. 2–3.

4 RECITATIVE
'Was ist der schnöde Mensch, das Erdenkind? Ein Wurm, ein armer Sünder' ('What is the worthless man, the earth-child? A worm, a poor sinner')
T. Vln i, ii, Vla, Cont

But the Lord grants him the protection of the Seraphim. The strings, with the first violins floating above, beautifully suggest the shining host.

5 ARIA
'Bleibt, ihr Engel, bleibt bei mir' ('Bide, ye angels, bide with me')
T. Tr, Vln i, ii, Vla, Cont
A prayer to the angels. The trumpet plays the melody of one
of the festival's hymns; the strings' and continuo's part recalls
the Pastoral Symphony in Bach's *Christmas Oratorio*.

6 RECITATIVE
'Lasst uns das Angesicht der frommen Engel lieben, und sie mit
unsern Sünden nicht vertreiben' ('Let us love the presence of the
holy angels, and with our sins not drive them away')
S. Cont

7 CHORALE
'Lass dein Engel mit mir fahren auf Elias Wagen rot, und meine
Seele wohl bewahren, wie Laz'rus nach seinem Tod' ('Let Thine
angels with me journey on Elijah's red chariot and keep my soul
well, as Lazarus's after his death')
SATB. Ob i, ii, Vln i, ii, Vla, Te, all with voices; Tr i, ii, iii, Timp, Cont
The ninth verse of the anonymous 'Freu' dich sehr, o meine
Seele' (1620) set to the melody of 'Ainsi qu'on oit le cerf'.

Man singet mit Freuden vom Sieg (Let songs of rejoicing be raised).
Cantata BWV 149. Leipzig, 1728.

1 CHORUS
(As above)
Tr i, ii, iii, Timp, Ob i, ii, iii, Fag, Vln i, ii, Vla, Cont
Cantata No. 19 plunged at once into the battle between Michael
and the angelic host and the evil forces of Satan. The text of this
chorus, drawn from Psalm CXVIII. 15, shows that the battle has
ended in victory. 'The right hand of the Lord does valiantly, the
right hand of the Lord is exalted.' Trumpets, therefore, ring out
at the start. The ritornellos, newly scored, are borrowed from the
concluding chorus of the delightful hunting cantata, *Was mir
behagt* (BWV 208), composed in 1716 in honour of the Duke Christian of Sachsen-Weissenfels, who was being entertained by Duke
Wilhelm Ernst of Weimar, but the vocal parts are re-written. The
adaptation is most skilfully done.

2 ARIA

'Kraft und Stärke sei gesungen, Gott, dem Lamme, das be-
zwungen und den Satanas verjagt' ('Strength and might be sung
[to] God, to the Lamb, who subdued and Satan drove away')
B. Violone, Cont

The aria reports the struggle described in the Epistle; not in the
powerful terms of the opening chorus in No. 19 but by a solo
bass accompanied only by the continuo! The declamatory vocal
part ranges widely, taking its combative first phrases from the
continuo ritornello. The reference to the Lamb becomes clear in
the text of the second section as 'Honour and victory ... through
the lamb's blood come'.

3 RECITATIVE

'Ich fürchte mich vor tausend Feinden nicht, denn Gottes Engel
lagern sich an meine Seiten her' ('I fear not a thousand enemies,
for God's angels encamp themselves by my side')
A. Cont

4 ARIA

'Gottes Engel weichen nie, sie sind bei mir aller Enden' ('God's
angels never waver, they are with me on all sides')
S. Vln i, ii, Vla, Cont

This is a most beautiful aria. One can only marvel that in his
noisy composer's room at St Thomas's School Bach could
tranquilly and tenderly contemplate the angels who guard us in
our waking and sleeping.

5 RECITATIVE

'Ich danke dir, mein lieber Gott, dafür' ('I thank Thee, my
beloved God, therefor')
T. Cont

A prayer that the soul's guardian angel may carry him to
Heaven when he dies.

6 DUET

'Seid wachsam, ihr heiligen Wächter, die Nacht ist schier dahin'
('Be wakeful, you holy watchers, the night is almost past')
A.T. Fag, Cont

The melody of the bassoon part in this duet is remarkably
evocative of the picture the words paint. It ends, just before the
voices enter, in canon, with an astonishing cadence. Whittaker
truly says that the choice of the bassoon is not fortuitous, '[it]

gives a feeling of loneliness, almost of awesomeness . . . and is as apt as Gluck's use of the flute in the Elysian scene in *Orpheus*.'

7 CHORALE
'Ach, Herr, lass dein lieb Engelein am letzten End die Seele mein in Abraham's Schoss tragen' ('Ah Lord, let Thy beloved angels at the latter end my soul into Abraham's bosom bear') SATB. Ob i, ii, iii, Fag, Vln i, ii, Vla, all with voices, Tr i, ii, iii, Timp, Cont

Bach reserves his trumpets and timpani for a master-stroke in the last two bars of the chorale as the voices sing 'eternally'. This is not only the 'consummate craftsmanship' the rationalists praise: it is religious inspiration.

Verse iii of Martin Schalling's 'Herzlich lieb hab ich dich, o Herr' (1571), set to its associated melody (1577).

NINETEENTH SUNDAY AFTER TRINITY

Epistle: Eph. IV. 22–28 (Put on the new man).
Gospel: Matt. IX. 1–8 (The sick of the palsy healed).

Ich elender Mensch, wer wird mich erlösen vom Leibe dieses Todes? (I wretched mortal, who will deliver me from the body of this death?).
Chorale Cantata BWV 48. Leipzig, 1723.

1 CHORUS
(As above)
SATB. Tr, Ob i, ii (unis.), Vln i, ii, Vla, Cont

The text is taken from Romans VII. 24, and comes in the sentence in which St Paul laments that though he wants to do right, evil lies close at hand, the law of his mind with another law making him captive to the law of sin that dwells in his members.

The main motif on the first violins, in the introductory ritornello, ascends phrase by phrase to a high point of impassioned questioning. Soprano and altos then come in, in canon, with the one line of text that suffices Bach in this masterly chorus, while trumpet and oboes, also in canon, begin the chorale, 'Herr Jesu Christ, ich schrei zu dir' ('Lord Jesus Christ, I cry to Thee'), the cry of the greatly troubled soul. In this way Bach gives expression to what was in St Paul's heart, the congregation of course recognizing the allusion.

2 RECITATIVE
'O Schmerz, o Elend, so mich trifft, indem der Sünden Gift, bei mir in Brust und Adern wütet' ('O pain, O misery, which strikes me, while sin's poison rages through me in breast and veins')
A. Vln i, ii, Vla, Cont

The strings, kept at a low pitch, add to the sombre atmosphere of this outcry in which the chromatic concluding phrases vividly depict the anguished state of the soul.

3 CHORALE
'Solls ja so sein, dass Straf und Pein auf Sünden folgen müssen' ('Shall it, yea, then be, that punishment and pain must on sins follow')
SATB. As No. 1. Insts. with voices

295

The fourth verse of the anonymous hymn 'Ach Gott und Herr' (1613) set to its original melody (1625). The chromatic harmonization is almost as amazing as that of the concluding chorale in cantata No. 60.

4 ARIA
'Ach, lege das Sodom der sündlichen Glieder, wofern es dein Wille, zerstöret darnieder' ('Ah lay the Sodom of sinful members, if it is Thy will, destroyed below')
A. Ob solo, Cont

The text refers here to the Gospel in which Jesus said to the paralytic man, 'Take heart, my son: thy sins are forgiven thee', before curing him. His joy is reflected in the melody of the oboe solo, taken up by the solo voice.

5 RECITATIVE
'Hier aber tut des Heiland's Hand auch unter denen Todten Wunder' ('Here, however, does the Saviour's hand among the dead ones [work] wonders')
T. Cont

And through Him are restored to health of body and soul, as the following aria confirms.

6 ARIA
'Vergibt mir Jesus meine Sünden, so wird mir Leib und Seel gesund' ('If Jesus forgives me, my sins, my body and soul become healthy')
T. Vln i and Ob (unis.), Vln ii, Vla, Cont

7 CHORALE
'Herr Jesu Christ, einiger Trost, zu dir will ich mich wenden' ('Lord Jesus Christ, sole comfort, to Thee will I myself turn')
SATB. As No. 1. Insts. with voices. Cont

The twelfth verse of the anonymous hymn above, 'Herr Jesu Christ, ich schrei zu dir' (1620) set to its own melody.

Wo soll ich fliehen hin? (Where shall I fly to?).
Chorale Cantata BWV 5. Leipzig, 1724.

1 CHORUS
(As above)
SATB. Ob i, ii, Vln i, ii, Vla, Tr da tirarsi with S. Cont

The libretto is based on Johann Heermann's hymn with the above title (1630) set in Nos. 1 and 7 to verses i and xi to a melody of secular origin. The remaining verses are paraphrased. The sopranos have the *cantus firmus* in long notes, with the lower parts deriving their thematic phrases from it. The orchestral ritornellos—also derived from the *cantus firmus*—express great unease, which gradually infects the lower voices, especially at the agitated cry, 'If all the world offers help it would not take away my agony'.

2 RECITATIVE
'Der Sünden Wust hat mich nicht nur befleckt, er hat vielmehr den ganzen Geist bedeckt' ('The sins' dirt has not only stained me it has rather covered my whole spirit')
B. Cont

3 ARIA
'Ergiesse dich reichlich, du göttliche Quelle, ach walle mit blutigen Strömen auf mich' ('Pour out thyself richly, thou divine spring, ah pour on me in streams of blood')
T. Vla solo, Cont
This is the only instance known of Bach's use of the viola as an obbligato instrument. He gives it a gloriously broad and warm-hearted melody, a veritable welling out of the divine spring. The melodious main motif, heard only in the voice part, expresses intense gratitude for newly found happiness.

4 RECITATIVE
'Mein treuer Heiland tröstet mich, es sei verscharrt in seinem Grabe' ('My faithful Saviour comforts me, let it be buried in His grave')
A. Ob i, Cont
The solo oboe plays the melody of the concluding chorale, 'Lead also my heart and my mind thither', in the course of the recitative which speaks of the inestimable blood of Jesus as the soul's highest good and treasure.

5 ARIA
'Verstumme, Höllenheer, du machst mich nicht verzagt' ('Silence, hell's host, thou makst me not disheartened')
B. Tr, Ob i, ii and Vln i (unis.), Vln ii, Vla, Cont
One of the finest of Bach's many grand battle arias for bass. The trumpet rings out and seems to mock, in the triplet figures follow-

ing, the scattered hosts of Hell. The bass spits out 'Silence, hell's host' over and over again and the disheartenment is all on the enemy's side.

6 RECITATIVE
'Ich bin ja nur das kleinste Teil der Welt, und da des Blutes edler Saft unendlich gross Kraft bewährt erhält, so lass dein Blut ja nicht an mir verderben, es komme mir nun gut, dass ich den Himmel kann ererben' ('I am indeed only the smallest part of the world, and as the blood's sublime sap boundlessly contains great strength itself . . . so let Thy blood not be lost in me, may it come to me for good that I can inherit Heaven')
S. Cont
An unexpectedly naïve and charming little recitative.

7 CHORALE
'Führ auch mein Herz und Sinn durch deinen Geist dahin, dass ich mög alles meiden, was mich und dich kann scheiden' ('Lead also my heart and mind through Thy spirit thither, that I may everything avoid that me from Thee can separate')
SATB. As No. 1. Insts. with voices. Cont

Ich will den Kreuzstab gerne tragen (I will the cross-staff gladly carry).
Solo Cantata BWV 56. Leipzig, 1726.

1 ARIA
(As above)
B. Ob i, ii with Vln i, ii, Te with Vla, Cont
The librettist, taking a hint from the Gospel for the day ('he entered into a ship and passed over') introduces the medieval conception of life as a voyage over the sea, used in various forms down the centuries and much loved by baroque writers. The ship and the storms it encounters represent the individual soul, its passions and emotions, and this cantata pictures the voyager setting out to the port from which he hopes to sail to Heaven. Bach makes it clear that the cross is a heavy burden by putting 'cross' on a C sharp in the singer's opening phrase. It is a burden gladly carried because 'it comes from God's dear hand'.
There are long-drawn descriptive phrases at 'carry' as the weary man makes his way, stumbling along, but very tender

ones as he remembers who imposed the cross on him and is leading him to the Promised Land. At these last words, in the middle section, his voice rises up in sequential phrases of great beauty but 'troubles' is given an extended phrase again full of pain. Then, before the *da capo*, comes a marvellous arioso. He will lay his sorrows in the grave where the Saviour will wipe away his tears. The 'tear motif' is woven into the orchestral part and the C sharp, at once flattened to C natural in the concluding phrase, is one of Bach's most subtle touches. It would take pages to describe the varied beauties of this wonderful movement.

2 RECITATIVE
'Mein Wandel auf der Welt ist einer Schiffahrt gleich' ('My wandering in the world is like a ship-journey')
B. V'cello, Cont

This is the direct application of the allegory. The cello illustrates the waves, the voice part the afflictions, crosses, and distress of the voyage, but God's pity is the anchor that holds him. God cries, 'I am with you, I will not forsake you.' Suddenly the raging sea of troubles ends, the waves die down and sustained chords alone accompany the concluding words, 'So step I out of the ship into my city, which is the heavenly kingdom where I am with the righteous'.

3 ARIA
'Endlich, endlich wird mein Joch wieder von mir weichen müssen' ('At last my yoke again from me must fall')
B. Ob solo, Cont

This aria is one of unrestrained joy. There are extended runs on 'yoke' and 'fall' with the oboe echoing the rejoicing and a prayer in the middle section, 'Oh that it might happen this day'.

4 RECITATIVE
'Ich stehe fertig und bereit, das Erbe meiner Seligkeit mit Sehnen und Verlangen von Jesu Händen zu empfangen' ('I stand ready and prepared, the inheritance of my blessedness with longing and yearning from Jesus's hands to receive')
B. Vln i, ii, Vla, Cont

The above words are sung to the accompaniment of sustained strings, after which Bach writes *adagio* as the now happy man recalls the day when, filled with sorrow for sins, he could only see the Promised Land from afar. The music is a variant of the arioso before the *da capo* in No. 1. He remembers his prayer that the

Saviour will wipe away his tears. In the last vocal phrase 'Saviour' is placed on the highest note in the section. The 'tear motif' on the strings concludes the movement, the cadence having the finality of the leading note falling to the tonic.

5 CHORALE
'Komm, o Tod, du Schlafes Bruder, komm und führe mich nur fort' ('Come, O death, thou sleep's brother, come and lead me only away')
SATB. As No. 1. Insts. with voices

The sixth verse of Johann Franck's 'Du, o schönes Weltgebäude' (1653) set to Johann Crüger's melody (1649).

The words are charming, 'Loose my little ship's rudder, bring me to safe port for through thee I come to the fairest Jesus'.

TWENTIETH SUNDAY AFTER TRINITY

Epistle: Eph. v. 15–21 (Avoid bad company).
Gospel: Matt. xxii. 1–14 (Parable of the marriage of the king's son).

Ach! Ich sehe, jetzt, da ich zur Hochzeit gehe (Ah! I see, now as I to the marriage go).

Solo Cantata BWV 162. Weimar, 1715. Libretto by Salomo Franck.

1 ARIA
(As above)
B. Cor da tirarsi, Vln i, ii, Vla, Fag, Cont

The text goes on to describe what is seen on the way to the marriage feast, 'weal and woe, soul-poison and life's bread, heaven, hell, life, death, heaven's splendour and hell's flames'. No wonder the last line is 'Jesu, help, that I endure'! The parable is consistent with the Gospel inasmuch as in the end bad, as well as good guests were impressed by the infuriated king's servants. The obsessive figure in the continuo, present almost throughout, the dense string parts and the declamatory voice part make a disturbing picture of one of those who had heard what had happened to the guests who were invited and stayed away. (The orchestral instruments do not play again until the concluding chorale.)

2 RECITATIVE
'O grosses Hochzeitsfest, dazu der Himmelskönig die Menschen rufen lässt' ('O great wedding feast to which heaven's King mankind calls')
T. Cont

It is the bride—that is the world—who speaks, at some length. The text pleads unworthiness and recalls the first verse of Psalm cx, 'Heaven is His throne, the earth serves as a stool for His feet, yet will He this world as bride and beloved kiss'. All is ready for the banquet: he who comes guided by faith is blessed, he who despises the meal is cursed.

3 ARIA
'Jesu, Brunnquell aller Gnaden, labe mich elenden Gast, weil du mich berufen hat' ('Jesu, spring of all mercies, lave me, poor guest, because thou hast called me')
S. Cont

301

One of Bach's lovely flowing 12/8 arias, endowed with a superb bass part. There is one very moving feature of the first section: each line of the text begins with 'Jesu' and to the Holy name Bach gives a little motif which breathes forth tender love.

4 RECITATIVE
'Mein Jesu, lass mich nicht zur Hochzeit unbekleidet kommen, dass mich nicht treffe dein Gericht' ('My Jesus, let me not come to the wedding unclad so that upon me thy judgement lights not')
A. Cont

The text tells the story of the unfortunate guest who had no wedding garment and was cast out. It goes on to pray that the speaker, though unworthy, be given the robe of salvation for the feast of the Lamb.

5 DUET
'In meinem Gott bin ich erfreut, die Liebesmacht hat ihn bewogen' ('In my God am I rejoiced, the love-might has moved Him')
A.T. Cont

This attractive, if lengthy duet, is an expression of joy by those clad in the garments of righteousness who will also be given a white robe of honour in Heaven. It carols happily along with sections in canon, parallel thirds and sixths, and extended runs on 'rejoiced'.

6 CHORALE
'Ach, ich habe schon erblicket diese grosse Herrlichkeit' ('Ah, I have already perceived this great glory')
SATB. As No. 1. Insts. with voices. Cont

The glory is being 'beautifully adorned with heaven's white robe and wearing a gold crown, standing before God's throne'.

The seventh verse of Johann Georg Albinus' 'Alle Menschen müssen sterben' (1652) to an anonymous melody.

**Schmücke dich, o liebe Seele, lass die dunkle Sünden-
höhle, komm an's helle Licht gegangen** (Adorn thyself,
O dear soul, leave the dark sin-hole, come forth into the
radiant light).
Chorale Cantata BWV 180. Leipzig, 1724.

Mendelssohn and Schumann went into raptures over the organ
chorale prelude Bach wrote on the melody by Johann Crüger set to
Johann Franck's hymn with the above title. They seem to have been
unaware of the existence of this lovely cantata in which Verses
i, iv and ix are set in their original form in Nos. 1, 3 and 7, the other
verses being paraphrased.

1 CHORUS
(As above)
SATB. Fl i, ii, Ob, Ob da cacc, Vln i, ii, Vla, Cont
   The melody, foreshadowed in long notes on the oboe at the
start of the movement, and by hints of it on the strings and
continuo, is sung by the sopranos in its proper rhythmic form,
but in notes of double the value of those in the concluding number.
Except for a reference to the 'dark sin-hole' this is a happy cantata
in which, as this verse relates, the guest invited by 'the Lord full
of salvation and mercy' does turn up and in a garment as beautifully woven, no doubt, as this movement.

2 ARIA
'Ermuntre dich: dein Heiland klopft, ach öffne bald die
Herzenspforte!' ('Arouse thyself, thy Saviour knocks, ah open
soon the heart's-door!')
T. Fl trav, Cont
   The libretto follows the chronology of the parable sufficiently
to picture the invitation to the feast being delivered by the King
—that is, by the Saviour Himself. Bach depicts the knocking less
realistically than in Cantata BWV 61 but none the less unmistakably. The flute expresses, in its wide-flung motif, the joy the
summons brings to the soul. The words in the middle section
suggest that the soul, overcome with joy, cannot find words to
reply to the Saviour, and this is reflected in a break in the vocal
part.

3 RECITATIVE
'Wie teuer sind des heilgen Mahles Gaben? Sie finden ihres

303

Gleichen nicht' ('How precious are the holy feast's gifts? There is not their equal')
S. V'cello picc, Cont

The recitative is followed by an arioso covering the fourth verse of the chorale but with the melody very attractively decorated. At this point the violoncello piccolo is brought in to represent the yearning to taste the Cup of Life.

4 RECITATIVE
'Mein Herz fühlt in sich Furcht und Freude' ('My heart is filled with fear and joy')
A. Fl i, ii, Cont

The usual Lutheran mixture but the presence of the flutes shows that the larger part is joy.

5 ARIA
'Lebens Sonne, Licht der Sinnen, Herr, der du mein Alles bist' ('Life's sun, light of the senses, Lord, Thou who my all art')
S. Fl i, ii, Ob, Ob da cacc, Vln i, ii, Vla, Cont

One of those enchanting arias with a little lift in the melody in orchestra and voice that rejoices the heart. All the instruments, except oboe ii and the viola, double the melody, giving a fine sonority to the introductory bars and in the ritornellos.

6 RECITATIVE
'Herr, lass' an mir dein treues Lieben . . . ja nicht vergeblich sein' ('Lord, let in me Thy true love . . . not be fruitless')
B. Cont

A prayer that the spirit kindled by Christ's love may not fail in faith and always remember that love.

7 CHORALE
'Jesu, wahres Brot des Lebens, hilf, dass ich doch nicht vergebens . . . zu deinem Tisch geladen . . . dass ich auch, wie jetzt auf Erden, mög ein Gast im Himmel werden' ('Jesus, true bread of life, help that I not vainly . . . to Thy table be invited . . . that as now on earth I may be a guest in Heaven')
SATB. Cont. Instrumentation not stated

Ich geh und suche mit Verlangen (I go and seek with longing).
Solo Cantata BWV 49. Leipzig, 1726.

It has long been established that the 'Song of songs, which is Solomon's' is not his at all, nor a continuous work, but an anthology of love poems compiled some time after his death. These erotic poems have been interpreted by Christian exegetes since the third century as a description of God's relations with the Church or the individual soul. St John of the Cross found in its language the only way of explaining the second of these relationships and the librettist of this cantata applies it in similar if more restrained—and commonplace—imagery to the same purpose.

1 SINFONIA
Ob d'am, Vln i, ii, Vla, Org obb. Cont

In Cantata 169 Bach used the first and second movements of his E major Clavier Concerto (BWV 1053) in the first and fifth numbers of that work and now starts off here with the third movement. It is no more relevant to what follows than in those other instances, unless it is taken to illustrate the general joy of a marriage feast.

2 ARIA
(As above)
B. Org obb. Cont

The organ, always independent of the continuo, announces a theme it maintains for most of the length of the aria. The soul, sought with longing, is described as 'my dove, my fairest Bride' in a charming duet of sequences between voice and organ.

3 RECITATIVE
'Mein Mahl ist zubereit' und meine Hochzeitstafel fertig, nur meine Braut ist noch nicht gegenwärtig' ('My meal is prepared, and my marriage-table ready, only my Bride is not yet present') S.B. Vln i, ii, Vla, Org, Cont

There is no question here of a reluctant guest. At Jesus's words her heart is rejoiced. The solo bass quotes the first phrases of the preceding aria—a very effective touch—and the soprano replies, 'My Bridegroom, I fall at Thy feet', in a phrase that precisely describes that action. The tempo changes to 3/8 for a

w

delightful little duet, 'Come most beautiful (one) come and let Thyself be kissed . . . Come, beloved Bride, and hasten the wedding garments to don', and so forth.

4 ARIA

'Ich bin herrlich, ich bin schön, meinen Heiland zu entzünden' ('I am glorious, I am beautiful, my Saviour to inflame')
S. Ob d'am, V'cello picc, Org, Cont

The middle section has the words, 'His salvation's justice is my ornament and honour garment and therewith will I endure when I shall to Heaven go'. The last words are the clue to the continually aspiring nature of the lovely melody of the aria.

5 RECITATIVE

'Mein Glaube hat mich selbst so angezogen' ('My faith has me myself so clothed')
S.B. Org, Cont

A duet, but this time in recitative. The Bridegroom replies, 'So remains my heart to thee affectionate, so shall I with Thee in eternity be wedded and affianced'. He ends, 'Be till death faithful, so place I on Thee the life-crown.' Here the leading note falls to the tonic with the finality the words imply.

6 DUET

'Dich hab ich je und je geliebet, und darum zieh ich dich zu mir' ('Thee have I ever and ever loved, and therefore draw I Thee to me')
S.B. Ob d'am with Vln i, Vln ii, Vla, Org obb. Cont

In this long but entrancing duet the soprano sings verse vii of Philipp Nicolai's hymn, 'Wie schön leuchtet der Morgenstern' (see p. 99) to words which begin, 'How heartily glad I am that my treasure is the A and O [Alpha and Omega]'. The words of the bass's part come from Jeremiah XXXI. 3 and Revelations III. 20.

TWENTY-FIRST SUNDAY
AFTER TRINITY

Epistle: Eph. vi. 10–17 (Put on the armour of God).
Gospel: John iv. 46–54 (The nobleman's son healed).

Ich glaube, lieber Herr, hilf meinem Unglauben! (I believe, Lord, help my unbelief).
Cantata BWV 109. Leipzig, 1723.

1 CHORUS
(As above)
SATB. Cor da cacc, Ob i, ii, Vln i, ii, Vla, Cont

The text comes from St Mark ix. 24, which concerns the healing of the epileptic boy whose father cried out the words quoted in answer to Jesus's saying, 'All things are possible to him that believeth'. It may be that the librettist chose this text and not that of the healing of the boy with a fever described in the Gospel for the day, whose father had no doubts, so as to link the hesitant man with St Paul's great passage from the Epistle for the day beginning 'Finally be strong in the Lord and put on the strength of His might' so as to resist the principalities and powers.

The antithesis draws from Bach a striking opening movement. The main motif in the orchestral part is a group of four notes, rarely absent from the score, but never used in the vocal parts.

When the ritornello ends the soprano bursts out with the first words of the text in a fine declamatory phrase. In the course of the movement, solo alto, bass and tenor all have similar entries. 'Unbelief' is set to extended phrases six times, 'believe' not even to one, which shows where Bach wishes to put the emphasis.

2 RECITATIVE
'Des Herren Hand ist ja noch nicht verkürzt, mir kann geholfen worden' ('The Lord's hand is indeed not yet shortened, I can be helped')
T. Cont

This line is marked *forte*, but the next one, a wavering of faith, *piano*. 'Ah no, I sink already to the earth from care, that it smites me to the ground'. This alternation, unique in Bach's recitatives, continues to the arioso at the end, 'Ah Lord! how long?'

3 ARIA

'Wie zweifelhaftig ist mein Hoffen, wie wankct mein geängstigt Herz' ('How doubting is my hope, how totters my anguished heart')

T. Vln i, ii, Vla, Cont

The text speaks of 'the bruised reed he will not break, the dimly burning wick he will not quench' (Isaiah XLII. 3). The 'tottering' heart is vividly illustrated, 'pain' is placed on a sustained note, followed by a pause-mark the first time it comes into the text, and given a run like that at 'totters' just before the *da capo*.

4 RECITATIVE

'O fasse dich, du zweifelhafter Mut, weil Jesus jetzt noch Wunder tut' ('O contain thyself, thou doubting mind, because Jesus now still does wonders')

A. Cont

Sanity begins to return and introspection to disappear. Faith's eyes should look at the salvation of the Lord and build on its promise.

5 ARIA

'Der Heiland kennet ja die Seinen, wenn ihre Hoffnung hilflos liegt' ('The Saviour knows, yea, His own, when their hope helpless lies')

A. Ob i, ii, Cont

This melodious aria falls gratefully on the ear and is peaceful up to the middle section, which speaks of the wrestling of flesh and spirit but ends with an assurance of faith conquering.

6 CHORALE

'Wer hofft in Gott und dem vertraut, der wird nimmer zu Schanden' ('Who hopes in God and Him trusts he will never be shamed')

SATB. As No. 1. Insts. with voices

The seventh verse of Lazarus Spengler's 'Durch Adams Fall ist ganz verderbt' (1529) set to its original melody in this splendid and extended chorale.

Aus tiefer Not schrei ich zu dir (From depths of woe cry I to Thee).

Chorale Cantata BWV 38. Leipzig, 1724.

1 CHORUS

(As above)

SATB. Trb i, ii, iii, iv, Ob i, ii, Vln i, ii, Vla, all with voices. Cont

The libretto is based on Luther's version of Psalm cxxx, 'Out of the depths I cry to Thee, O Lord'. Verses i and v are set to the original melody in Nos. 1 and 6. Verses ii–iv are paraphrased in Nos. 2, 3 and 5; No. 4 refers to the Gospel. Bach, with sure instinct, cast the opening chorus in the strict form of those of Pachelbel's organ chorale preludes in which the lower parts anticipate the entry of the *cantus firmus*, sung in the top part. There is no instrumental prelude, the basses at once begin a fugue on the melody. The chorale, sung at Luther's funeral, makes an overwhelming impression in this motet-like movement. The emotion reaches its height in the chromatic phrases in the underparts at the words, 'Whatever sin and wrong is done, who can, Lord, before Thee remain?'

2 RECITATIVE

'In Jesu Gnade wird allein der Trost für uns und die Vergebung sein' ('In Jesu's mercy will alone the comfort for us and the pardon be')
A. Cont

Without that, the text continues, mankind would be wholly subject to Satan.

3 ARIA

'Ich höre mitten in dem Leiden ein Trostwort, so mein Jesu spricht' ('I hear in the midst of suffering a comfort-word, which my Jesus speaks')
T. Ob i, ii, Cont

This aria has been severely criticized for its faulty declamation —which shows at once in the opening vocal phrase—but the music does reflect in general the spirit of the words and in view of the succeeding movements offers the contrast of melodiousness and simplicity.

4 RECITATIVE

'Ach! dass mein Glaube noch so schwach, und dass ich mein

309

Vertrauen auf seichtem Grunde muss erbauen' ('Ah! that my faith is still so weak, and that I my confidence on a shallow foundation must build')
S. Cont

This recitative is marked 'battuta', that is, strict tempo, and the reason for the direction will be found in the continuo part, which is given the melody of the chorale throughout but without any pauses. This is unique in the cantatas.

5 TERZETT
'Wenn meine Trübsal als mit Ketten ein Unglück an den andern hält' ('When my affliction as with chains one misfortune with the others links')
S.A.B. Cont

Bach emphasizes, in this trio—one of the five in the cantatas —the 'chains' with extended phrases. The three phrases with repeated notes in the introductory bars for the continuo point to the certainty that the Saviour will come to the rescue of the heavily burdened soul, expressed later in the text.

6 CHORALE
'Ob bei uns ist der Sünden viel, bei Gott ist viel mehr Gnade' ('Although among us is sin abundant, with God is much more grace')
SATB. As No. 1. Insts. with voices

To illustrate the opening line Bach begins with a discord which even in our time produces a dramatic effect, but the remainder of the verse puts its trust in the Good Shepherd, redeemer of all sins.

Was Gott tut, das ist wohlgetan (What God doth, surely that is right).
Chorale Cantata BWV 98. Leipzig, 1726.

1 CHORUS
(As above)
SATB. Ob i, ii, Te with S.A.T., Vln i, ii, Vla, Cont

This is Bach's first setting of Samuel Rodigast's hymn with the above title. The other two cantatas that use it will be found on pp. 268 and 270. The only words repeated are those of the opening line in which the sopranos have the melody in the original rhythm. The movement is in the form of an extended chorale with the first violins alone given a melodic part of any consequence.

310

2 RECITATIVE
'Ach Gott! wann wirst du mich einmal von meiner Leiden Qual,
von meiner Angst befreien?' ('Ah God! when wilt Thou me from
my sorrow's torment, from my anxiety free?')
T. Cont

3 ARIA
'Hört, ihr Augen, auf zu weinen, trag ich doch mit Geduld mein
schweres Joch' ('Cease, ye eyes, to weep, I carry yet with patience
my heavy yoke')
S. Ob solo, Cont

In spite of the confidence in God proclaimed at the end of the
expressive recitative above, this aria is bedewed with tears,
depicted in Bach's familiar two-note groups, but a more cheerful
note comes into the vocal part in the middle section at the words,
'God the Father lives, yet of His own leaves'. Here the vocal line
is enlivened by some triplet phrases but the oboe brings in the
'tear motif' towards the end of the section and so leads to the *da
capo*.

4 RECITATIVE
'Gott hat ein Herz, das des Erbarmens Überfluss' ('God has a
heart, that [is] pity's abundance')
A. Cont

The text includes the line, 'He keeps His word; knock, so will
to you be opened', which is a paraphrase of St Matthew VII. 7,
'Seek, and ye shall find; knock, and it shall be opened unto you.'

5 ARIA
'Meinen Jesum lass ich nicht, bis mich erst sein Angesicht wird
erhören oder segnen' ('My Jesus leave I not till first His presence
will hear or bless me')
B. Vln i, ii, (unis.), Cont

Terry first suggested that Bach clearly had in mind, in this
aria, Andreas Hammerschmidt's melody (1658) with the above
title but he makes use only of its first phrase and this is well
concealed in the florid vocal line. The violins have a delightful
lilting part in which the opening phrase is constantly repeated and
indeed is the truly joyous element.

Bach did not include the chorale which we can be sure would
have been sung as he does not write his usual *Fine S.D.G.* ('End,
to God alone the glory') at the close of the aria, but it is easy to
add the verse of a suitable hymn when the cantata is performed.

Ich habe meine Zuversicht auf den getreuen Gott gericht (I have my confidence on the faithful God placed).
Solo Cantata BWV 188. Leipzig, 1728. Libretto by Picander.

A note on the only copy of the score of this cantata indicates that Bach meant the first movement of the D minor Clavier Concerto, which he had adapted for the Sinfonia at the start of Cantata 146, to be played in the same place in this one.

1 ARIA
(As above)
T. Ob, Vln i, ii, Vla, Cont

There is no wavering of faith in this cantata. The melodious tenor aria is an affirmation of complete trust, for in God, 'my hope rests secure'. The text of the middle section asserts that this trust will hold firm 'when all breaks, when all falls, when nobody faithfulness and belief holds', words illustrated by detached falling arpeggios for the oboe and agitation in the strings until the last line before the *da capo*, 'So is yet God the best of all'.

2 RECITATIVE
'Gott meint es gut mit jedermann, auch in den allergrössten Nöten' ('God means it well with everyman even in the all-greatest need')
B. Cont

God may seem to conceal His love but 'even if he killed me I would still hope in Him'. His anger is like a dark cloud that hides the sun. The recitative ends with a short arioso in 6/8 time. 'Therefore I cling to Him then so that He may bless me.'

3 ARIA
'Unerforschlich ist die Weise, wie der Herr die Seine führt' ('Unfathomable is the way in which the Lord His own guides')
A. V'cello, Org obb.

Whittaker considers that the addition of the vocal part makes the number sound laboured. A look at the score shows how true this is, the more the pity, for it is quite a long aria. This is a case of a faulty adaptation of a previously existing movement.

4 RECITATIVE
'Die Macht der Welt verlieret sich, wer kann auf Stand und Hoheit bauen? Gott aber bleibet ewiglich. Wohl allen, die auf ihn vertrauen' ('The might of the world loses itself, who can on

rank and position build? But God abides eternally, it is well for all who in Him trust')
S. Vln i, ii, Vla, Cont

You never know with Bach. He comes up here with a fine dramatic picture of the passing of the world's might (double-stopping reiterated chords in the strings) and a radiant conclusion in the closing bars.

5 CHORALE
'Auf meinen lieben Gott trau ich in Angst und Not' ('On my beloved God I rely in anguish and need')
SATB. Cont. Instrumentation not stated

This is the first verse of Sigismund Weingärtner's hymn (1607) with the above title set to its melody (1609). The latter is adapted from a secular song, 'Venus, du und dein Kind', one of many instances of the kind familiar in the Masses of sixteenth-century polyphonic and later composers.

TWENTY-SECOND SUNDAY
AFTER TRINITY

Epistle: Phil. I. 3–11 (Paul's love for the Philippians).
Gospel: Matt. xviii. 23–35 (Parable of the unmerciful servant).

Was soll ich aus dir machen, Ephraim? (What shall I of thee make, Ephraim?).
Solo Cantata BWV 89. Leipzig, 1723.

1 ARIA
(As above)
B. Ob i, ii, Cor, Vln i, ii, Vla, Cont

The tremendous, indeed terrifying, outburst of God's anger against Ephraim and Israel was occasioned by their worship of false gods. The text comes from Hosea xi. 8, and is related to the parable of the unjust servant, except that he was tortured until he had paid his due whereas the second half of the aria shows that, 'God is of another mind'. He is reluctant to treat Ephraim and Israel and their people as He did the cities of Admah and Zeboim (two of the cities of the plain destroyed with Sodom and Gomorrah). His heart recoils, his compassion grows warm and tender. 'I am God and not man; the Holy One in the midst of thee.'

This middle section would be something of an anti-climax if Bach had radically changed the character of the music, but he has not. The question lingers in the mind: did He think Israel worth preserving—or will He if they offend again?

Three themes appear in the opening ritornello: (*a*) in the continuo, a figure symbolic of God's anger, (*b*) the rise and fall of the terrible question on the strings, (*c*) the cries of the threatened on the oboes. The voice part, which repeats the question twice, with an awesome pause after each one, is declamatory but softens somewhat at 'But my heart is of another mind', seven times repeated. The muttering in the orchestra, however, only ceases as God speaks of His 'burning compassion'. The repeat of the orchestral introduction leaves no room for complacence.

2 RECITATIVE
'Ja, freilich sollte Gott ein Wort zum Urteil sprechen, und seines Namens Spott an seinen Feinden rächen' ('Yea, verily God should

speak a word of judgement and avenge His name-mocking on His enemies')
A. Cont

The unjust servant is mentioned in the course of this recitative as oppressing the neighbour for his debt and thus calling down judgement on himself.

3 ARIA
'Ein unbarmherziges Gerichte wird über dich gewiss ergehn' ('An unpitying judgement will on thee surely fall')
A. Cont

The creditor is unmercifully trounced in this austere aria in which James II. 13 is quoted for the line, 'For judgement is without mercy to one who has shown no mercy', and 'God's anger will destroy such, as He destroyed Sodom'.

4 RECITATIVE
'Wohlan! mein Herze legt Zorn, Zank, und Zwietract hin; es ist bereit, dem Nächsten zu vergeben' ('Well then! My heart puts anger, quarrel and discord away; it is ready the neighbour to pardon')
S. Cont

5 ARIA
'Gerechter Gott, ach, rechnest du? So werde ich zum Heil der Seelen die Tropfen Blut von Jesu zählen' ('Righteous God, ah reckonest Thou? So shall I for the salvation of souls the drops of blood from Jesus count')
S. Ob, Cont

A beautifully flowing and tuneful aria in the major key with a very grateful melodic line for the singer. The image of the angry and vengeful God of the Old Testament so powerfully drawn in the first section of the opening aria is effectually banished.

6 CHORALE
'Mir mangelt zwar sehr viel, doch, was ich haben will ist alles mir zu Gute' ('Indeed I lack very much, yet, what I wish to have is everything good for me')
SATB. As No. 1. Insts. with voices. Cont

Verse vii of Johann Heermann's hymn, 'Wo soll ich fliehen hin' to the melody of the chorale sung at the close of Cantata BWV 188 (p. 312).

Mache dich, mein Geist, bereit (Make thyself, my spirit, ready).

Chorale Cantata BWV 115. Leipzig, 1724.

1 CHORUS

(As above)

SATB. Fl trav, Ob d'am, Vln i, ii and Vla (unis.), Cor with S. Cont

The libretto is based on Johann Burkhard Freystein's hymn (1697) set in Nos. 1 and 6 to the anonymous melody (1694) to 'Straf mich nicht in deinem Zorn'. The other verses of the hymn are paraphrased.

Christ concluded the parable of the wicked servant (the Gospel for the day) who was delivered up to the jailers until he paid all his debt with 'So also shall my heavenly Father do unto you, if ye do not forgive your brother from your heart'. Hence the choice of this chorale with its emphasis on the Last Judgement. The soul is warned to watch and pray, to beware of Satan's wiles, and always to be ready for the Last Judgement. It is refreshing to find that the music expresses trust, not threats. This is conveyed in the opening prelude by the strong little figure in the continuo part above which the widely ranging and lively theme, at first on the strings, is the spur to spirited activity.

The sopranos have the melody of the chorale doubled by the horn.

2 ARIA

'Ach, schläfrige Seele, wie? ruhest du noch? Ermuntre dich doch' ('Ah, sleepy soul, what? resteth thou yet? Rouse thyself then')

A. Ob d'am, Vln i, ii, Vla, Cont

The soul has not heeded the warning. One is reminded of St Augustine's words, 'Wake me up, Lord, but not just yet'! In the second section of the aria the tempo changes from *adagio* to *allegro* and urgent runs, on the voice and orchestra, repeat the warning to watch, not be awakened by punishment and, as a few measures of the *adagio* return, not be enwrapped in the sleep of death.

3 RECITATIVE

'Gott, so für deine Seele wacht, hat Abscheu an der Sünden Nacht' ('God, who for Thy soul watches, has abhorrence of the sin-night')

B. Cont

No threats. God, in His mercy and according to His promises, sends light to open the eyes of the blind spirit, which is attached to worldly values.

4 ARIA

'Bete aber auch dabei, mitten in der Wachen' ('Pray yet also in the midst of watching')

S. Fl trav, V'cello picc, Cont

Molto adagio is the tempo of this beautiful aria, expressive of God's patience. He asks only that the soul, however guilty of sin, will pray and so be freed by his Maker of his sins. An interesting and significant feature in the parts of the accompanying instruments is a slide from a lower to an upper note, emphasizing the pleading of the now really awakened soul.

5 RECITATIVE

'Er sehnet sich nach unserm Schreien, er neigt sein gnädig Ohr hierauf' ('He troubles Himself about our crying, He bends His merciful ear to this')

T. Cont

The recitative ends with an arioso, '[He] will as a helper come'.

6 CHORALE

'Drum so lasst uns immerdar wachen, flehen, beten' ('Therefore so let us perpetually watch, implore, pray')

SATB. As No. 1. Insts. with voices. Cont

The two final lines are grim. 'The time is not far when God will judge us and annihilate the world.'

Ich armer Mensch, ich Sündenknecht (I wretched man, I, slave of sin).

Solo Cantata BWV 55. Leipzig, 1726.

1 ARIA

(As above)

T. Fl trav, Ob d'am, Vln i, ii, Cont

The libretto dwells on the theme of a guilt-ridden sinner, picturing himself in this aria before the judgement seat of God.

As in the tenor aria 'Ach, schlage doch bald, sel'ge Stunde' in Cantata 95 (see p. 274) Bach keeps his singer at the top of the stave, and above, for the best part of this aria, which is poignant, whereas the other is severe. Both arias depend for their effect on a voice able to scale these heights without strain. The orchestral introduction pictures the sinner in phrases eloquent of his unhappy condition. He repeats his self-accusation five times and then at 'I go before God's countenance with fear and trembling to judgement' his voice rises in phrase by phrase of awe, as he, the unrighteous, faces the righteous.

2 RECITATIVE
'Ich habe wider Gott gehandelt' ('I have against God acted')
T. Cont

He bewails not having followed the path God prescribed and cries out for wings to fly to Heaven, where dwells the God who speaks to him of judgement. Bach places 'God' on a high B flat with startling effect.

3 ARIA
'Erbarme dich, lass die Tränen dich erweichen, lass sie dir zum Herzen reichen' ('Have mercy, let the tears Thee soften, let them to Thy heart reach')
T. Fl trav, Cont

This number can be placed alongside the alto aria in the St Matthew Passion, which begins with the same words and almost the same opening phrases. The tear motif comes here into both the voice and flute parts, and prominently in the second section after the ritornello. The many agitated arabesques for the flute betoken the anguish in the sinner's soul. There is no *da capo* to this superb aria.

4 RECITATIVE
'Erbarme dich! jedoch nun tröst ich mich, ich will nicht vor Gerichte stehen, und lieber vor den Gnadenthron zu meinem frommen Vater gehen' ('Have mercy! Yet now I comfort myself, I shall not before judgement stand and rather go before the mercy-throne to my righteous Father')
T. Vln i, ii, Vla, Cont

The strings put a tender glow of tone round the very different sentiments, and as the singer ends they play an 'Amen' cadence at a high pitch.

318

5 CHORALE
'Bin ich gleich von dir gewichen, stell ich mich doch wieder ein'
('Although I have turned aside from Thee, yet I return')
SATB. Fl. trav, Ob, Vln i, ii, Vla, all with voices, Cont

This is the sixth verse of Johann Rist's 'Werde munter, mein
Gemüte' (1642) set to Johann Schop's melody of that date.

TWENTY-THIRD SUNDAY
AFTER TRINITY

Epistle: Phil. III. 17–21 (Follow not carnal things, as many do).
Gospel: Matt. XXII. 15–22 (The Pharisees and the tribute to Caesar).

Nur jedem das Seine (Only to each his due).
Solo Cantata BWV 163. Weimar, 1715. Libretto by Salomo Franck.

1 ARIA
(As above)
T. Ob d'am, Vln, Vla, V'cello, Cont

Franck's libretto makes excellent use, as we shall see, of both the Epistle and Gospel. The text of this aria paraphrases Christ's answer to the Pharisees' cunningly devised question as to whether it was lawful to pay taxes to Caesar, or not. 'Pay what thou owest to highest and lowest but render your heart only to God.'

The melody, begun by cello and continuo and taken up by the oboe d'amore, seems to represent a cheerful giver, so it is amusing to remember how annoyed Bach was to have duty levied by Customs and Excise on a present of wine during his residence at Leipzig. The text speaks of not refusing the obligation to pay tax, adding after the sentence a mark of exclamation, either by Franck or, more likely, by Bach himself.

2 RECITATIVE
'Du bist mein Gott, der Geber aller Gaben, wir haben, was wir haben, allein von deiner Hand' ('Thou art my God, the giver of all gifts, we have what we have alone from Thine hand')
B. Cont

Hence we must render as tribute the money of gratitude we owe Him but, at the end of the recitative, this coinage is denounced as false, stamped with Satan's image: a typical application, contradicted in the aria following.

3 ARIA
'Lass mein Herz die Münze sein, die ich dir, mein Jesu, steu're' ('Let my heart the coin be, that I to Thee, my Jesu, pay')
B. V'cello obb. i, ii, Cont

The cellos and the voice go cheerfully and melodiously along and when the words in the second section which ask God to

320

restore the tarnished coin to its original lustre are reached, the first cello underlines the word 'shining' with a sustained note followed by a joyous run of triplets, and the voice has delightful detached phrases addressed to the angelic minters, 'Come, work, melt and stamp'.

4 RECITATIVE
'Ich wollte dir, o Gott, das Herze gerne geben, der Will ist zwar bei mir' ('I would to Thee, O God, the heart gladly give, the will is indeed in me')
S.A. Cont

This is really an extended arioso duet expressing the fear that flesh and blood will strive to tarnish the shining coin—here the libretto takes another cue from the Epistle and its denunciation of the worldly, but ends with a prayer that God will fill the heart with grace and empty it of worldly desires.

5 DUET
'Nimm mich mir und gib mich dir . . . deinen Willen zu erfüllen' ('Take me from myself and give me to Thee . . . Thy will to fulfil')
S.A. Vlns i, ii, Vla (unis.) Cont

Bach introduces into this endearing duet the melody by Andreas Hammerschmidt (1658), to Christian Keimann's hymn, 'Meinen Jesum lass ich nicht' (1658), the point of which would be understood by the congregation as referring to the words of the first verse, which speak of Jesus being crucified for our sakes. The melody is played by the strings. Bach repeats over and over again the opening words of the duet in lovely phrases, one voice responding to the other.

6 CHORALE
Bach provided only the figured continuo part in the score, marking it 'Chorale. *In simplice stylo*.' Various chorales have been suggested to end the cantata.

Wohl dem, der sich auf seinen Gott recht kindlich kann verlassen! (Well for him, who on his God right childlike can depend).
Chorale Cantata BWV 139. Leipzig, 1724.

1 CHORUS
(As above)
SATB. Ob d'am i, ii, Vln i, ii, Vla, Org, Cont

The libretto is based on Johann Christoph Rübe's hymn (1692) with the above title set in Nos. 1 and 6 to Johann Hermann Schein's 'Mach's mit mir, Gott, nach deiner Güt' (1628). Verses i and v are set in their original form in Nos. 1 and 6, the rest (ii–iv) are paraphrased. The libretto has only a tenuous connection with the Epistle and Gospel of the day.

The text in this amiable movement dwells on the contentment that the friendship of God brings. The sopranos have the melody of the chorale in long notes, the under parts, one or the other, beginning their entries with the ascending first phrase of the chorale in diminution.

2 ARIA
'Gott ist mein Freund; was hilft das Toben, so wider mich ein Feind erhoben' ('God is my friend; what avails the rage which against me an enemy [has] set up')
T. Vln i concertante, Cont

The soul, having God for friend, is comforted when faced with envy and hatred. There are long runs on 'rage' and a great deal of activity in the violin solo and the continuo part, but the text does not really engage Bach's attention after the initial line.

3 RECITATIVE
'Der Heiland sendet ja die Seinen, recht mitten in der Wölfe Wut' ('The Saviour sends, yea, His own [ones] right into the middle of the wolf's fury')
A. Cont

4 ARIA
'Das Unglück schlägt auf allen Seiten um mich ein centner schweres Band' ('Misfortune wraps on all sides around me an exceedingly heavy band')
B. Ob d'am i, ii, Vln, Cont

Bach is wholly involved in this magnificent movement which should properly be described as a dramatic *scena*. It makes one wonder, not for the first time, what he might have given us if he had turned to *opera seria*.

This aria divides up into eleven sections, some very brief, involving many changes of tempo. It is one of those movements which can best be fully appreciated by following the score. A long prelude has the main material of the first section in which the upper instruments picture the unhappy state of the man. The fragmented vocal part, echoed by the dotted figure in the continuo, suggests his struggle to free himself. The second section (*vivace*) greets the appearance of a helping hand in smooth vocal lines. In the third (*andante*), with continuo only, consolation's light appears from afar. The opening section is repeated, the *vivace* also following it, and then both of these to the same words, the aria closing with a coda. (This description does not take account of very brief sections.)

5 RECITATIVE

'Ja, trag ich gleich den grössten Feind in mir, die hohe schwere Last der Sünden, mein Heiland lässt mich Ruhe finden' ('Yea, bear I even the greatest enemy in myself, the heavy load of sins, my Saviour lets me rest find')
S. Vln i, ii, Vla, Cont

6 CHORALE

'Dahero Trotz der Höllen Heer! Trotz auch des Todes Rachen' ('Therefore defiance to the Hell's hosts, defiance also of death's jaws')
SATB. As No. 1. Insts. with voices. Cont

Verse v of the chorale. The last line sums up the message of the cantata, 'Well for Him who has God as friend'.

Falsche Welt, dir trau ich nicht (False world, I do not thee trust).
Solo Cantata BWV 52. Leipzig, 1726.

1 SINFONIA

Cor i, ii, Ob i, ii, iii, Fag, Vln i, ii, Vla, Org, Cont
Bach begins the cantata with an adaptation of the opening movement of the first Brandenburg Concerto, in F major (BWV 1046), omitting the violino piccolo from the original score and altering only a few bars of the horns' part. The movement has absolutely no relevance to the libretto.

2 RECITATIVE

(As above)
S. Fag, Org, Cont
This embittered and utterly pessimistic outburst jars, coming as it does after the lively orchestral movement. The soul pictures herself surrounded by 'scorpions and false serpents'. The text refers to Joab's treacherous murder of Abner (2 Samuel III. 27) called 'Armer' ('poor man') in the text.

323

3 ARIA
'Immerhin, immerhin, wenn ich gleich verstossen bin' ('I care
not, even if I am repudiated')
S. Vln i, ii, Fag, Org, Cont

The ascending phrases of the violins at the start of the aria
are a welcome relief after the above diatribe. The repudiation is
by the world. The source of happiness, in this delightful aria, is
the joy of God's friendship. The florid phrases on 'repudiated'
are full of contempt for the world.

4 RECITATIVE
'Gott ist getreu, er wird, er kann mich nicht verlassen' ('God is
faithful, He will, He can me not leave')
S. Cont

The opening words are emphasized by short florid phrases in
the voice and also in the continuo. The three repetitions of the
words at the close make a moving effect.

5 ARIA
'Ich halt es mit dem lieben Gott, die Welt mag nur alleine bleiben' ('I hold to the dear God, the world may merely alone
remain')
S. Ob i, ii, iii, Fag, Org, Cont

Themes that recall those by a contemporary composer offer a
trap to the commentator, but the opening theme on the orchestra
in this aria irresistibly reminded me, in shape and rhythm, of
Cleopatra's far better-known aria, 'V'adoro pupile' in Handel's
opera *Giulio Cesare*, produced two years before this cantata. It
is not inconceivable that Bach knew of it or had perhaps heard
it in Hamburg. The voice part has its own, and lovely, melody
in the middle section, beginning with the words, 'God with me and
I with God, therefore can I drive away the mockery of false
tongues'. 'Mockery' is given two extended runs as contemptuous
as in 'repudiated' in No. 3.

6 CHORALE
'In dich hab ich gehoffet, Herr, hilf, dass ich nicht zu Schanden
werd' ('In Thee have I hoped, Lord, help that I come not to
shame')
SATB. Ob i, ii, iii, Vln i, ii, Vla, all with voices; Cor i, ii, Fag, Org, Cont

The first verse of Adam Reissner's hymn (*c.* 1533) as above, set
to Seth Calvisius's melody (1581).

TWENTY-FOURTH SUNDAY
AFTER TRINITY

Epistle: Col. I. 9–14 (Prayer for increase of grace).
Gospel: Matt. IX. 18–26 (Raising of Jairus's daughter).

O Ewigkeit, du Donnerwort (Eternity, thou thunder-word).
Solo Cantata BWV 60. Leipzig, 1723.

1 DUET
(As above)
A.T. (Cor with T.), Ob d'am i, ii, Vln i, ii, Vla, Cont

The libretto of this cantata is a dialogue between Fear (alto)
and Hope (tenor). Bach uses only the first verse of Johann Rist's
hymn with the above title, which he had set much more fully
in the previous year for the first Sunday after Trinity (BWV 20).
The connection with Epistle and Gospel in the present cantata is
tenuous.

The thudding notes in the strings and continuo, heard throughout a large part of the duet, express Fear's terror of death, the
background to her singing of the first verse of the chorale to its
appointed melody. Hope, represented instrumentally by the
oboes d'amore, suddenly comes in, about half-way through, with
the words, 'I await Thy salvation', constantly reiterating them in
florid phrases to the end of the duet.

2 RECITATIVE
A: 'O schwerer Gang zum letzten Kampf und Streite'. T: 'Mein
Beistand ist schon da, mein Heiland steht mir ja mit Trost zur
Seite' (A: 'Oh heavy going to the last combat and struggle')
(T: 'My help is already there, my Saviour stands with me, yea,
with comfort at my side')
A.T. Cont

Bach gives a realistic extended phrase to 'tortures' (these
limbs) and in another arioso at the close Hope declares that God
is not of that mind.

3 DUET
A: 'Mein letztes Lager will mich schrecken'. T: 'Mich wird des
Heilands Hand bedecken' (A: 'My last halting-place will me
frighten') (T: 'Me will the Saviour's hand cover')
A.T. Ob d'am i, Vln i solo, Cont

Bach was unable to set the opposed sentiments that are exchanged throughout this duet to music that would convincingly express both and so compromises by giving the tenor and solo violin more ornate parts than the alto and oboe d'amore.

4 RECITATIVE
A: 'Der Tod bleibt doch der menschlichen Natur verhasst'.
B: 'Selig sind die Toten' (A: 'Death remains yet to human nature hateful') (B: 'Blessed are the dead')
A.B. Cont

Hope has done all he can, and departs. Fear, who speaks always in recitatives, is in a state of acute terror. Then comes the voice of Christ with the comforting words from Revelation XIV. 13, in a most beautiful phrase. Fear breaks out again, this time with gruesome allusions to worms devouring the body. Christ's voice completes the sentence from Revelation, 'Blessed are the dead' with 'who die in the Lord', but Fear is still not comforted. There follows a closing arioso of far greater length which ends with an exquisite phrase at 'who in the Lord die from henceforth', and now, learning those last words, Fear is able to reply, 'I shall henceforth be blessed, I can hope again, my body can sleep in peace and my spirit rejoice'.

5 CHORALE
'Es ist genug: Herr, wenn es dir gefällt, so spanne mich doch aus' ('It is enough: Lord, if it pleases Thee, so set me then free')
SATB. As No. 1. Insts. with voices. Cont

Verse v of Franz Joachim Burmeister's hymn 'Es ist genug, so nimm, Herr, meinen Geist' (1662) set to Johann Rudolph Ahle's melody. The first phrase of the melody rises in three whole tones and the remarkable harmonization in the first two bars still has power to startle, the chromatic harmonies six bars before the end to amaze.

These latter are echoed in Chopin's C minor Prelude (No. 20). It should also be mentioned that this is the chorale which Alban Berg chose for the last movement of his Violin Concerto to commemorate the death of a beloved friend.

Ach wie flüchtig, ach wie nichtig, ist der Menschen Leben (Ah, how fleeting, ah, how fading is the life of mortals).
Chorale Cantata BWV 26. Leipzig, 1724.

1 CHORUS
(As above)
SATB. Fl trav with Ob i, Ob ii, iii, Vln i, ii, Vla, Cor with S. Org. Cont

The libretto is based on Michael Franck's hymn set to his own melody (1652) in Nos. 1 and 6. Other verses are paraphrased in the intermediate numbers.

The Gospel account of the raising of the ruler's daughter perhaps leads to this discourse on the mortality of man. Bach, with his partiality for tonal symbolism, paints a picture in the orchestral and vocal parts (except for the sopranos who have the melody), of cloud-wreaths forming and quickly dissolving in the brief life of man. As the voices cease the orchestra recapitulates the opening ritornello.

2 ARIA
'So schnell ein rauschend Wasser schiesst, so eilen unser's Lebens Tage' ('As quickly as rushing water gushes, so hasten on our life's days')
T. Fl trav solo, Vln solo, Cont

The flute, violin, and voice are given phrases, rather than a developed melody, to depict the rushing waters. The tenor is kept hard at it in the lengthy first section with numerous runs on 'quickly' and 'hasten'. In the middle section Bach realistically depicts drops of water suddenly dividing before falling into the abyss. It is a splendid aria.

3 RECITATIVE
'Die Freude wird zur Traurigkeit, die Schönheit fällt als eine Blume' ('Joy turns to mournfulness, beauty falls like a flower')
A. Org, Cont

4 ARIA
'An irdische Schätze das Herze zu hängen ist eine Verführung der törichten Welt' ('To earthly treasures the heart to attach is a temptation of the foolish world')
B. Ob i, ii, iii, Org, Cont

Another fine aria, Handelian in the texture of the melody. The text derides 'the pomps and vanities of this wicked world' and in

327

the middle section warns how easily consuming flames or boiling floods can engulf. This is graphically illustrated first in the florid phrases of the continuo, then by the voice. The opening section returns, written out, and the *da capo* is confined to the opening ritornello.

5 RECITATIVE
'Die höchste Herrlichkeit und Pracht umhüllt zuletzt des Todes Nacht' ('The greatest splendour and pomp envelops, at last, death's night')
S. Org, Cont

Rightly styled a very fine piece of declamation, with every significant word assigned to its inevitable note or notes. The man, so great in this world, is now quite forgotten. The voice alone utters that last word, 'vergessen'.

6 CHORALE
'Ach wie flüchtig, ach wie nichtig, sind der Menschen Sachen' ('Ah, how fleeting, ah how fading are men's affairs')
SATB. As No. 1. Insts. with voices. Org, Cont

Verse xiii of the hymn.

TWENTY-FIFTH SUNDAY
AFTER TRINITY

Epistle: 1 Thess. IV. 13–18 (Christ's second coming).
Gospel: Matt. XXIV. 15–28 (Christ's prediction of His second coming).

Es reifet euch ein schrecklich Ende, ihr sündlichen Verächter, hin (There ripens a dreadful ending for you, ye scornful sinners).
Solo Cantata BVM 90. Leipzig, 1723.

1 ARIA
(As above)
T. Vln i, ii, Vla, Cont

To appreciate to the full the two powerful arias in this cantata the listener will be well advised to look up the appointed readings from the Epistle and Gospel for this Sunday, the first of which speaks of the Lord descending from heaven 'with a cry of command . . . and with the sound of triumph of God'. The Gospel has terrifying predictions of such tribulation coming as the world has never before seen, false Christs and false prophets arising, and the abominations in the Holy Place spoken of by the prophet David.

As the dramatic prelude ends the tenor bursts in with an extended phrase to the denunciatory opening words, which the first violin afterward punctuates with a wild upward rush of demisemiquavers. The words of the middle section accuse the guilty sinners of forgetting their Judge.

2 RECITATIVE
'Des Höchsten Güte wird von Tag zu Tage neu, der Undank aber sündigt stets auf Gnade' ('The Highest's goodness is renewed day by day, but ingratitude always sins against mercy')
A. Cont

3 ARIA
'So löschet im Eifer der rächende Richter, den Leuchter des Wortes zur Strafe doch aus' ('So the avenging Judge extinguishes in zeal the light of the word as a punishment then')
B. Tr, Vln i, ii, Vla, Cont

The text of this tremendous aria is made up of quotations from Revelations II. 5 and St Luke XIX. 46 (the latter describes the desecration of the Temple at Jerusalem denounced by Christ). The fanfares at the start seem to indicate the trumpet, though the very quick runs that follow would need a very skilled player. This is a finely declamatory aria with rushes up and down the scale suggestive of dissolution. The words of the middle section accuse sinners of defiling the holy place, making it a place of murder. The first utterance of the text is followed by successive phrases of rapid notes in the continuo, then in the second violin and viola parts, which intensify the horror of the scene.

4 RECITATIVE
'Doch Gottes Auge sieht auf uns als Auserwählte' ('For God's eye looks on us as the chosen')
T. Cont

The Father's power is manifested in danger and gratefully acknowledged by His own.

5 CHORALE
'Leit uns mit deiner rechten Hand, und segne unser Stadt und Land' ('Lead us with Thy right hand and bless our town and land')
SATB. Cont. Instrumentation not stated

Verse vii of Martin Moller's 'Nimm von uns, Herr, du treuer Gott' (1584) set to the associated melody of 'Vater unser im Himmelreich', Luther's version of the Lord's Prayer.

Du Friedefürst, Herr Jesu Christ (Thou Prince of Peace, Lord Jesus Christ).
Chorale Cantata BVM 116. Leipzig, 1724.

1 CHORUS
(As above)
SATB. Ob d'am i, ii, Vln i, ii, Vla, Cor with S. Cont

The libretto is based on Jakob Ebert's hymn with the above title (1601) in Nos. 1 and 6 set to Bartolomäus Gesius's melody of the same date. The other verses are paraphrased in the intervening numbers.

The second coming of the Lord casts no shadow over the confident introduction, at the end of which the chorus sing the opening lines of the chorale in massive harmonies, the second line, 'true man and true God', being separated from the first, in the customary manner, by an orchestral ritornello. Two fugal expositions follow: the first to the line, 'a strong help in need Thou'; the second, 'in life and in death. Therefore we alone in Thy name', has detached phrases for the lower voices. Then, at 'to Thy Father cry' comes full harmonization of the line.

2 ARIA
'Ach, unaussprechlich ist die Not und des erzürnten Richters Dräuen!' ('Ah, unspeakable is the need and the menace of the angered Judge!')
A. Ob d'am solo, Cont
This poignant aria is the cry of a soul terrified of the judgement and entirely lacking the confidence heard in the movement above. The chromatic nature of all the parts betokens acute distress and Bach even put a trill for the voice, two bars long, at 'anguish'. But the soul *does* cry out to Jesus even though her mind is filled with the terrible vision of God's anger.

3 RECITATIVE
'Gedenke doch, o Jesus, dass du noch ein Fürst des Friedens heissest' ('Remember then, O Jesus, that Thou still a Prince of Peace art called')
T. Cont

4 TERZETT
'Ach, wir bekennen unsre Schuld und bitten nichts als um Geduld und um dein unermesslich Lieben' ('Ah, we confess our guilt and ask for nothing but patience and Thine immeasurable love')
S.T.B. Cont
This is the longest and perhaps the loveliest of Bach's trios in the cantatas. The middle section, to the words, 'Thy pitying heart broke, that it was grief for every fallen one that drove Thee into the world', is deeply moving. All through Bach uses, in continuo and voices, a variation of the little motif heard at the start of the movement.

5 RECITATIVE
'Ach, lass uns durch die scharfen Ruten nicht allzu heftig bluten' ('Ah, may the sharp rods not cause us too violently to bleed')
A. Vln i, ii, Vla, Cont
The recitative ends with a prayer for peace to come to the land and its people. The strings, high up in their compass, endorse the words in lovely sounds betokening that peace is now approaching.

6 CHORALE

'Erleucht' auch unsern Sinn und Herz, durch den Geist deiner
Gnade' ('Enlighten also our mind and heart, through the spirit
of Thy grace')

SATB. As No. 1. Insts. with voices. Cont

Verse vii of the chorale.

TWENTY-SIXTH SUNDAY
AFTER TRINITY

Epistle: 2 Pet. III. 3–13 (Christ's second coming).
Gospel: Matt. xxv. 31–46 (The Last Judgement.)

Wachet, betet, seid bereit (Watch, pray, be prepared).
Cantata BWV 70. Weimar, 1723. Additions Leipzig, 1731.

The libretto of Nos. 1, 3, 5, 8, 10 is by Salomo Franck and intended for use at Weimar on the second Sunday in Advent. It is thought that the text of the remaining six numbers was added by Bach for the Leipzig performance on this Sunday in 1731.

PART I

1 CHORUS
(As above)
SATB. Tr, Ob, Vln i, ii, Vla, Fag, Cont
 The libretto, as regards the Gospel, concentrates on the Son of Man coming in His glory and all the angels with Him on the Day of Resurrection when all men will be gathered together. More prominence is given in the chorus to Peter's warning of the solemn event in the Epistle. The trumpet sounds, in the opening ritornello, with the oboe and strings conveying the awe of the tremendous moment. With his keen sense of drama, Bach leaves the entry of the chorus, with the first line of the text, unaccompanied, 'Pray' is given sustained notes, then comes a vivid picture of the trembling multitude expressed in a series of trills. There is a fearful urgency in the setting of 'be prepared'. This is one of Bach's greatest choruses.

2 RECITATIVE
'Erschrecket, ihr verstockten Sünder' ('Tremble, ye hardened sinners')
B. As No. 1
 Clarion calls ring out again here but the direful text ends by turning to the joy of the elect expressed by the bass in a superb extended phrase. The echoes of the last trump gradually die away, leaving the trumpet sounding alone in the last two bars.

3 ARIA
'Wann kommt der Tag, an dem wir ziehen aus dem Ägypten dieser Welt' ('When comes the day when we go out of the Egypt of this world')
A. V'cello obb., Fag, Cont

The righteous are depicted in the Epistle and in the Gospel fleeing from Sodom, and so they are in this aria, which does not, however, seem to have inspired Bach.

4 RECITATIVE
'Auch bei dem himmlischen Verlangen hält unser Leib den Geist gefangen' ('Even in our heavenly longing our body holds the spirit imprisoned')
T. Fag, Cont

5 ARIA
'Lass der Spötter Zungen schmähen, es wird doch, und muss geschehen' ('Let the mockers' tongues jeer, it will yet, and must happen')
S. Vln i, ii, Vla, Fag, Cont

Bach here unmistakably adapted a bass solo aria from Handel's early opera *Almira* but the theory that the material of the whole cantata is based on this source has been shown to be erroneous.

6 RECITATIVE
'Jedoch bei dem unartigen Geschlechte denkt Gott an seine Knechte' ('Yet in this wicked generation God thinks of His servants')
T. Fag, Cont

7 CHORALE
'Freu dich sehr, o meine Seele, und vergiss all Not und Qual' ('Rejoice thee greatly, oh my soul, and forget all need and torment')
SATB. As No. 1. Insts. with voices. Cont

Verse x of the anonymous hymn, 'Freu' dich sehr, o meine Seele' (1620) set to Louis Bourgeois' melody to Psalm XLII (1551).

PART II

8 ARIA
'Hebet euer Haupt empor und seid getrost, ihr Frommen' ('Lift up your heads on high and be comforted, ye pious')
T. Ob, Vln i, ii, Vla, Fag, Cont

This delightful aria is Handelian in idiom, but is certainly signed by Bach.

9 RECITATIVE
'Ach, soll nicht dieser grosse Tag, der Welt Verfall und der Posaunen Schall' ('Ah, shall not this great day, the world's fall, and the trumpet call')
B. Tr, Vln i, ii, Vla, Fag, Cont

As in No. 2, but at greater length, the terrors of the Last Judgement are graphically expressed here with a thudding bass in the continuo part and frightening phrases of dissolution in the string parts. Then, on the trumpet, comes the melody of the Advent Chorale, 'Es ist gewisslich an der Zeit', which is associated with Luther's hymn, 'Nun freut euch, lieben Christen, g'mein', reflected in the text of the second half of the recitative.

10 ARIA
'Seligster Erquickungstag, führe mich zu deinen Zimmern' ('Blessed Resurrection day, guide me to Thy chambers')
B. As No. 9

The simplicity of the beautiful melody set to these words makes an overwhelming effect. It is followed by a final dramatic outburst picturing the destruction of the world, and even of the heavens! Then comes the utter peacefulness of the words, 'Jesus guides me to calm, to the place where delight abounds' set to an even more lovely *adagio* melody.

11 CHORALE
'Nicht nach Welt, nach Himmel nicht meine Seele wünscht und sehnet' ('Not after the world, not after heaven does my soul desire and long')
SATB. As No. 1. Insts. with voices. Cont

The soul desires only Jesus, who reconciles him with God. The trumpet and oboe have the melody, the strings are independent. This is verse v of Christian Keimann's 'Meinen Jesum lass ich nicht' (1658) set to its associated melody (1658).

TWENTY-SEVENTH SUNDAY
AFTER TRINITY

Epistle: 2 Cor. v. 1–10 (Assurance of Salvation).
Gospel: Matt. xxv. 1–13 (Parable of the wise and foolish Virgins).

Wachet auf, ruft uns die Stimme der Wächter sehr hoch auf der Zinne (Wake up, cries the voice of the watchers very high on the battlements).
Chorale Cantata BWV 140. Leipzig, 1731.

1 CHORUS
(As above)
SATB. Ob i, ii, Te, Vln i with Vln picc, Vln ii, Vla, Cor with S. Cont

The best-known and loved of all Bach's church cantatas needs little description. The picture he paints of the summons in the night, the agitated scene that follows among the suddenly awakened virgins, the great hymn and melody by Philipp Nicolai (1599)—used in Nos. 1, 4, and 7—ringing out on the heights, the exultant Alleluias, make an unforgettably vivid impression.

2 RECITATIVE
'Er kommt, er kommt, der Bräut'gam kommt! Ihr Töchter Zions, kommt heraus' ('He comes, He comes, the Bridegroom comes! Ye daughters of Zion, come out')
T. Cont

3 DUET
S: 'Wann kommst du, mein Heil?'. B: 'Ich komme, dein Teil'
(S: 'When comest thou, my salvation?') (B: 'I come, thy portion')
S.B. Vln picc, Cont

Bach uses one of his favourite motifs in the main theme of this duet, very different in the context from its use in 'Have mercy, Lord' in the St Matthew Passion or 'It is enough' in the 'Simeon' Cantata No. 60. The language of this love duet between the Soul and Christ, as with such great spiritual writers as St John of the Cross, cannot be other than that which is used by ordinary lovers.

The violino piccolo wreathes exquisite arabesques round the tender exchanges. It is, alas, rare indeed to hear this duet, or the one in No. 6, sung with true spiritual understanding.

4 CHORALE
'Zion hört die Wächter singen, das Herz tut in ihr vor Freuden springen' ('Zion hears the watchmen sing, the heart in her for joy doth spring')
T. Vln i, ii, Vla (unis.), Cont

Those who think of counterpoint as an academic device should listen to the superb orchestral countermelody to the chorale. This glorious movement cannot but hearten the weak and uplift the strong. The marvellous inspiration should shame those who regard Bach merely as a consummate craftsman, and no more religious than the Cantor in the next town.

5 RECITATIVE
'So geh herein zu mir, du mir erwählte Braut. Ich habe mich mit dir in Ewigkeit vertraut' ('So come within to me, my chosen Bride. I have thee eternally wedded')
B. Vln i, ii, V'cello picc, Vla, Cont

The line 'I will set Thee as a seal on my heart, on my arm', is a quotation from 'The Song of Solomon' VIII. 6.

6 DUET
S: 'Mein Freund ist mein!' B: 'Und ich bin dein' (S: 'My friend is mine') (B: 'And I am thine')
S.B. Ob solo, Cont

An even more beautiful duet than No. 3. It sums up the depth of love between Christ and the Soul which the music so well expresses.

7 CHORALE
'Gloria sei dir gesungen mit Menschen- und englischen Zungen, mit Harfen und mit Cymbeln schon' ('Gloria be to Thee, sung with men's and angels' tongues, with harps and cymbals too')
SATB. As No. 1. Insts. with voices. Cont

The church year ends fittingly with those words and this magnificent setting of the third verse of the hymn. Among the lost cantatas there may have been one or more for this Sunday but there could not have been one more perfect than this.

Ein' feste Burg ist unser Gott (A strong citadel is our God).
Chorale Cantata BWV 80. Leipzig, ?1724.

In 1715, when at Weimar, Bach set a libretto by Salomo Franck
for the third Sunday in Lent. It consisted of six numbers in the first of
which, a duet for soprano and bass, Franck introduced the second
verse of Luther's *Ein' feste Burg* and used the same verse again for the
concluding chorale. Bach retained these six numbers in BWV 80 but
added in this revised version the first and third verses of the chorale
as Nos. 1 and 5 and ended with the last verse. Franck's libretto is
based on St Luke's Gospel xi. 14–28, which speaks of Jesus casting
the devil out of a dumb man and so is related to the dominant theme
of Luther's hymn.

1 CHORUS
(As above)
SATB. Tr i, ii, iii, Timp, Ob i, ii, Vln i, ii, Vla, V'cello, Violone, Org

Luther's great hymn, inspired by Psalm xLvi and composed in
1529 was the battle-song—and has been called the 'Marseillaise'—
of the Reformation, and in the long and tremendous chorale
fantasia, spread over 228 bars, Bach's profound love for and
loyalty to the founder of his religion and his faith are expressed
with burning conviction and consummate technique. The influ-
ence Pachelbel had over Bach is conspicuous in the great contrapuntal structure he erects over the free continuo in which the
organ part is put on two bass staves, one marked manual, the
other pedal, with a 16-foot trombone stop. The brass, woodwind
and timpani are never allowed to obscure the familiar lines of the
melody. As Whittaker says, 'They are always unmistakably
prominent; to his congregation it must have been like meeting a
bewilderingly large crowd in which every face is known.' The
chief entries of the melody lines are in canon at the octave. These
entries decorate the melody of the chorale but, well spaced out,
the unadorned melody of the continuo stands out rock-like, on the
first trumpet above in canon with the violone below, as if span-
ning heaven and earth.

2 DUET
S: 'Mit unsrer Macht ist nichts getan' ('By our might is nothing
done')

338

B: 'Alles, alles was von Gott geboren ist zum Siegen auserkoren'
('All, all that of God is born is to victory chosen')
S.B. Ob, Vln i, ii, Vla (unis.), Cont

The soprano sings a decorated version of the melody to the words of the second verse, which goes on to proclaim that the man chosen to strive for us is Jesus Christ. The oboe plays the melody, in duet with the voice, in an even more decorated style. The florid bass part has Franck's text which continues 'Who by Christ's blood-banner in baptismal faith is pledged, conquers in spirit for ever and ever', and the militant phrases for the strings underline the fighting spirit of the text.

3 RECITATIVE
'Erwäge doch, Kind Gottes, die so grosse Liebe, da Jesus sich mit seinem Blute dir verschriebe' ('Consider then, Child of God, the so great love with which Jesus pledged himself to you with his blood')
B. Cont

The second half of this expressive recitative is a beautiful arioso in which a rising motif of three notes is constantly repeated by voice and continuo.

4 ARIA
'Komm in mein Herzens-Haus, Herr Jesus, mein Verlangen' ('Come into my heart's house, Lord Jesus, my desire')
S. Cont

The use of bass and tenor clefs in the continuo part seems to indicate that Bach wished the 'cello alone to accompany the singer in this touching aria. The lovely phrase with which the 'cello begins runs almost throughout and just before the close the soprano is given an extended phrase on the middle syllable of 'longing'.

5 CHORALE
'Und wenn die Welt voll Teufel wär' und wollte uns verschlingen' ('And if the world were full of devils and would devour us')
SATB. Tr i, ii, iii, Timp, Ob d'am i, ii, Te, Vln i, ii, Vla, Cont

Another splendid battle piece with the text of verse iii. It reassures the faithful that the Prince of this World will not succeed in his wiles, 'a little word [i.e. the Word of God] can fell him'. A unique feature of the choral writing here is that the voices are in unison and thunder out each line to the blazing and triumphant orchestral accompaniment in which the descending notes of the first melody line are a constant feature. Bach puts the melody in this number in 6/8 time and this lends it a greater rhythmic liveliness.

6 RECITATIVE
'So stehe denn bei Christi blutgefärbter Fahne, o Seele, fest, und glaube' ('So stand then beside Christ's blood-bespattered banner, O Soul, firm, and believe')
T. Cont

Joyfully the Soul is exhorted, in a vigorous phrase, to go to war, to hear and follow truly the Word of God—and then the foe will be repelled. As in No.3 an arioso follows, here eloquently stressing that the Saviour is the Soul's hope and strength.

7 DUET
'Wie selig sind doch die, die Gott im Munde tragen' ('How blessed are then they who God in their mouths carry')
A.T. Ob da cacc, Vln, Cont

The fact that the oboe da caccia was not in use at Weimar suggests that this movement was re-composed at Leipzig. The voices charmingly unite now in thirds, now in sixths, and have many canonic phrases of which the long-drawn one at 'carry' when the opening line is repeated is specially attractive. The middle section, rather declamatory, tells of the unconquered heart being crowned when Death is overthrown.

8 CHORALE
'Das Wort sie sollen lassen stahn und kein' Dank dazu haben' ('The Word they shall let abide, yet they no thanks shall merit')
SATB. No instrumentation given

Verse iv has one of Bach's finest 4-part harmonizations. One can imagine with what enthusiasm the huge congregation, gathered for this supremely important Festival (which fell on 31 October, whether or not a Sunday) must have joined in this concluding chorale, more particularly because it would have been difficult for them to do so in the unison chorus of No. 5.

Gott, der Herr, ist Sonn und Schild (God, the Lord, is Sun and Shield).

Cantata BWV 79. Leipzig, 1725.

1 CHORUS
(As above)
SATB. Cor i, ii, Timp, Fl trav i, ii with Ob i, ii, Vln i, ii, Vla, Cont

Verse 11 of Psalm LXXXIV, which provides the text for the chorus, inspired Bach to compose music even more thrilling and magnificent than that of the opening chorus of the preceding cantata (BWV 80) and now, not having to consider the clearest enunciation of the words as in Luther's hymn 'Ein feste Burg', he makes the fullest use of his orchestra.

Terry followed Spitta in ascribing the first performance of the Cantata to 30 October 1735 when the War of the Polish Election was near its close, this accounting, in part, for the dominantly martial character of Bach's opening chorus: but later research gives the date as ten years earlier and so disposes of that theory. The Reformation Festival was, as Whittaker says, 'the celebration of earthly victories in the cause of national religion' and so there is no need, in any case, to look further than this to account for this stupendous battle scene.

The two principal themes appear in the long orchestral prelude. The fanfare-like theme on the horn is accompanied by relentlessly beating drums, vigorous passages for oboes, doubled by transverse flutes, first violins, with detached notes for second violins, viola and continuo suggesting the tramp of the soldiers. Horns and timpani cease at the entry of the second theme, on first oboes and first violins, as the subject of a three-part fugato, after which the first theme returns scored as before but newly accompanied, for now, as later, Bach combines his two themes. There follows the massive and dramatic entry of the chorus—the tenors noticeably high-pitched—with both themes in the accompaniment, to the words 'God the Lord, is Sun and Shield, the Lord gives mercy and honour'.

The remaining two lines of the psalm verse are 'He will allow no good thing to be lacking from the pious'. These words at their first repetition are set to the second theme, the material also of its orchestral accompaniment (horns and timpani again being silent), in the form of a four-part fugue. The opening two sections are recapitulated, and the two themes finally combined as the chorus end with the last two lines of the psalm. Words are more than usually inadequate to describe the overwhelming effect of this marvellous chorus.

2 ARIA
'Gott ist unser Sonn und Schild' ('God is our Sun and Shield')
A. Oboe or Fl trav solo, Cont

The text begins with a paraphrase of the first lines of the psalm verse in No. 1. In the original score Bach assigns the obbligato part to an oboe but on the part sheet to the transverse flute. This perhaps suits the character of the music better but not the words of the middle section, which speak of God protecting the faithful from 'sharp arrows and the blasphemous barking of a dog'. Oboe tone would be more appropriate here—but it is not suggested that the instruments should share out the accompaniment of the aria! The charming alto melody is foreshadowed in the instrumental introduction.

3 CHORALE
'Nun danket Alle Gott mit Herzen, Mund und Händen' ('Now thank we all God with heart and mouth and hands')
SATB. Cor i, ii, Timp, Fl trav i, ii, Ob i, ii, Vln i, ii, Vla, all with voices, Cont

The first verse of Martin Rinkart's hymn (1636) to the melody by Johann Crüger (1648). Bach lays out the chorale in square-cut blocks of minims with occasional crotchet passing notes and accompanies it throughout with the horn theme and timpani of No. 1, and the continuo detached notes so suggestive of marching armed men. The effect is splendid and gives a fine unity to the cantata. At this point Bach might well have ended for what comes after is not of great interest, but just as the pastor had to preach for at least an hour—so Bach's cantatas had to last for approximately half an hour. Thus a bad tradition made him spoil what could have been a very satisfying three-movement cantata—and this is not the only example.

4 RECITATIVE
'Gott Lob! wir wissen den rechten Weg zur Seligkeit' ('To God be praise! We know the right way to blessedness')
B. Cont

That way is contrasted, in the latter part of the recitative, with those 'who must go under the strange yoke of blindness' and prays God to 'pity them and lead them in the right way'.

5 DUET

'Gott, ach Gott, verlass die Deinen nimmermehr' ('God, ah God, forsake thy people nevermore!')

S.B. Vln i, ii (unis.), Cont

The most attractive feature of this over-long duet is the violins' part, characterized by descents of an octave and then of a seventh. The figuration of the part continues practically unchanged throughout. There is a line in the text 'though sorely against us the enemies rage', which ignores the victory so obviously won in the great chorale movement (No. 3).

6 CHORALE

'Erhalt uns in der Wahrheit, gieb ewigliche Freiheit zu preisen deinen Namen durch Jesum Christum, Amen' ('Sustain us in the truth, give everlasting freedom to praise thy name, through Jesus Christ, Amen!')

SATB. As in No. 3

This is verse viii of Ludwig Helmbold's hymn, 'Nun lasst uns Gott dem Herren' (1575), set to an anonymous melody, and plainly harmonized by Bach.

SCORES

Vocal Scores

Breitkopf and Härtel. Nos. 1 to 199 (Church Cantatas), 201–216 (Secular Cantatas).

The order of this standard edition is that of the Bach *Gesellschaft* (The Bach Society edition) and so is not chronological but numerical. A fair number of the scores have English translations. The standard of editorship varies considerably in regard to the reduction to the piano of the instrumental parts of the scores, and though the later printings give details of scoring they make no reference to the Gospel or Epistle for the relevant Sunday or Feast Day.

(For the origins of the German cantata form from Italian sources the reader is referred to the bibliography. The wonderful variety of treatment Bach brought to it is described in the commentaries on the cantatas in this book and at length in W. G. Whittaker's *The Church Cantatas of Johann Sebastian Bach* (2 vols).)

Miniature Orchestral Scores

All the cantatas, sacred and secular—except No. 199 which did not come to light until 1911—reproduced from the *Bach Gesellschaft* are now to be had in the sixty-six volumes of the Kalmus Study Scores. There are three cantatas, on average, to a volume. One disadvantage in them is the use of the old vocal clefs, not only for tenor and alto voices but also for the soprano. This is not a great impediment to listening with these scores but raises a difficulty for those who want to play the vocal parts at the piano. The Lea Pocket Scores, comprising forty-one cantatas in fourteen volumes, are also reproduced from the *Bach Gesellschaft* and here also the average is three cantatas to a volume. No references are made in either of these publications to the Epistle and Gospel of the day.

There are forty-four scores, with modern clefs, in the Eulenburg Edition, one in each volume. Most of these have introductions by various musicologists and include a leaflet with the German text and the English translation below it. In addition they give particulars of the relevant Gospel and/or Epistle and any other biblical material, which is of great importance.

345

The New Bach Edition is reprinting all Bach's works, newly edited, and at this date ten of the church cantatas have been issued in miniature scores with introductory matter but no English translations.

SELECTED BIBLIOGRAPHY

David, H. T. and Mendel, A. *The Bach Reader: a Life of J. S. Bach in Letters and Documents*. Dent, 1966.

Day, J. *The Literary Background to Bach's Cantatas*. Dobson, 1961.

Dürr, A. *Zur Chronologie der Leipziger Vokalwerke J. S. Bachs*. Bach-Jahrbuch, 1957.

Dickinson, E. F. *The Art of Bach*. Hinrichsen, 1950.

Geiringer, K. *The Bach Family*. Allen & Unwin, 1954.

——*The Culmination of an Era*. O.U.P., 1966.

Parry, C. H. H. *J. S. Bach*. Putnam, 1946.

Scheide, W. H. *J. S. Bach as a Biblical Interpreter*. Princeton Theological Seminars, New Jersey, 1952.

Schmeider, W. *Thematisch-systematisches Verzeichnis der musikalischen Werke von J. S. Bach*. Breitkopf & Härtel, 1966. (The standard thematic catalogue, comprising 1,080 works.)

Schweitzer, A. *J. S. Bach*. English translation by E. Newman. 2 vols. Black, 1962.

Spitta, P. *J. S. Bach*. English edition by Clara Bell and J. A. Fuller-Maitland. Novello, 1951.

Terry, C. S. *The Four-part Chorales of J. S. Bach*. O.U.P., 1964.

—— *Bach, a Biography*. O.U.P., 1949.

—— *Bach's Orchestra*. Revised by Thurston Dart. O.U.P., 1961.

—— *The Music of Bach*. Constable, 1964. Dover Books, N.Y., 1963.

—— *Johann Sebastian Bach: Cantata Texts, Sacred and Secular*. New ed, Holland Books, 1964.

Whittaker, W. G. *The Cantatas of J. S. Bach*. 2 vols. O.U.P., 1959.

INDEX

A. THE CANTATAS IN NUMERICAL ORDER

B. THE CANTATAS IN ALPHABETICAL ORDER

Warum betrübst du dich, mein Herz? (138), 266
Was frag' ich nach der Welt und allen ihren Schatten wenn ich mich nur
    an dir, mein Jesu, kann ergötzen (94), 233
Was Gott tut, das ist wohlgetan (98), 310
Was Gott tut, das ist wohlgetan (99), 268
Was Gott tut, das ist wohlgetan (100), 270
Was mein Gott will, das g'scheh allzeit (111), 62
Was soll ich aus dir machen, Ephraim? (89), 314
Was willst du dich betrüben, o meine liebe Seel' (107), 220
Weinen, Klagen, Sorgen, Zagen (12), 126
Wer da glaubet (37), 140
Wer Dank opfert, der preiset mich (17), 263
Wer mich liebet, der wird mein Wort halten (59), 153
Wer mich liebet, der wird mein Wort halten (74), 154
Wer nur den lieben Gott lässt walten (93), 204
Wer sich selbst erhöhet, der soll erniedriget werden (47), 281
Wer weiss, wie nahe mir mein Ende! (27), 277
Wie schön leuchtet der Morgenstern (1), 99
Wir müssen durch viel Trübsal in das Reich Gottes eingehen (146), 129
Wo gehest du hin? (166), 132
Wo Gott, der Herr, nicht bei uns hält, wenn unsre Feinde toben (178), 226
Wohl dem, der sich auf seinen Gott recht kindlich kann verlassen! (139),
    321
Wo soll ich fliehen hin? (5), 296